DISCOVERING WHETHER PROGRAMS WORK:

A Guide to Statistical Methods for Program Evaluation

The Scott, Foresman Public Policy Analysis and Management Series
Arnold J. Meltsner and Mark H. Moore, Editors

Designing Public Policy: A Casebook on the Role of Policy Analysis
Laurence E. Lynn, Jr.

Getting the Facts: A Fieldwork Guide for Evaluators and Policy Analysts
Jerome T. Murphy

DISCOVERING WHETHER PROGRAMS WORK:

A Guide to Statistical Methods for Program Evaluation

Laura Irwin Langbein

The American University

Scott, Foresman and Company

Glenview, Illinois

Dallas, TX   Oakland, NJ   Palo Alto, CA   Tucker, GA   London, England

Library of Congress Cataloging in Publication Data

Langbein, Laura Irwin.
    Discovering whether programs work.

    (The Scott, Foresman public policy analysis and management
series)
    Bibliography
    Includes index.
        1. Social sciences—Statistical methods.   2. Evaluation research—
(Social action programs)   I. Title.   II. Series: Scott, Foresman public
policy analysis and management series.
HA33.L34   361.6'07'2   79-27878
ISBN 0-673-16260-5

CONTENTS

PREFACE

This volume had its genesis as a series of lectures for graduate public administration students in statistics and program evaluation courses. Reflecting the unique needs of this audience, the disciplinary origins of the formal methods comprising the course content disappeared as the lectures became increasingly practical. In time, the lectures began to blend the development of systematic quantitative research designs with the political and administrative considerations typical in evaluation research settings.

Such a merger is essential. Program evaluation is unquestionably political because results can affect the allocation of budgets. Agencies also use evaluation research to answer urgent questions from voters, legislators, and chief executives who want to know whether public programs work. In addition to the political considerations, program evaluation utilizes formal statistical methods; determining if public programs work makes causal inferences unavoidable. Program evaluation thus inextricably links the political process to scientific methods.

This volume acknowledges this link and seeks a middle ground among existing texts on program evaluation. These texts are either far too methodologically advanced for most practitioners and students, or so centered on the environment of evaluation that they ignore important statistical problems of valid causal inference.

The following pages consider a variety of quantitative approaches for making causal inferences regarding the social and economic impact of public programs. The volume compares the accuracy and utility of alternative research designs in circumstances that practicing evaluators (with little statistical training) will probably encounter. Some of these designs are described in detail, including the randomized field experiments and quasi experiments pioneered by social psychologists, and the regression techniques utilized by economists. Rather than defend any single approach, evaluators are advised instead to select the mix of methods most appropriate for the specific situation they confront. The text thus outlines strategies for attaining findings that are general, but it simultaneously recognizes that generality is not always essential. Methods for isolating the impact of a single program from the multiplicity of other influences on human behavior are also considered and weighed against the need for generality, the size of the evaluator's budget, the availability of data, the need for quick results, and the need for precision.

This text is designed for practicing evaluators and for use in advanced undergraduate and graduate classrooms. Its contents assume that readers have had one semester of statistics. The volume explains some statistical methods, but it is not a statistics text. Instead it considers only those aspects of research design and statistical method most likely to be encountered by practicing program evaluators. This practical orientation also makes it useful for sophisticated quantitative analysts whose disciplinary training leaves them unfamiliar with political and practical constraints surrounding evaluation.

Many people have contributed to the production of this book. Detailed comments from Lorraine Blank, Linda Ingram, Cornelius Kerwin, David H. Koehler, Ron Landis, Walter B. Langbein, Allan J. Lichtman, and Nick Matalas were particularly helpful. Students who read and questioned the manuscript and who asked questions in class about evaluation research were unwitting but nonetheless important contributors. Mary Wason's typing was consistently correct despite my handwriting. The most critical intellectual contribution comes from numerous works by Hubert M. Blalock, Jr., regarding the theory and practice of causal inference. I am entirely responsible for the remaining flaws.

Laura Irwin Langbein
July, 1979

Chapter 1

INTRODUCTION

PROGRAM EVALUATION: SOCIAL SCIENCE AND POLITICS

The early 1960s were the apogee of America's faith in the ability of government to solve the pressing social and economic problems of the day. Americans did not question their belief that schools educated, that government spending reduced unemployment, that education and training led to jobs, that community action reduced poverty, that community development could stimulate economic growth. Once identified, problems could be solved by governmental action. Although no one believed that problems would disappear overnight, most citizens were confident that with enough time and money, government programs could have a significant and beneficial impact on even the most severe ills of American society.

The war in Vietnam and the violent protests of urban blacks crumbled the foundations of America's faith in government. The event that first began to erode these foundations was the release in 1966 of a thick government report entitled *Equality of Educational Opportunity*. Mandated by Congress and sponsored by the U.S. Office of Education, the report is replete with statistical terms such as variable, mean, standard deviation, sampling error, explained variance, within-group variance, and between-group variance. What emerged from this technical and lengthy analysis was a carefully worded but myth-shattering conclusion:

> . . . it is clear that schools are not acting as a strong stimulus [on achievement scores measuring reading ability] independent of the child's background or the level of the student body. . . . This is not to say, of course, that schools have no effect, but rather that what effects they do have are highly correlated with the individual student's background, and with the educational background of the student body in the school; that is, the effects appear to arise not principally from factors that the school system controls, but from factors outside the school proper. (Coleman et al. 1966: 311–312)

1

This conclusion startled both the American public and the report's authors alike. It was particularly devastating because America's public schools were thought to be a critical avenue for upward mobility. Schools, we believed, taught the "3 Rs" to all Americans and thereby gave everyone an equal chance to succeed and prosper. Public schools were thus the lynchpin of assimilation and egalitarianism in America.

Equality of Educational Opportunity came to be known as the Coleman Report, named after its principal author, James Coleman, a sociologist. The Coleman Report was unique in two ways. First, it applied the methods of the social sciences to the analysis and evaluation of government programs. Previously, evaluation of government programs had been largely journalistic and episodic rather than scientific and systematic. The use of research methods drawn from the social sciences went far to assure that conclusions from the Coleman Report were both as accurate and general as possible. These properties, in turn, gave the report credibility that previous evaluations lacked.

Second, the Coleman Report centered not just on the process of public education but also on its impact. Earlier studies had examined curricula, libraries, science labs, teaching methods, class size, and the like. These studies assumed that improving the quality and quantity of educational inputs also increased what students learned. No study had produced any empirical evidence with which to justify this proposition. By questioning the assumption that more inputs produced better education, the Coleman Report also raised a larger issue, for it was no longer possible simply to assume that government programs actually achieved their intended goals. Instead, scientifically gathered evidence would now be necessary to buttress statements regarding program impact.

Reflecting this new requirement, this book outlines and compares the principal strategies that social scientists have used in the past to determine whether public programs have their intended impact. Chapter 2 considers the goals and criteria according to which impact is most often judged. The chapter suggests that the multiplicity of program goals raises the costs of studying program impact, while conflict among goals makes the findings ambiguous. Chapters 3–5 introduce the general criteria by which investigations of program impact can be evaluated. Chapter 3 considers the meaning of accuracy or validity in the context of analyzing program impact. Chapter 4 describes how different methodologies for attaining accurate findings correspond to each of the predominant strategies that analysts use to study program impact. The chapter also defines the main characteristics of these strategies. Experiments use random procedures to assign persons to programs. Quasi experiments compare persons in one program to similar persons in another, while so-called "nonexperiments" use statistical procedures to make these comparisons. Chapter 5 introduces two important properties by which analyses of program impact can be judged—generality and precision. When findings are general, they can be applied in other times and settings. When findings are precise, investigators can separate program impact from random influences.

Chapters 6–9 consider experiments, quasi experiments and nonexperiments in depth. Each of these chapters provides examples and depicts the practical problems that investigators are likely to encounter as they strive for evidence which is valid, general, and precise. The final chapter summarizes the most critical issues of impact analysis and suggests some directions that impact analysis may need to take in the future.

Concern for the issues of research design that this book introduces has increased considerably since Coleman began his research on the impact of schools. Even before the Coleman Report was released, the evaluation of program impact became an institutional component of the U.S. Office of Economic Opportunity. Today virtually every federal agency in every executive department has an evaluation branch responsible for using scientific methodology to determine whether agency programs have their intended impact. Congress has also incorporated program evaluation into its oversight activities. Both the Government Accounting Office and the Congressional Budget Office have evaluation responsibilities. Program evaluation is also a rapidly growing industry, particularly in Washington, D C., and the industry has branches in towns surrounding major universities. Both Congress and the executive department help support the industry by commissioning evaluative studies.[1]

Like the Coleman Report, succeeding evaluations have continued to produce findings that are inconsistent with prevailing myth.[2] These evaluations also share experience from the Coleman Report, since their use of scientific methodology does not shield their findings from controversy.

Most often, the controversy surrounding evaluative findings is methodological.[3] Detractors argue that the methods the investigator used were inadequate, inappropriate, and biased. Defenders may often agree to these charges, but retort that alternative and possibly superior methods were considered and rejected as impractical, too costly, or too time-consuming. To the technically untrained but financially interested and politically concerned taxpayer, these charges and countercharges must seem arcane and irrelevant. Yet methodological issues are critical in program evaluation. Using improper or inappropriate methods can lead investigators to erroneously conclude that programs are effective when in fact they are ineffective. The reverse error—concluding that programs are not effective when in fact they are—may be even more likely. Equally disturbing is the fact that no single methodology is ever guaranteed to be error-free, especially in the context of program evaluation.

Program evaluation is party scientific and partly political. While this text centers on the scientific aspects of program evaluation, readers should be aware that "scientific" program evaluation requires judgment as well as statistics, and political sensitivity as well as quantification. Consider the Coleman Report. Readers will discover that this study used a "nonexperimental" research design. However, its conclusions might have been less controversial had Coleman undertaken randomized experiments to measure the impact on achievement of factors that the school system controls relative to factors which lie outside the control of the school system itself, such as a student's family background. Such a design would probably be a political impossibility even today and certainly was politically infeasible in the early 1960s. Nonetheless, randomized experiments are desirable because they are capable of producing reasonably conclusive evidence regarding program impact. Recent experience with ongoing experiments suggests that this approach is still no guarantor of scientific verisimilitude.

People charged with designing their own evaluation or with applying the results of someone else's evaluation must recognize that good evaluations never emerge from a cookbook. Instead, good evaluations with useful findings must cleverly marry political awareness, cost-consciousness, and administrative ability with scientific and statistical expertise.

An understanding of the basic elements of program evaluation suggests why such a marriage may sometimes be stormy. Specifying the criteria for evaluation is the first step of any evaluation. The evaluator must understand what the elements of program "success" are. Lists of these criteria rarely exist, and an evaluator cannot simply make up a set of criteria reflecting his own priorities and preferences. Instead, the goals and criteria emerge from the political process in which the voices of both proponents and opponents can be heard. Sometimes the political process produces well-defined goals, but more often program intent is vague or glib; yet to determine whether programs have been successful, the meaning of success must be clarified. Because politicians, administrators, and managers comprise the audience for evaluation research, evaluators must be sensitive to the political, administrative, and managerial issues surrounding programs they study. If evaluators ignore how their audiences define "success," even the most scientifically elegant evaluations will be consigned to irrelvance.

Hand-in-hand with selecting the goals and criteria by which the program is to be evaluated, evaluators must also specify exactly what aspects of the program are to be studied. This, too, is a nonscientific task. Evaluators can examine a program in its entirety; they can also compare the relative effectiveness of different program elements. As in the specification of goals, the evaluator's audience should have a major role in selecting which of these issues is to be the focus for study. Answering the wrong question makes an evaluation useless to its audience.

Having defined precisely what is to be evaluated and the criteria that are to be used, the evaluator must next select an appropriate research strategy. While this choice is largely scientific, the evaluator's audience and environment frequently constrain the range of alternative methods from which he can select. Sometimes the audience specifies the precise methodological approach, but more often, political, administrative, and budgetary considerations simply narrow the range of feasible approaches. These possibilities are likely to be reduced further because program managers and administrators frequently resist evaluation. In evaluation, the subject may also turn out to be the enemy.

Finally, when the field operations and data analysis are complete, the evaluator must submit a report. The evaluator must continue to be cognizant of his audience. Rarely will politicians, administrators, or managers be willing or able to assimilate the details in a lengthy report filled with scientific jargon and tentative conclusions. Simple answers and summary reports are more suitable for the evaluator's audience, which ordinarily will be preoccupied with numerous and more pressing issues than the results of a single evaluation. The need for simplicity only increases the likelihood that the evaluator's findings will be misinterpreted.

This sketch of the elements of evaluation suggests that evaluation research differs from academic social science research. While social science research uses scientific methods to answer questions posed by social scientists, evaluation research uses methods that are as scientific as possible to answer questions that the evaluator believes his nonscientific audience has posed. The fundamental ambiguity of this task guarantees that the results from evaluation research will nearly always be controversial. The Coleman Report actually encountered each of these issues. First of all, the goals by which to evaluate public education were only vaguely specified by the legislation that commissioned and funded the research. According to the legislation, the study was to examine "the lack of availability of equal educational opportunities for individuals by reason of race, color, religion, or national origin. . . ."[4] Nowhere did Congress define "equal educational opportunity." Instead, specific definitions had to be supplied by the evaluators.

In contrast to their failure to specify the criteria for evaluation, Congress constrained the subject and the methods that Coleman and his associates could use. They were asked to study the public elementary and secondary educational system as a whole. Accordingly, the investigators could not compare the relative effectiveness, for instance, of school libraries and science labs, even though a narrow focus often provides more useful information. The congressional instructions also specified a survey approach, even though other research strategies could possibly produce more conclusive evidence.

While evaluation research uses the methods of social science to determine whether programs are successful, experience suggests that the boundary between the scientific and the political is neither clear nor immutable. Nonetheless, the merger of social science and practical politics that characterizes evaluation research means that evaluation research encompasses the methodological concerns of science and the normative concerns of politics. The following section outlines these aspects of evaluation and places evaluation in the larger context of policy analysis.

POLICY ANALYSIS AND EVALUATION RESEARCH

As a scientific enterprise, evaluation research uses both causal and descriptive methodologies. Causally oriented evaluations assess issues of cause and effect. Coleman's study of the effects of schooling on pupil achievement is fundamentally causal because it strives to determine whether attending school causes achievement to improve. Although this text centers on causal evaluations, descriptive evaluations are equally important. Descriptive studies enumerate conditions or portray needs; they do not make causal claims. Coleman's study, though basically causal, was also partly descriptive. Its assessment of the quantitative difference between facilities in predominantly black as opposed to predominantly white schools is largely descriptive because the assessment entails no attribution of causality.

Descriptive studies are basically enumerative; they depict the target population or the recipient population; they may contrast one with the other. Descriptive studies seek to discover whether a particular program is reaching all who qualify. Descriptive investigations also evaluate the adequacy of benefit levels authorized by a program, or determine whether a program's actual beneficiaries are among those in the target group who are most needy or least needy. Issues like these can best be answered by descriptive research.

Many issues, by contrast, demand causal research. Causal studies examine whether a particular outcome occurred because of a particular program, or inquire whether a particular program caused a particular effect. When a chief of a municipal police force asks if neighborhood team policing reduces crime, his question must be answered by causal rather than descriptive research. The question itself is one of causation because the chief wants to know whether a particular program (neighborhood team policing) causes a particular goal (the reduction of crime).

Causal issues abound in popular debates about public policy. Proponents of capital punishment believe that it is a deterrent and thereby causes a reduction in crime. Detractors of tuition tax credits for parents of elementary and secondary school children argue that the credits would cause a long-run decline in the quality of public schools, while proponents argue the reverse. Critics of housing allowances aver that increasing the demand for housing among the poor will only cause an increase in the price they pay. Even the statement, "large police forces are more efficient than small forces," is an implicit causal claim that increasing the size of a force causes operations to be more efficient. Allegations regarding the effects of public programs are usually causal claims even though the word "cause" does not appear explicitly and only causal research can ascertain their empirical validity.

Evaluation research can also be characterized in terms of its normative focus. While all evaluation research examines program success, some studies define success in terms of the outcome or impact of a program, while other studies focus on the process by which programs are implemented. Auditors examine programs in terms of their adherence to procedural and administrative guidelines; their definition of success is based on the process by which programs are carried out. Other evaluations measure the success of a program according to its social or economic outcome. Coleman's decision to judge schools according to their impact on achievement indicates that he used an outcome measure of success.

Defining program success in terms of process alone can convey an incomplete picture. A community mental health center may do little to reduce alcoholism among the poor even though it is efficiently operated. The rapidity with which the Farmers' Home Administration processes loans to businesses may have little impact on employment in rural areas. Evaluations based on measures of outcome alone can also produce misleading evidence. Preliminary investigations of Title I of the Elementary and Secondary Education Act revealed that it had little or no impact on the achievement levels of educationally disadvantaged students. Subsequent process evaluations disclosed that investigators could have anticipated such an outcome since only a portion of Title I funds actually reach educationally disadvantaged children (National Institute of Education, 1978). Thus, process evaluations should often precede or accompany outcome evaluations. Because processes can actually affect outcomes, evaluators should not ignore issues of process even when they employ measures of success based on program outcomes.

The distinction between process and outcome and that between descriptive and causal research is not always clear-cut since these dimensions are really continua rather than categories. Individual studies often include process as well as outcome measures of success, and the same study might contain both descriptive and causal elements. Nonetheless, cross-tabulating the two dimensions maps the range of issues that evaluation research encompasses. Figure 1.1 suggests the principal questions that characterize the three basic kinds of evaluation research.

FIGURE 1.1

Types of Evaluation Research[5]

	Definitions of Success	
Method	*Process*	*Outcome*
Descriptive	Was the program implemented according to guidelines? What facilities, resources did the program use? How were they used?	Who participated in the program? Did the program reach all who were eligible?
Causal		Did the program produce the intended (or unintended) outcomes? Which means of implementing the program produced the best outcomes?

This book considers causal evaluations alone, and thus does not span the entire field of evaluation research.[6] Although descriptive evaluations are as important as causal evaluations, causal investigations are methodologically more complex and therefore deserve special and detailed attention. Classical scientific methodology makes it difficult to have great confidence in causal claims about program impact. To show that a manpower program increased employment requires the investigator to rule out other explanations for the observed increase in employment. Many factors besides the manpower program could account for greater employment: the composition of the population could change; the economy could improve; persons affected by the manpower program might have been employed even without the program; the employment rise could be seasonal, random, temporary or part of a long-term trend. No evaluation can rule out all of these explanations, but the best designs will rule out the most plausible alternative explanations. Subsequent chapters consider these designs according to the canons of science and suggest adaptations necessitated by the interdisciplinary, practical, and action-oriented context of program evaluation.

Like evaluation research, policy analysis is a related field that also applies systematic analysis to the consideration of public issues. These similarities make it easy to assume that policy analysis and evaluation research are identical. The outline in Figure 1.2 reveals that evaluation research is just one of several analytical techniques that policy analysts might select.[7] Policy analysis includes the application of any systematic methodology to the resolution of public problems. Evaluation research is part of policy analysis because it applies statistical methods to public problems. Cost-benefit analysis and linear (and nonlinear) programming are also part of policy analysis; they use optimizing techniques for allocating scarce resources to produce maximum benefits. While these techniques rely heavily on economic theory, other techniques, such as decision theory, game theory, and queuing models, rely on the mathematical theory of probability. Probabilistic techniques indicate how to make decisions in the presence of uncertainty about the future, little information, and unpredictable human behavior. Modeling is a set of procedures designed to represent policies and their impact as a set of mathematical equations. Formal models allow investigators to simulate what is likely to happen when policies change.

These methods may best be applied in combinations. Cost-benefit analyses often use decision theory to measure the value of benefits that accrue in the future. By using decision theory, the analyst explicitly recognizes that the future benefits of public programs are both uncertain and contingent.

FIGURE 1.2
Methods of Policy Analysis

I. Statistical techniques
   A. Evaluation research

II. Optimization techniques
   A. Cost-benefit analysis
   B. Linear/nonlinear programming

III. Decision making under risk and uncertainty
   A. Decision theory
   B. Games
   C. Queues

IV. Simulation and modeling techniques
   A. Difference equations
   B. Markov processes
   C. Diffusion processes

Evaluation research is also used in combination with the other techniques of policy analysis. Because methods of optimization and decision making under uncertainty often rely on the results of evaluation research, evaluation must precede their use. Evaluation is particularly important in cost-benefit analysis. Cost-benefit calculations compare the costs of a program (or project) with the dollar value of the benefits that accrue as a result of the program. Only a benefit (or cost) that the program actually causes can be counted as a program benefit (or cost). If a benefit could occur even in the absence of the program, it should not appear in the program's cost-benefit calculation. To determine whether the program causes the particular benefit requires evaluation research. Attaching a monetary value to the benefit is a task for economic analysis.[8]

Evaluation research can also be used to estimate the parameters in a queuing problem or a decision tree. The so-called "arrival rate" is a parameter of a typical queuing problem. In the judicial system, the arrival rate is the number of cases that enter the system each month. An analyst could use queuing theory to predict how a procedural change affects the size of the judicial backlog or the average waiting time before a case comes to trial. To use queuing theory in this fashion, the analyst must first estimate the impact of the procedural change on the arrival rate. Securing such an estimate requires evaluation research techniques.

Evaluation research can also be used in conjunction with modeling. Causally based evaluations have verified a diffusion model of the impact of a measles vaccine on the incidence of measles among young children (Albritton 1978).

The results of an evaluation are thus a necessary basis, but not sufficient alone for systematic policy choice. Demonstrating that a particular program is effective does not justify the program. Estimates indicating that one project has a larger beneficial impact than another does not constitute conclusive support for the former. Parameter estimates like these are nonetheless necessary to solve optimization problems, to apply techniques for decision making under uncertainty, and to validate mathematical models. Evaluation research is therefore critical because it incorporates statistical techniques appropriate for generating these estimates.

The pages that follow describe some of these statistical techniques in a nontechnical fashion. All of these techniques can be understood by reading a variety of statistical textbooks, but not without great difficulty. Statistical texts introduce issues that are appropriate for academic research but somewhat tangential for evaluators. Many statistics texts are too technical to be read comfortably by individuals who actually do evaluation research. Statistics texts also fail to indicate how evaluators must blend statistics with political reality and tight budgets to produce useful evidence regarding the efficacy of public programs.

The political and statistical issues that policy analysts must consider before undertaking causal evaluations make this book most appropriate for students who have had at least one semester of social statistics. Students who need their statistics knowledge refreshed can refer to the Appendix which includes brief descriptions and formulas for measures of the association between two variables that the text itself does not consider.

Readers of this text will probably find themselves at once more skeptical and more sympathetic to the enterprise of evaluation. It may be impossible to design and implement evaluations that produce accurate, general, and uncontroversial findings all at once; but the alternatives are surmise and popular mythology. Politicans, administrators, and managers may surmise that their programs are effective. Popular mythology increasingly supports a contravening hypothesis. Only empirically based evaluations can separate the facts from everybody's favorite fiction.

FOOTNOTES

1. Numerous texts on program evaluation have accompanied the flow of federal support for evaluation research. Among the first of these was Campbell and Stanley (1963), Suchman (1967), and Weiss (1972). Campbell and Stanley discuss experiments and quasi experiments in the context of academic research. In a seminal work, Campbell (1971) adapted quasi experimentation to program evaluation. The volumes by Suchman and Weiss center more on the environment of evaluation than on its methodology. Many specialized texts and readers also exist. Among them is Clark (1976), which centers on experiments and quasi experiments; Cook and Campbell (1979) and Caporaso and Roos (1973) consider quasi experiments; Bennett and Lumsdaine (1975) and Riecken and Boruch (1974) compare experiments to quasi experiments; Glass, Willson, and Gottman (1975) examine time-series quasi experiments; while Tufte (1970 and 1974) considers statistical approaches. Some of these volumes are quite technical, while some are accessible to persons with no statistical training at all. Other readers and texts examine the general field of evaluation research. Among these are Rutman (1977), Rossi and Williams (1972), Nachmias (1979), and Rossi, Freeman, and Wright (1979). The first two are readers and may seem disjointed to persons unfamiliar with the field of evaluation research. The others are more comprehensive.

2. Among these are Cicirelli et al. (1969), Peltzman (1975), and Kershaw and Skidmore (1974).

3. Debates about the validity of Coleman's study of the impact of busing on white flight are a contemporary instance of controversy surrounding the methodology of scientifically based program evaluation. See Pettigrew and Green (1976) and Rossell, Ravitch, and Armor (1978).

4. Mosteller and Moynihan (1972:4).

5. The question that corresponds to the empty cell is: what causes organizations to adopt the implementation strategies that they do? This is a question that academic researchers who study organizations frequently ask. It is not ordinarily a question that evaluators consider. According to Elmore (1978), evaluation research should encompass this issue since implementation strategies affect outcomes. See also Pressman and Wildavsky (1973).

6. For an excellent text that gives detailed consideration to descriptive methodologies, see Rossi, Freeman, and Wright (1979).

7. This list is illustrative and not necessarily comprehensive. It represents a reordering of many of the topics listed in Part II of the Table of Contents in Stokey and Zeckhauser (1978). Curiously, Stokey and Zeckhauser omit evaluation research as a method of policy analysis. For other general treatments of the field of policy analysis, see Poister (1978), Fairley and Mosteller (1977), and Nagel and Neef (1979).

8. For an empirical example of this contention, see Gray, Conover, and Hennessy (1978).

LIST OF REFERENCES

Albritton, Robert B. "Cost-Benefits of Measles Eradication: Effects of a Federal Intervention." *Policy Analysis* 4 (1978): 1–22.

Bennett, Carl A., and Lumsdaine, Arthur A., eds. *Evaluation and Experiment.* New York: Academic Press, 1975.

Campbell, Donald T. "Reforms as Experiments." *Urban Affairs Quarterly* Vol. 7. (1971): 133–171.

Campbell, Donald T., and Stanley, Julian C. *Experimental and Quasi-Experimental Designs for Research.* Chicago: Rand McNally and Co., 1963.

Caporaso, James A., and Roos, Leslie L., Jr. *Quasi-Experimental Approaches: Testing Theory and Evaluating Policy.* Evanston, Ill.: Northwestern University Press, 1973.

Cicirelli, V. G., et al. *The Impact of Head Start: An Evaluation of the Effects of Head Start on Children's Cognitive and Affective Development* Vol. I. U.S. Dept. of Commerce, National Bureau of Standards, Institute for Applied Technology. Springfield, Va.: Clearinghouse, 1969.

Clark, Lawrence P. *Designs for Evaluating Social Programs.* Croton-on-Hudson, N.Y.: Policy Studies Associates, 1976.

Coleman, James S.; Campbell, Ernest Q.; Hobson, Carol J.; McPartland, James; Mood, Alexander M.; Weinfeld, Frederic D.; and York, Robert L. *Equality of Educational Opportunity.* U.S. Dept. of Health, Education and Welfare, Office of Education. Washington, D.C.: U.S. Government Printing Office, 1966.

Cook, Thomas D., and Campbell, Donald T. *Quasi-Experimentation: Design and Analysis Issues for Field Settings.* Chicago: Rand McNally and Co., 1979.

Elmore, Richard F. "Organizational Models of Social Program Implementation." *Public Policy* 26 (1978): 185–228.

Fairley, William B., and Mosteller, Frederick. *Statistics and Public Policy.* Reading, Mass.: Addison-Wesley Publishing Co., 1977.

Glass, Gene V.; Willson, Victor L.; and Gottman, John M. *Design and Analysis of Time-Series Experiments.* Boulder: Colorado Associated University Press, 1975.

Gray, Charles M.; Conover, C. Johnston; and Hennessy, Timothy M. "Cost Effectiveness of Residential Community Corrections: An Analytical Prototype." *Evaluation Quarterly* 2 (1978): 375–400.

Kershaw, David N., and Skidmore, Felicity. *The New Jersey Graduated Work Incentive Experiment.* Mathematica Policy Analysis Series, no. 1. Princeton, N.J.: Mathematica Inc., 1974.

Mosteller, Frederick, and Moynihan, Daniel P. "A Pathbreaking Report." Ch. 1 in Mosteller, Frederick, and Moynihan, Daniel P., eds. *On Equality of Educational Opportunity.* New York: Random House, 1972.

Nachmias, David. *Public Policy Evaluation: Approaches and Methods.* New York: St. Martins Press, 1979.

Nagel, Stuart S., and Neef, Marian. *Policy Analysis in Social Science Research.* Beverly Hills: Sage Publications, Inc., 1979.

National Institute of Education. *Compensatory Education Study: A Final Report to Congress from the National Institute of Education.* U.S. Dept. of Health, Education and Welfare, Office of Education. Washington, D.C.: U.S. Government Printing Office, 1978.

Peltzman, Sam. "The Effects of Automobile Safety Regulation," *Journal of Political Economy* 83 (1975): 677–725.

Pettigrew, Thomas F., and Green, Robert L. "School Desegregation in Large Cities: A Critique of the Coleman 'White Flight' Thesis." *Harvard Educational Review* 46 (1976): 1–53.

Poister, Theodore H. *Public Program Analysis: Applied Research Methods.* Baltimore, Md.: University Park Press, 1978.

Pressman, Jeffrey L., and Wildavsky, Aaron. *Implementation: How Great Expectations in Washington Are Dashed in Oakland*. Berkeley: University of California Press, 1973.

Riecken, Henry W., and Boruch, Robert F. *Social Experimentation: A Method for Planning and Evaluating Social Intervention*. New York: Academic Press, 1974.

Rossell, Christine H.; Ravitch, Diane; and Armor, David J. "Busing and 'White Flight'." *The Public Interest* 53 (1978):109–115.

Rossi, Peter H.; Freeman, Howard E.; and Wright, Sonia R. *Evaluation: A Systematic Approach*. Beverly Hills: Sage Publications, Inc., 1979.

Rossi, Peter H., and Williams, Walter. *Evaluating Social Programs: Theory, Practice and Politics*. New York: Seminar Press, 1972.

Rutman, Leonard, ed. *Evaluation Research Methods: A Basic Guide*. Beverly Hills: Sage Publications, Inc., 1977.

Stokey, Elizabeth, and Zeckhauser, Richard. *A Primer for Policy Analysis*. New York: W. W. Norton and Co., 1978.

Suchman, Edward Allen. *Evaluative Research: Principles and Practice in Public Service and Social Action Programs*. New York: Russell Sage Foundation, 1967.

Tufte, Edward R. *Data Analysis for Politics and Policy*. Englewood Cliffs, N.J.: Prentice-Hall, 1974.

——. *The Quantitative Analysis of Social Problems*. Reading, Mass.: Addison-Wesley Publishing Co., 1970.

Weiss, Carol H. *Evaluation Research: Methods for Assessing Program Effectiveness*. Englewood Cliffs, N.J.: Prentice-Hall, 1972.

Chapter 2

GOALS AND CRITERIA FOR EVALUATING PUBLIC PROGRAMS

IDENTIFYING GOALS AND CRITERIA

A fundamental purpose of evaluation is to ascertain the degree to which publicly funded programs have attained their goals. This chapter introduces a conceptual framework which evaluators can use to enumerate the entire set of goals or expected outcomes associated with particular programs. Investigators concerned with ascertaining the outcome of a public program must first identify the goals and criteria by which the program could be judged. Because most programs have multiple goals, such a determination may be quite difficult to make. Often there is no consensus surrounding the goals of a program, and frequently there is little agreement about the relative importance of each goal. For instance, some people believe that education should stress the "3 Rs," while others believe with equal fervor that education should foster personal development or interpersonal skills. Evaluators who examine the impact of schooling on just one of these goals are likely to be criticized by advocates of the other goals.

The multiple goals and criteria by which citizens judge public programs can also be mutually incompatible or inconsistent, so that successful attainment of one goal precludes attainment of another. One strategy to obtain equitable law enforcement is to allocate police so that the probability of being a victim is equal among all citizens (Thurow 1976). But since probable offenders are not equally distributed throughout the population, the probability of being caught will not be equal for all criminals. The police will also be unable to concentrate their resources on particular crimes or in particular neighborhoods where the probability of successfully apprehending criminals is relatively high. Equity for citizens is thus inconsistent with equity for criminals; attaining either type of

13

equity also reduces the effectiveness with which policemen can apprehend criminals. Even if everyone agreed on these goals, it would be impossible to attain all
of them at once.

Program goals may also be so poorly defined that their meaning is completely vacuous. One legislative goal of programs funded by the Farmers' Home
Administration is to "promote rural development," and one purpose of our
nation's federally funded urban housing programs is to assure that all Americans
have a "safe and suitable living environment." Such legislative vagueness frequently buys the political support of representatives who vote for the same
program for very diverse reasons. Housing programs have the allegiance of liberals
who want to house the poor adequately, of savings and loan bankers who want
to make mortgages a relatively more attractive investment, and of builders who
want to reap the benefits of an augmented demand for new housing. Actual
goals are thus often more specific than stated goals.

Legislative obfuscation demands that evaluators be politically sensitive to
the variety of interests that surround public policies. It is not, however, an
excuse for failing to evaluate public programs. This chapter outlines a general
structure for considering the entire range of goals and criteria which diverse
groups are likely to use in judging the merit of particular programs. The goals,
purposes, and criteria that others use to judge the merit of public programs must
also become the evaluator's standard. If one group wants government housing
subsidies to augment the consumption of housing, then evaluators should examine the influence of housing subsidies on the demand for housing. If another
group wants housing subsidies to eliminate substandard housing among the
nation's poor, then evaluators should scrutinize housing subsidies from this per-
spective as well. Evaluators should not arbitrarily neglect the values of one group
in favor of the values of another.[1]

ECONOMIC GROWTH

Figure 2.1 depicts an inventory of politically important goals. The inventory
lists the two most global criteria by which to judge public programs—the degree
to which they promote economic growth and the degree to which they are dis-
tributionally equitable.[2]

The goal of many programs is economic growth, and evaluators should
examine whether those programs actually bring about economic growth. Programs that stimulate economic growth either augment resource productivity or
allocate resources to their best use. The outline encompasses these elements of
economic growth respectively by the terms, "promote resource productivity,"
and "promote economic efficiency/remove market failures." Programs designed
to assure that productive resources are not idle employ otherwise unemployed or
underemployed land, labor, or capital. Programs designed to attain efficiency
are directed at altering or removing "market failures" that impede competition.

FIGURE 2.1

Goals and Criteria for Judging the Outcomes of Public Programs

I. Economic growth
    A. Promote resource productivity
    B. Promote economic efficiency/remove market failures
        1. Provide nonprivate goods
            a. Toll goods
            b. Common pool resources
            c. Public goods
        2. Provide information/reduce costs of poor information
        3. Spread risk
        4. Promote market entry

II. Distributional equity
    A. Adequacy
    B. Horizontal equity
    C. Vertical equity

III. Citizen preference
    A. Level of satisfaction
    B. Correspondence between citizen preferences and public policy

According to economic theory, stimulating market competition simultaneously allocates resources so they yield the highest possible return.

Achievement of one of these aspects of economic growth does not imply that the other will also be reached; in fact, they may at times be mutually inconsistent. Consider programs to promote development in rural areas or in central cities. One purpose of these programs is to ensure that potentially productive resources are not idle, and evaluators should investigate the success with which these programs employ idle resources. Manpower programs train unemployed workers for the ostensible purpose of increasing their employability. Rural development programs fund the construction of highways, hospitals, sewers, and waste-water treatment facilities to stimulate the use of rural land, labor, and capital that might otherwise go unused. Historically, the government's involvement in the construction of canals and, later, railroads was designed to promote the development of idle resources in the West.

Policies that employ idle resources do not necessarily foster the most productive use of these resources. Programs designed to use resources that would otherwise be idle or underemployed may actually impede efficiency by drawing resources from other more productive activities. Rural land is often idle because the labor and capital needed to develop that land are being used in more productive ways. Resources used to train unemployed workers may also be more productively used by, for instance, retraining space scientists and astronomers.

Employing idle resources may not be efficient, but it is undeniably a major purpose of many federal programs. Measuring the degree to which these programs actually reduce the amount of unemployed resources is consequently an appropriate component of evaluation research. This task requires causal inference. To examine whether manpower training reduced unemployment necessitates a causal determination: does training cause employment? The answer is not obvious, because trainees might have found employment even without the publicly funded program. To the degree that employment could occur without the program, the more difficult it becomes to credit the program with being the cause of employment. If rural population and employment growth (or stability) can occur even without public support, it is incorrect to credit the public program with causal impact.

Another major purpose of many publicly funded programs is to promote economic efficiency by encouraging market competition and removing market "failures." The rationale for this goal originates in conventional economic theory, which states that, in a competitive economy, rational consumers and producers will voluntarily agree only to those exchanges that make all parties involved in the exchange "better off" and none "worse off." When the market is not competitive, the public sector may be called upon to eliminate the obstacles to competition. Because there are many instances in which the market fails to be competitive, a variety of public programs are justified. The items listed in Figure 2.1 under the general topic "promoting efficiency" indicate that the notion of efficiency incorporates many different goals. Each goal corresponds to an element of inefficiency in private markets.

In order to understand why public programs can promote economic efficiency, we must first examine the sources of market failures. One of the most important reasons for market inefficiency is the existence of goods and services that are not private. Markets are efficient only when the goods and services exchanged are private. Private goods have two characteristics. First, with regard to their consumption, one person's use of the good precludes its use by another. If A consumes a loaf of bread, B cannot also consume it; if A catches fish from the ocean, B cannot simultaneously capture the same fish. Second, private goods have unique properties with regard to their production. When goods are private, it is possible to exclude persons who have not paid for the good from its use. People cannot consume a loaf of bread for which they have not paid, nor can they attend a theater without first paying. In these instances, exclusion is possible. These two characteristics of purely private goods are called "subtractibility of consumption" and "exclusion in production."

Figure 2.1 lists three types of nonprivate goods.[3] Toll goods are not private because consumption is not subtractible. A person's use of a telephone line, toll road, library, or movie at a particular time does not subtract from someone else's concurrent use of that good. Unlike hamburgers, one person's consumption of a "toll good" does not prevent another from simultaneously enjoying the same good. Like hamburgers, the good can be consumed only by those who pay; exclusion is possible. The fact that many people can concurrently consume toll goods differentiates them from private goods and exposes them to inefficiencies of congestion. Too many people at once may drive on the toll road, use the telephone service, go to the library, or attend a movie. When toll roads become crowded, travel costs increase with no commensurate increase in benefits. Attending a crowded movie reduces one's enjoyment with no reduction in cost. Congestion makes everyone "worse off," whereas economic theory posits that smoothly functioning markets make people "better off."

The private sector responds to most congestion costs by adjusting prices accordingly. Telephone companies charge lower rates for party lines since party lines get congested. To prevent congestion, theaters raise prices when they anticipate a crowd. The public sector adopts other responses to congestion. Restricting certain highway lanes to buses and carpools is a common response to rush-hour congestion. Controlling municipal growth is a response to congested water and sewer facilities. The public sector also regulates the conditions under which the private sector provides toll goods. The public sector may even induce congestion by failing to charge for the use of swimming pools, parks, and other services. Policies like these affect both congestion and the efficiency with which resources are used. Evaluators should therefore examine how municipal growth controls affect both the burden on water and sewer facilities and the efficiency with which they are used. Evaluators should also estimate the impact of user fees on both congestion and efficiency.[4]

Other public policies are designed to make the use of "common pool resources" more efficient. Although the consumption of these goods is subtractible, exclusion is not possible. When people fish from a fishery, extract oil from an oil pool, pump water from a ground water basin, or let their cattle graze on the "commons," the portion of the common resource that they use is no longer available to others. Two persons cannot catch the same fish, extract the same oil, pump the same water, or graze the same grass; but two persons can use two boats to fish from the same fishery, build their own oil rigs over the same oil pool, construct their own pumps over the same ground water basin, and let their cattle graze on the same commons. As long as the costs of extracting additional "common pool resources" are less than the value of the resources extracted, people will continue to extract fish, oil, water, and grass from the "commons." No individual has any voluntary incentive to conserve the "commons," because others will benefit while he alone bears the cost. In the long run, people will exhaust common pool resources.[5] When these resources are depleted, everyone will be "worse off"; there will be no fish, oil, water, or grazing lands.[6] With common pool resources, the pursuit by each individual of his short-term economic interests harms everyone in the long run.

There are two conventional ways to make the use of common pool resources more efficient. One is to make exclusion technologically feasible at reasonable cost. When exclusion becomes economically feasible, the rationale for public involvement disappears because the use of devices to exclude people transforms a common pool resource into a private good. Fences, for example, turned common grazing lands into private property. Individual owners of grazing lands will not permit their cattle to overgraze. Private owners thus use common pool resources efficiently.

When exclusion is either technologically impossible or economically infeasible, we resort to public law. Public laws control access to common pool resources by defining artificial "property rights" which allow legitimate access to some and not to others. Other policies regulate the prices that can be charged for goods extracted from the commons (e.g., oil and water). Public laws also regulate the quantity of resources that can be extracted (e.g., limits on the size of tuna and salmon catches). One purpose of these policies is to remove the incentive that individual "extractors" have to exhaust the commons. Evaluators should therefore examine the impact of these laws on the efficiency with which common pool resources are used.

Market efficiency is also a primary purpose of policies that affect the production and consumption of so-called "public" goods.[7] In the case of public goods, exclusion is infeasible and consumption is not subtractible. Clean air is a public good. One person's consumption of clean air does not preclude others from concurrently enjoying the same air. Also, a producer of clean air cannot exclude anyone from consuming it, even if the person does not pay. Protection from crime is also a public good. Protection provided to one person does not prevent another from availing himself of the same protection; both will be protected even if one fails to pay. A public good is like a toll good because its consumption is not subtractible; two individuals can concurrently consume the same good. Public goods, like toll goods, are also subject to congestion. Too many concurrent users of clean air or protection from crime reduce the benefits that accrue to each with no commensurate reduction in costs. Public goods also resemble common pool resources because it is impossible to prevent nonpayers from receiving benefits. When exclusion is impossible, the private market will fail to produce even a single good.

The failure of voluntary decisions by individual consumers and producers to provide public goods is understandable since no individual retains exclusive rights to the benefits produced as a result of his actions. Because private voluntary decisions fail to produce public goods, government frequently intercedes to produce these goods itself. In the U.S., the federal and state governments produce many public goods, from protection from crime and fraud to national defense, public health, fire protection, and weather forecasts. Other public goods, such as clean air, are actually produced by the private sector, but their production is required by the government as a condition of doing business.

No matter how public goods are produced, their purpose is the same—to remove a "market failure" by ensuring that consumers can purchase as much (or as little) of the public good as they wish at the given price. Evaluators should therefore determine if public programs actually produce public goods. Investigators should study the impact of environmental regulations on air and water quality as well as the influence of police on protection from crime. Evaluators can also compare the efficacy of alternative policies and alternative institutional arrangements in producing public goods. Evaluators have examined the relative efficiency of public and private provision of fire protection (Ahlbrandt 1973).

Investigators have also studied the public provision of police protection by measuring the impact of jurisdictional size on efficiency (Ostrom et al. 1973).

Classifying nonprivate goods into toll goods, common pool resources, and public goods suggests that a broad range of policies is directed at their allocation. Each of these policies has economic efficiency as an important goal that evaluators should not ignore.

Figure 2.1 indicates that market efficiency also requires perfect information about the price and quality of goods and services. Investments in efficient markets must also be riskless, and producers must be able to enter efficient markets freely.[8] The purpose of numerous government programs is to foster market efficiency by eliminating these additional sources of market failure.

Consider the need for perfect information. Many programs are designed to provide information directly, while other programs are designed to decrease the costs of imperfect information. Regulations requiring accurate labeling of package contents as well as efforts by the Department of Agriculture to provide the latest data on crops to farmers exemplify the direct provision of information. Public education provides information directly; it should also enhance the ability of consumers to assimilate and understand information. The success with which programs such as these actually produce informed consumers should therefore be a concern for evaluators. Investigators could estimate the impact of labeling the nutritional content of food on consumer information. Researchers could also study the effect of information on consumption and production behavior.

Information is sometimes too technical for the average consumer to comprehend. Consequently, many programs are devised to mitigate the impact of imperfect knowledge on purchases. Agencies of the government license doctors, lawyers, beauticians, and cabdrivers to guarantee that they meet some minimum standards. Health and safety standards also assure minimum quality levels for many products, including the toys we buy, the food we eat, the drugs we ingest, the places we work, the homes in which we live, and the cars we drive. Both licensing and standards should avert the consequences of poor information by diminishing accidents, sickness, and death.[9]

Efficient markets also necessitate the absence of risk. Risk makes individuals reluctant to undertake a project or investment when potential losses are extremely high relative to the individual's own income or assets. Extremely risky investments will be foregone in favor of less productive but more secure investments. Since it is impossible to eliminate risk, many government programs try to equalize risk by forcing many people to share it. When a government undertakes an investment or makes or underwrites a loan, each person within the polity bears only a small share of risk. Risk-sharing is one rationale for the direct loan and loan guarantee programs sponsored by agencies such as the Department of Housing and Urban Development, the Small Business Administration, and the Farmers' Home Administration. Evaluators should therefore examine whether these programs stimulate investments in risky projects that would not otherwise have been undertaken.

Efficient markets also minimize restrictions on exit or entry. Restricting entry is inefficient because it prevents resources from attaining their most productive use. Racial discrimination in housing markets prevents blacks from making optimal housing choices. Discrimination in the workplace based on race or sex prevents both employees and employers from making optimal occupational choices. Public programs to circumvent discriminatory practices therefore have an efficiency rationale, and their success can be evaluated accordingly.

Many different goals can thus be subsumed under a single general goal—economic growth. Economic growth has many elements, however, and some of these elements can be mutually inconsistent. Many programs also have unintended effects that may or may not be consistent with their intended effects. Requiring the installation of seat belts on cars has numerous goals. Underlying this policy is the assumption that technological information regarding automobile safety is too complex for the average consumer to comprehend. Seat belts are one means to ensure that autos will be minimally safe. Another goal of the seat belts policy is to reduce the number of traffic accidents, which waste resources by causing unnecessary sickness and death.

Seat belts can also be justified as a means by which to produce a public good—automobile safety. Voluntary decisions by individuals will produce "too little" automobile safety. Seat belt legislation should produce the amount of safety that consumers would demand if safety were a private good. These three purposes suggest three different, but compatible, criteria that an evaluator could use to examine the effectiveness of seat belt legislation. Seat belts should reduce traffic accidents, reduce illness and death due to traffic accidents, and produce these results at a price commensurate with the benefit gained.

Seat belt legislation may also have unintended effects that are inconsistent with some of these criteria. Because the installation of seat belts reduces the risk that the driver and passengers incur, drivers might increase the carelessness with which they drive. Seat belts could thus increase the number of accidents involving pedestrians.[10]

This consideration of seat belts illustrates how evaluators can use the inventory in Figure 2.1 to identify the intended as well as the unintended effects that public programs can have. Any comprehensive evaluation must recognize that most programs have multiple purposes, which may not be internally consistent. Programs also have unintended consequences which can complement as well as contravene any of the intended effects.

DISTRIBUTIONAL CRITERIA

We have considered so far only effects whose rationale is economic growth. The task of evaluation in this regard is primarily one of causal research. When goals stem from economic growth, evaluators must examine whether a particular program caused idle resources to become productive or whether a particular program caused resources to be more productively used. The issue of causality is important. If an observed outcome would have occurred even in the absence of the program, the outcome cannot causally be attributed to the program.

Questions about growth do not span the entire range of issues that evaluators frequently address, because they ignore the distributional aspects of public programs. Many public programs are designed primarily to redistribute income from one sector of society to another, while other programs unintentionally or secondarily redistribute income. Programs designed to redistribute income may also either encourage or inhibit economic growth. Regardless of the impact of income redistribution on economic growth, programs intended to transfer monies from the "better off" sector of society to those who have less constitute a significant portion of public budgets. Evaluators must therefore be cognizant of the major criteria by which the distributional properties of public programs can be analyzed.[11]

One of the most important criteria for judging many programs is the adequacy of their benefit levels. Even though there are no objective measures of adequacy upon which everyone would agree, adequacy is still important. Sometimes there is relative consensus; many people agree, for example, that "adequate" housing for low- and moderate-income families should conform to the Census Bureau's definition of "standard" housing. In contrast, there is no consensus regarding an "adequate" level of health care. Even when there is little agreement, concerned people wish to know what the average level of benefits from public programs actually are. Comprehensive evaluations of public programs should therefore determine the cash value of benefits accruing to the average recipient.

The degree to which programs treat all eligible beneficiaries equally is another important distributional issue. Programs that fail to reach all who are eligible for its benefits and programs that fail to treat all eligibles equally are said to be horizontally inequitable. Programs for low- and moderate-income housing are horizontally inequitable because they reach only a small proportion of those who are eligible. Welfare payments are also horizontally inequitable because two eligible families with precisely the same needs living in different states receive vastly different cash benefits. Even the courts have been concerned with horizontal equity. The U.S. District Court in the decision of *Hobson* v. *Hansen* ordered the District of Columbia public schools to spend the same amount of money on each student, no matter what school the student attended.[12]

Vertical equity is another criterion by which transfer programs can be evaluated. Programs that distribute benefits to people not in the specified target group are said to be vertically inequitable. The Department of Health, Education and Welfare (HEW) attempted to eliminate vertical inequity by ordering state and local public assistance agencies to purge all persons who were legally ineligible for benefits from the welfare rolls. Legal instances of vertical inequity are considerably more common. Persons who deliver services are ineligible beneficiaries, yet they frequently benefit. Federal programs concomitantly house low- and moderate-income families and help the housing industry. Medicaid provides substantial benefits to the health care industry as well as to the poor. Children from upper middle-class families obtain assistance from programs designed to help students from middle-income and low-income families finance their college education.[13] These unintended beneficiaries are receiving legal benefits. The structure and rules by which transfers are made frequently encompass more beneficiaries than the primary target group. Okun (1975) invites us to regard transfers like these as "leaky buckets." These leaks are often a necessary cost of political support.

Criteria for evaluating transfer programs are also useful for describing programs whose primary purpose is to stimulate some aspect of economic growth. Consider a national program to train workers who have been unemployed for a significant length of time. One of the most important purposes of such a program is to foster economic growth by reemploying resources that would otherwise be idle. Accordingly, suppose that an evaluator finds that the program has reached 10% of all formerly unemployed persons. After some sort of job training, suppose that each of the people in this 10% group steps into a reasonably well-paying job, and that none of them would have obtained his position without the training program.

This example provides a realistic portrayal of programs that successfully foster economic growth but have inequitable distributional effects. While the benefits received by each of the trainees were "adequate," the distribution of benefits was horizontally inequitable. Of the millions of persons who were eligible, only 10% actually received any benefits. Although there are additional criteria by which to evaluate a manpower training program, the example suggests that programs designed to bring about economic growth can be judged in distributional terms as well.

Distributional programs also affect economic growth.[14] Programs to aid the poor are typically evaluated in terms of the adequacy of their benefits, the degree to which they treat all eligibles equally, and the degree to which the nonpoor benefit. But programs to help the poor also reduce the incentive to work, and thereby retard the productivity of resources. Unemployment compensation raises the wages that an employer must pay in order to induce idle labor to return to work. Poor people can frequently amass more benefits from housing, food, welfare, and medical programs than they could by working at the low-paid jobs for which they qualify. Programs designed to transfer income can thus be judged according to both distributional and economic criteria.

Citizen satisfaction is also a relevant criterion by which evaluators can judge programs. In a democracy, the preferences of citizens should be an important determinant of policy and program outcomes. There should be some correspondence between citizens' desires and the programs that governments undertake. Because the electoral process alone is insufficient to guarantee this outcome, programs that successfully promote economic growth and have desirable distributional impacts may simultaneously produce irate citizens. Both evaluators and politicians must therefore take citizen satisfaction into account before they judge the overall merit of a particular program.[15]

TWO ILLUSTRATIONS OF THE GOALS
AND CRITERIA INVENTORY

The inventory of goals and criteria presented in this chapter should prevent evaluators from unwittingly overlooking important aspects of programs they investigate. Consistent with the purposes of this text, the list ignores issues of process and presents outcome measures alone. One set of outcome measures depicts the dimensions of economic growth and indicates that even noneconomic programs may affect economic growth. Evaluating the impact of programs on economic growth is largely a task for causal research. Causal research can also indicate whether a program fostered one aspect of economic growth while impeding another. Citizen satisfaction and distributional effects are also important. Investigations based on these criteria alone ordinarily require only descriptive methods of research. Most often, evaluators should use economic as well as distributional criteria, even though not every goal and criterion in the inventory is equally relevant. Some elements of the inventory will sometimes be inapplicable or unimportant. The relevance of each element therefore depends on the program the inventory is applied to.

To illustrate how the entire inventory can be applied to a particular program, consider the National High Blood Pressure Education Program (NHBPEP). Sponsored by the Department of Health, Education and Welfare, this program provides information and education to adults regarding the detection and consequences of high blood pressure. Figure 2.2 outlines the goals and criteria an investigator could use to evaluate the success of this program. Unlike many evaluations, the example centers on measures of outcome rather than "workload." Nowhere in the inventory of outcome measures are there indicators of process like "number of movies about hypertension shown" and "number of brochures mailed."

One purpose of the NHBPEP is to promote resource productivity by reducing the time lost from work due to illnesses associated with high blood pressure. The NHBPEP also has efficiency goals. Improving health by reducing hypertension provides a common pool resource because health insurance makes it impossible to exclude the healthy from bearing the costs of hypertension. Reducing hypertension is not a public good or a toll good because consumption is subtractible. One person's relief from hypertension cannot simultaneously be captured by another. Another efficiency goal of the NHBPEP is to provide information. The success of the NHBPEP can also be judged according to distributional criteria. The adequacy of the information that it provides is subsumed by the efficiency goal of supplying information. Horizontal and vertical equity are important for a variety of reasons. Defining these terms requires identifying the target groups

FIGURE 2.2

Outcome Measures: National High Blood Pressure Education Program

Goals and Criteria	Specific Indicator	Explanation
I. Economic Growth		
A. Promote resource productivity	Hours and income lost from work due to sicknesses attributable to hypertension	One purpose of the program is to cause reductions in these losses. This indicator may be very difficult to measure.
B. Promote economic efficiency		
1. Provide nonmarket goods		
a. Toll goods	Not relevant	
b. Common pool resources	Number of sicknesses and deaths due to hypertension; amount that high blood pressure is reduced; medical costs of sicknesses attributable to hypertension	Medical insurance makes sickness due to hypertension a common pool resource. In the case of hypertension, insurance rates of the healthy go up as more persons become ill. Persons have too small an incentive to keep well because they bear all of the costs of prevention; should they get sick, insurance mechanisms spread risk so that the sick do not bear the full cost of their illness. The hypertension program also corrects a market failure attributable to another government policy—support of health insurance.
c. Public goods	Not relevant	
2. Provide information/ reduce costs of poor information	Level of information that hypertensives have regarding detection and treatment of hypertension	The program should make information levels increase.
3. Spread risk	Not relevant	
4. Promote market entry	Not relevant	

FIGURE 2.2 (continued)

Goals and Criteria	Specific Indicator	Explanation
II. Distributional characteristics		
A. Adequacy	Redundant—see under providing information	
B. Horizontal equity	Number (and characteristics) of hypertensives with no information and with misinformation regarding hypertension; also, the number of hypertensives not reached by the program.	
C. Vertical equity	Number of physician visits by hypertensives caused by program	Note that this particular vertical inequity may in fact be desirable.
	Number of nonhypertensives reached by the program	Nonhypertensives are not in the target group.
III. Citizen satisfaction	Percent of citizens who rank spending for the prevention/detection of hypertension above other spending alternatives	Evaluators should be concerned with the correspondence between citizen preferences and public policy.

of the NHBPEP. Persons with hypertension are the most likely targets. Considerations of horizontal equity require that black and white hypertensives be equally well-informed. Similar concerns dictate that the program reach as many hypertensives as possible.

The indicators in Figure 2.2 are not fully operational. The example does not give precise directions for measuring and gathering data on the "number of sicknesses and deaths due to hypertension." Yet measurement issues are critically important, and the measurement procedures that evaluators use should capture the meaning of the corresponding indicator as accurately as possible. "Number of complaints received" is rarely an adequate measure of citizen satisfaction. Nor is the number of brochures read and TV spots viewed an adequate measure of the level of information regarding hypertension that citizens actually have.

Accurate measurement is also costly. Using "citizen complaints" to measure satisfaction is much less expensive than a scientific survey of citizens' opinions. It is also simpler to count brochures and TV spots than to measure the amount of information that people actually assimilate. Evaluators must weigh the advantages against the costs of accuracy. High costs can also force evaluators to reduce the number of indicators they use to evaluate a program. Citizen satisfaction is a relevant but tangential indicator of outcome in many program areas. The costliness of accurate measurement may make it necessary to delete the indicator entirely or to substitute less costly indicators. Evaluators should reserve the most costly procedures to measure the most important outcomes.

The high blood pressure program has national scope. The list of criteria in Figure 2.1 can also be used to develop outcome measures for evaluating the success of locally administered programs. The Neighborhood Youth Corps (NYC) is a federally funded but locally administered employment program. In one community, the program provides manual labor for underprivileged youths in the community's parks. Figure 2.3 lists the goals and criteria against which an evaluator might judge the success of the community's NYC program.

The list reflects multiple goals. Some are probably more important than others, and resources should be concentrated on measuring the most important. A major purpose of NYC is to reduce unemployment among underprivileged youths in the community. The program should not merely provide employment for youths who would be employed even without the program; NYC should also improve future job prospects. This goal may be secondary, and measuring it could critically delay the results of an evaluation. Most investigators would probably decide to omit this goal from an evaluation of NYC. Other goals of NYC are to improve the community's parks and to reduce juvenile delinquency. In each of these instances, the investigator must rely on causal research to determine how the program affected the outcome measure. By contrast, descriptive tools are appropriate for assessing the distributional aspects of NYC.

Despite their programmatic differences, these illustrations share a common theme. Measures like "Number of clients served," "Number of TV spots shown," and "Number of youths enrolled" are measures of workload and reflect program

FIGURE 2.3

Outcome Measures: Neighborhood Youth Corps Program[16]

Goals and Criteria	Specific Indicator	Explanation
I. Economic Growth		
A. Promote resource productivity	Unemployment rate of under-privileged youths	One purpose of the program is to employ underprivileged youths.
	Future employment and wages	Another purpose of the program is to increase future employability.
B. Promote economic efficiency		
1. Provide non-market goods		
a. Toll goods	Not relevant	
b. Common pool resources	Improvement in park appearance, services	Youths work in the parks, which are a common pool resource.
c. Public goods	Incidence of juvenile delinquency among underprivileged youth	NYC program should reduce crime, a public "good."
2. Provide information/reduce costs of poor information	Not relevant	
3. Spread risk	Not relevant	
4. Promote market entry	Not relevant	
II. Distributional Characteristics		
A. Adequacy	Not relevant	
B. Horizontal equity	Number of eligible youths not reached by the program	
C. Vertical equity	Salaries of the NYC staff members	
	Number of ineligible youths reached by the program	
III. Citizen satisfaction	Percent of citizens who rank spending for NYC above other spending alternatives	

inputs rather than outputs. In the case of the high blood pressure program, providing information is not useful unless it induces people to alter their medical behavior. Similarly, enrolling as many youths as possible is not the purpose of NYC unless those youths would otherwise be unemployed. Investigators should thus refrain from using workload measures to gauge program impact.

FOOTNOTES

1. The process of specifying the goals of public programs is even more complicated than the following pages indicate. For a comprehensive discussion of those complications, see Ostrom (1979).

2. While many persons believe that public funds should not be used for these purposes, it is impossible to ignore the fact that many programs actually do have these purposes. This text regards goals as given and does not question their legitimacy.

3. These terms and definitions of nonprivate goods in Figure 2.1 come from Ostrom and Ostrom (1977). For a similar discussion of public sector purposes, see Steiner (1977: 27-70).

4. We consider the distributional aspects of public policies below.

5. This will happen only if cheaper substitutes do not develop. We are particularly unlikely to develop cheap substitutes for water.

6. This scenario inspired Garrett Hardin's phrase, "The Tragedy of the Commons" (Hardin 1968).

7. There are few purely public goods. Most are more aptly termed "quasi-public goods," but the shorter term is more convenient.

8. According to microeconomic theory, the decision to invest reflects a person's willingness to forego present consumption while gaining future benefits. In theory, this decision is riskless. Although the requisite for risk-free investment could be subsumed under the need for perfect information, we discuss it separately because so many policies are designed to reduce or spread risk.

9. Licensing and standards can also have undesirable effects by raising prices and constricting the range of consumer choice, illustrating again how programs designed to foster one goal may simultaneously impede the attainment of others. In contrast, reducing accidents, sickness, and death by licensing and standards may be compatible with the goal of promoting resource productivity.

10. Peltzman (1975) produced empirical evidence to support this contention.

11. Assessing the degree to which particular programs are consistent with distributional criteria usually requires techniques of descriptive research. Because this text centers on causal research, it cites the economic effects of public programs as illustrative concerns for evaluators. The text therefore tends to neglect distributional issues, but this omission is methodological and not ideological. Distributional criteria for evaluating income transfer programs are more completely discussed in Marmor (1971), Weisbrod (1977), Aaron (1973), and Brown (1978).

12. *Hobson* v. *Hansen*, 269 F. Supp. 401 (D.D.C. 1967).

13. See Hansen and Lampman (1977).

14. See Okun (1975) for a detailed discussion.

15. Citizen satisfaction is a particularly important outcome measure in respect to public services that nearly everyone consumes. These services include defense, police, education, water supply, and refuse collection and disposal.

16. I am indebted to John O'Connell for this example.

LIST OF REFERENCES

Aaron, Henry J. *Why Is Welfare So Hard to Reform?* (Washington, D.C.: The Brookings, Institution, 1973).

Ahlbrandt, Rogers, Jr. "Efficiency in the Provision of Fire Services." *Public Choice* 16 (1973):1-15.

Albritton, Robert B. "Cost-Benefits of Measles Eradication: Effects of a Federal Intervention," *Policy Analysis* 4 (1978):1-22.

Brown, Lawrence D. "The Scope and Limits of Equality as a Normative Guide to Federal Health Care Policy." *Public Policy* 26 (1978):481-532.

Hansen, W. Lee, and Lampman, Robert J. "Basic Opportunity Grants for Higher Education: Good Intentions and Mixed Results." Ch. 19 in Haveman, Robert H., and Margolis, Julius. *Public Expenditures and Policy Analysis.* 2d ed. Chicago: Rand McNally and Co., 1977.

Hardin, Garrett. "The Tragedy of the Commons." *Science* 162 (1968):1243-1248.

Marmor, Theodore. "On Comparing Income Maintenance Alternatives," *American Political Science Review* 65 (1971):83-96.

Okun, Arthur M. *Equality and Efficiency, The Big Tradeoff.* Washington, D.C.: The Brookings Institution, 1975.

Ostrom, Elinor. "Purposes, Performance Measurement, and Policing." Paper read at TIMS/ORSA Meeting, May 1979, New Orleans, La.

Ostrom, Elinor; Baugh, William H.; Guarasci, Richard; Parks, Roger B.; and Whitaker, Gordon P. *Community Organization and the Provision of Police Services.* Beverly Hills: Sage Publications, Inc., 1973.

Ostrom, Vincent, and Ostrom, Elinor. "Public Goods and Public Choices." In *Alternatives for Delivering Public Services: Toward Improved Performance*, edited by E. S. Savas, pp. 7-49. Boulder, Col.: Westview Press, 1977.

Peltzman, Sam. "The Effects of Automobile Safety Regulation." *Journal of Political Economy* 83 (1975):677-725.

Steiner, Peter O. "The Public Sector and the Public Interest." Ch. 1 in Haveman, Robert H., and Margolis, Julius. *Public Expenditures and Policy Analysis.* 2d ed. Chicago: Rand McNally and Co., 1977.

Thurow, Lester C. "Equity versus Efficiency in Law Enforcement." Ch. 8 in Amacher, Ryan C.; Tollison, Robert D.; and Willett, Thomas D. *The Economic Approach to Public Policy.* Ithaca: Cornell University Press, 1976.

Weisbrod, Burton A. "Collective Action and the Distribution of Income: A Conceptual Approach." Ch. 4 in Haveman, Robert H., and Margolis, Julius. *Public Expenditures and Policy Analysis.* 2d ed. Chicago: Rand McNally and Co., 1977.

Chapter 3

THE PRINCIPLES OF CAUSAL INFERENCE

REQUISITES OF CAUSAL INFERENCE

Although evaluation research encompasses both causal and descriptive elements, inferences regarding the impact of a program are always causal. Causal inference requires the investigator to assess how much impact an influencing or independent variable (X) has on a dependent variable (Y). The independent variable is a hypothetical cause, while the dependent variable is the effect. In evaluation research, the cause is a set of program, policy, or management options among which managers can choose. The effect is a set of outcome measures that the investigator can derive according to the inventory developed in the last chapter. To assess whether a manpower training program increases the expected earnings of its trainees requires causal research. The independent variable or causal agent is the manpower training program (X); the outcome measure or dependent variable is earnings (Y).[1] Causal research is also required to determine whether school desegregation (X) causes white flight (Y). Arguments regarding the probable impact of national health insurance (X) on the price of medical care (Y) entail causal questions. Recent evidence reporting the efficacy of monies authorized by Title I of the Elementary and Secondary Education Act (ESEA) of 1965 (X) in raising the achievement scores (Y) of educationally disadvantaged students is based on causal research.

The prevalence of causal issues like these challenges our ability to answer critical questions of public policy. The challenge arises both from the principles and from the practice of causal inference. In this chapter, we consider the principles essential for making valid causal inferences, while the following chapter outlines some practical considerations that investigators must address before implementing the principles. Together, these two chapters indicate why evaluators so often find it difficult to accurately measure the impact of public programs. At the same time, each chapter develops a general framework that evaluators can use to anticipate and avert some of these difficulties.

The general framework within which program evaluation can be understood relies on the concept of causality. From an empirical point of view, causality entails three conditions.[2] First, changes in the program (independent variable) must correspond or covary with changes in the outcome measure (dependent variable). Second, change in the independent variable must precede change in the dependent variable. Finally, the analyst must rule out alternative explanations of changes in the outcome measure; he must attribute change in the dependent variable to change in the program itself instead of to change in some other variable. Each of these conditions must be empirically verified before deciding that X causes Y.

Consider the requirement that X, the independent or causal variable, must covary with Y, the dependent or effect variables. When both X and Y change concomitantly, they are said to covary. Because the idea of causation means that change in X brings about change in Y, it follows that both X and Y must change. Sometimes an independent variable, X, changes, but Y, the dependent variable, does not. An investigator might observe that the pump price of gasoline (X) increases during a time period, but that gasoline consumption (Y) remains unchanged during the same period. The investigator could not argue that the observed change in X actually changed Y, because Y did not in fact change. Instead, the investigator can conclude that the observed change in X did not bring about a change in Y.[3]

When Y changes but X does not, the investigator can make no causal inference at all. Invariance in X makes it impossible to determine if a change in X would in fact affect Y. One cannot attribute an observed reduction in the number of loan delinquencies (Y) among college students who received Basic Equal Opportunity Grants to a change in federal lending policy (X) if in fact federal lending policy had not truly changed.[4]

The second requirement for valid causal inference is evidence that X precedes Y. When change in X causes change in Y, the change in X must occur before the change in Y. If employment in a municipality improves before an infusion of federal Comprehensive Employment and Training Act (CETA) funds, it would be difficult to credit the improvement to CETA because an effect cannot antedate its cause.[5]

The final requirement for valid causal inference is the most difficult to satisfy. The investigator must show that no third variable, Z, can account for the observed association of X and Y. Covariation is thus said to be a necessary but not a sufficient condition for valid causal inference. In other words, covariation must be present if we are to claim that a causal relationship exists, but its presence does not in and of itself warrant the claim that causality exists. To claim that an observed decrease in municipal crime rates (Y) was caused by an observed increase in the number of patrolmen on duty (X) requires more than concomitant change as evidence. A critic could argue that a reduction in the proportion of young men (Z) rather than the larger force (X) accounts for the lower crime rate (Y).

Observers might also detect covariation between the number of days that a certain group of adults were ill (Y) and the type of medical care (X) they received. If persons who visit physicians have less illness than persons who receive care from paraprofessionals, then X and Y can be said to covary. But covariation alone provides insufficient evidence to justify concluding that physicians provide superior care. People who use them tend to be wealthier than those who rely on paraprofessionals, and wealthy people have less illness. Their income (Z) rather than the type of care they receive, accounts for their superior health.

The association between education and earnings could also depend on a third variable, family background. Employees with college degrees often have higher earnings than those without, but covariation does not prove that graduating from college causes earnings to increasse. College graduates come from relatively wealthy families, and people from upper class families may have higher earnings. Family background and not college graduation could account for the higher earnings of college graduates. The abundance of examples like these makes it necessary for investigators to avoid confusing covariation with causal inference.

SPURIOUS AND CONFOUNDING VARIABLES

Two types of variables account for observed covariation between X and Y: spurious and confounding. In the simplest case of three variables, any variable that affects both X and Y and entirely explains their covariation is said to be spurious. A variable that jointly influences both X and Y but fails to account entirely for their covariation is said to be confounding. Unless the investigator can eliminate the impact of spurious and confounding variables, he risks the threat of invalid causal inference. An undetected spurious variable, depicted by variable Z in Figure 3.1(a), is particularly troublesome because its presence leads an investigator to erroneously conclude that X has a direct effect on Y when in fact it has no impact at all. The presence of undetected confounding variables, represented by the variable Z in Figure 3(b), threatens accurate causal inference by producing overestimates or underestimates of the impact of X on Y.

FIGURE 3.1
Spurious and Confounding Variables

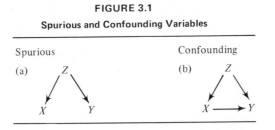

Consider first how an investigator might mistakenly conclude that X affects Y when in fact X has no effect on Y at all. (See Figure 3.2.) To determine accu-

FIGURE 3.2

Z as Spurious Variable

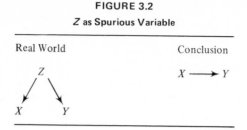

rately whether X influences Y, the investigator must be certain that no source of spurious association between X and Y is present. In studying the effects of a manpower training program on the earnings of participants, suppose an investigator has already ascertained that the average earnings of program participants increased more than those of nonparticipants and that the increase occurred after the job training program and not before. Even though the investigation has met the first two requisites for valid causal inference, it is still possible that a third variable affects both program participation (X) and earnings (Y). Those who choose to participate in manpower training programs are frequently more motivated than those who do not participate, and higher motivation alone can often account for higher earnings. Level of motivation is possibly a spurious variable whose influence must be removed to secure valid causal inference.[6] (See Figure 3.3.)

FIGURE 3.3

Motivation as Spurious Variable

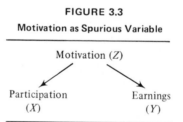

To test whether motivation is actually spurious requires a conceptual experiment. If motivation is spurious, variation in Z (motivation) causes variations in both X (program participation) and Y (earnings). (See Figure 3.1(a).) All of the covariation between X and Y is thus attributable to their joint dependence on Z. When Z is confounding, variation in Z also brings about covariation between X and Y. But only when Z is confounding is there a direct causal arrow from X to Y, as in Figure 3.1(b). The arrow means that variation in X alone is sufficient to bring about variation in Y, even when Z is invariant. This difference between the models in Figure 3.1(a) and 3.1(b) defines the test for spuriousness. When Z is spurious, variations in Z account for variation in both X and Y. Consequently, removing variation in a spurious (Z) variable also eliminates the covariation of X and Y. When Z is confounding, variation in Z makes X and Y covary, but variation in X alone will also affect the value of Y. Eliminating the variation in a confounding (Z) variable will consequently fail to make the covariation between X and Y disappear.

To determine if motivation is spurious, the investigator must compare the earnings of participants and nonparticipants who share the same level of motivation. If the earnings of identically motivated participants and nonparticipants are equal, then X and Y do not covary when Z is invariant. The investigator can conclude that Z is spurious and that the training program failed to influence earnings.

Third variables are not always spurious or confounding. Figure 3.4 reveals that third variables can impinge on X or Y even when they are not spurious or confounding. Whenever Z intervenes between X and Y, it is neither spurious nor confounding, as Figure 3.4(a) and 3.4(b) show. Figure 3.4(c) and 3.4(d) also disclose that if Z has a direct effect on X or Y alone, it is neither spurious nor confounding. Figure 3.4(e), 3.4(f), and 3.4(g) reveal that Z could depend on both X and Y. Third variables like these are not spurious or confounding; they threaten the accuracy of causal inference only when they have a direct effect on both the causal agent (X) and the outcome measure (Y).

The ubiquity of confounding and spurious variables cannot be overestimated. The Rand Corporation evaluated one of the key presuppositions that justifies the regulation of television. Regulation rests on the assumption that viewing local news on TV will increase the public's awareness of local events (Lucas and Possner 1975). The amount of local affairs broadcasting that respondents

FIGURE 3.4
Nonspurious and Nonconfounding Third Variables

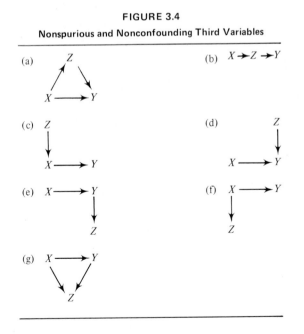

watched is the independent variable (X), and their awareness is the dependent variable (Y). The researchers recognized that persons of high socioecononomic status (SES) are likely to watch more local affairs broadcasts than persons of lower status. High status persons are also more aware of local events. The researchers therefore removed the effect of variations in SES among the individuals they studied in order to estimate the influence of local affairs viewing on the awareness of local news.

More than one confounding or spurious variable is usually present, and the accuracy of causal inferences depends on identifying and removing their influence. Suppose that an investigator erroneously believes that Z_1 is the only confounding or spurious influence on X and Y when in fact Z_1 and Z_2 are both spurious influences. Even though X has no effect on Y, the investigator will still observe covariation between X and Y after he removes the influence of Z_1, and he will incorrectly conclude that X affects Y. Only by removing the influence of both Z_1 and Z_2 will the investigator draw the correct conclusion. (See Figure 3.5.)

FIGURE 3.5
Ignoring Spurious Variables

Evaluators usually recognize that there are many possible confounding and spurious variables. The Westinghouse Corporation's evaluation of Head Start removed the influence of age, sex, race, ethnicity, previous kindergarten attendance, and socioeconomic status before estimating the impact of Head Start participation on achievement (Cicirelli et al. 1969). Rosenstone and Wolfinger (1978), in their study of the impact of voter registration laws on turnout, controlled for race and education before concluding that the stringency of registration laws has only a marginal effect on turnout.

Not only can the failure to remove all spurious influences produce the misleading conclusion that X influences Y, but the failure to remove all confounding variables can also produce errors. Even when X actually does influence Y, the presence of uncontrolled confounding variables can lead investigators to overestimate or underestimate its influence. When the Head Start evaluators failed to remove the influence of prior achievement levels on participation and achievement, critics charged that they underestimated the impact of Head Start (Williams and Evans 1972). Figure 3.6 examines this charge in greater detail.

Assume that participation in Head Start does indeed increase achievement scores, as the arrow and the "+" sign between X and Y in Figure 3.6 indicate.

FIGURE 3.6

Effect of Prior Achievement

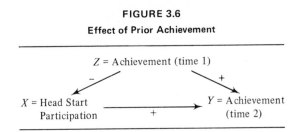

To estimate the amount of the increase in achievement due to participation, it is necessary to adjust for the fact that Head Start participants had lower achievement scores to begin with, indicated by the "$-$" sign on the arrow between Z and X. The "$+$" sign on the arrow between Z and Y means that students whose achievement is low at the beginning of one school year will probably continue to have low scores the next year.

The observed estimate of the difference in achievement between participants and nonparticipants at the program's end consists of two components. One component is the difference in achievement scores between participants and nonparticipants that is due to Head Start itself; the other is the difference due to prior ability. Symbolically, let the total difference in achievement scores between participants and nonparticipants be $T_P - T_{NP}$. If the difference attributable to participation is $P_P - P_{NP}$ and the difference attributable to prior achievement is $A_P - A_{NP}$, then $(T_P - T_{NP}) = (P_P - P_{NP}) + (A_P - A_{NP})$. In the Westinghouse study, $T_P - T_{NP}$ was a small positive number, since participants slightly outscored nonparticipants. According to Williams and Evans (1972), pupils with the lowest achievement scores were more likely to be assigned to Head Start, so that $(A_P - A_{NP})$ is negative. Since $(T_P - T_{NP}) > 0, (P_P - P_{NP}) > 0$ and $(A_P - A_{NP}) < 0$, it follows that $(T_P - T_{NP}) < (P_P - P_{NP})$.[7] Failure to adjust for prior achievement means that the observed difference in achievement scores between Head Start participants and nonparticipants $(T_P - T_{NP})$ is actually less than the true difference $(P_P - P_{NP})$. Head Start may thus have been considerably more effective than the evaluators claimed it was.

The failure to adjust for confounding influences can frequently lead investigators to underestimate program impact. Like Head Start funds, CETA monies are targeted at areas most in need. The largest CETA programs are thus associated with areas of high unemployment for the purpose of reducing unemployment. Neglecting the influence of prior unemployment may yield underestimates of program impact. Similarly, investigations of the impact of housing or business loans on the incomes of a low-income target group can easily underestimate program impact if they fail to account for prior income.

Failure to control for confounding variables can also result in overestimates of program impact. Investigators who study the impact of training programs on future earnings should remove the possibly confounding variables of worker motivation and prior earnings. Only some of the observed difference in earnings between trainees and nontrainees may be attributable to the program itself; the remainder may be due to the tendency, aptly called "creaming," for manpower programs to enroll the most able of those who are eligible. The most able have the best motivation and the highest prior earnings. They are also likely to have higher earnings even without training. Failure to remove these preexisting differences between trainees and nontrainees could well inflate estimates of program impact.

SUMMARY

This chapter has shown that evaluating the impact of public programs incorporates two tasks: establishing causal impact and estimating its magnitude. These tasks entail three steps. No step alone is adequate, but together they are necessary and sufficient for inferring causal relationships. First, the investigator must determine whether there is covariation. There must be variation in the treatment as well as variation in the outcome; both X and Y must change. Second, the treatment must precede the outcome because causes always antedate their effects. Finally, investigators must strive to eliminate as many confounding and spurious influences as possible in order to determine whether the program alone, rather than some other variable, brought about the observed outcome. The presence of spurious variables may yield evidence that the program has an impact when in fact it does not. Even when the program actually is effective, confounding variables can mislead evaluators by producing estimates of program impact that are either too high or too low.

Removing spurious and confounding variables is probably the most difficult methodological task facing evaluation research. The next chapter discloses that there are three basic approaches to this task: the true experimental design; the quasi-experimental design, and the nonexperimental design. The distinction among these approaches hinges on the means by which spurious and confounding influences are removed. Each approach has its own strengths and weaknesses, advocates and detractors. It is therefore important to consider each type of design according to its ability to measure covariation, establish time order, and remove confounding and spurious influences.

FOOTNOTES

1. Most evaluations have more than one outcome measure. A single program (X) can thus have more than one effect ($Y_1, Y_2, \ldots, Y_k$). Referring to a single effect and thus to one Y simplifies the presentation with no loss of generality. See Ostrom (1975) on the importance of multiple measures of program outcomes.

2. The formulation as well as the notation of causal inference that this chapter develops were originally presented in a seminal work by Blalock (1964). This and subsequent chapters apply the concepts originated by Blalock to the special instance of estimating program impact.

3. This statement has two exceptions which subsequent chapters consider in detail. It is always possible that a larger change in X than the investigator actually observed could

effect a change in Y. It is also possible that the observed invariance of Y would not occur in other times and settings.

4. The Appendix discusses three techniques for measuring the association or covariation between X and Y. One—the percent difference—is appropriate when X and Y are both categories; another—the simple (or bivariate) regression coefficient—is appropriate when X and Y are both continuous variables; the third—the difference of means—is appropriate when X is categorical and Y is continuous. The Appendix also reviews the significance tests that correspond to these measures of association. Significance tests estimate the probability that the association between X and Y which the investigator actually observes could occur if the true association were zero. A measure of association is said to be statistically significant if there is only a small chance of drawing the measure from a population in which the true association is zero.

5. Anticipation of CETA monies could account for the employment increase, but not the funding itself. There are many examples of anticipatory reactions. One study of Professional Standards Review Organizations (PSRO's) showed that hospital costs dropped prior to the inception of PSRO's. Anticipation of the PSRO's could account for the decline rather than the PSRO's themselves. (See Department of Health, Education and Welfare, 1978.) Similarly, whites may flee a school district in anticipation of school desegregation. Anticipation of an event, rather than the event itself, is sometimes a causal agent.

6. The actual measurement of motivation could be troublesome. This text does not address issues of measurement in great detail. In this example, motivation could be measured in a number of alternative ways. For instance, a question or set of questions in a survey questionnaire could be designed to tap the concept of motivation to work. Alternatively, some indicator of past performance could be used as indicative of motivation. For a more detailed consideration of measurement strategies, see Nachmias (1979: Ch. 4).

7. This assumes that T, P, and A are > 0.

LIST OF REFERENCES

Blalock, Hubert M., Jr. *Causal Inferences in Nonexperimental Research.* Chapel Hill: University of North Carolina Press, 1964.

Cicirelli, V. G., et al. *The Impact of Head Start: An Evaluation of the Effects of Head Start on Children's Cognitive and Affective Development.* Vol. 1. U.S. Dept. of Commerce, National Bureau of Standards, Institute for Applied Technology. Springfield, Va.: Clearinghouse, 1969.

Department of Health, Education and Welfare, Office of Planning, Evaluation and Legislation, *PSRO: An Initial Evaluation of the Professional Standards Review Organization.* Vol. V. *A Comprehensive Case Study: The Colorado Experience.* Washington, D.C.: U.S. Goverment Printing Office, 1978.

Lucas, William A., and Possner, Karen B. *Television News and Local Awareness: A Retrospective Look.* Santa Monica, Calif.: The Rand Corporation, October, 1975.

Nachmias, David. *Public Policy Evaluation: Approaches and Methods.* New York: St. Martins Press, 1979.

Ostrom, Elinor. "The Need for Multiple Indicators in Measuring the Output of Public Agencies." Ch. 2 in Scioli, Frank P., Jr., and Cook, Thomas J. *Methodologies for Analyzing Public Policies.* Lexington, Mass.: Lexington Books, Inc. 1975.

Rosenstone, Steven J., and Wolfinger, Raymond E. "The Effect of Registration Laws on Voter Turnout." *American Political Science Review* 72 (1978): 22–45.

Williams, Walter, and Evans, John W. "The Politics of Evaluation: The Case of Head Start." Ch. 11 in Rossi, Peter H., and Williams, Walter. *Evaluating Social Programs: Theory, Practice and Politics.* New York: Seminar Press, 1972.

Chapter 4

THE PRACTICE OF CAUSAL INFERENCE

MAXIMIZING VARIATION IN X

Systematic evaluation of program impact incorporates the elements of causality by establishing covariation and time order and by eliminating all possible spurious and confounding influences. Conclusions from an evaluation that successfully incorporates these three elements are said to be internally valid.[1] This chapter considers some practical aspects of internal validity and shows that the successful measurement of covariation and time order is difficult in practice, while the elimination of confounding influences is difficult in both principle and practice.

Consider the problem of establishing covariation. To determine whether X, a program, causes Y, an outcome, requires X to truly vary. An evaluator who underestimates or overestimates the magnitude of variation in X is likely also to produce misleading evidence regarding the impact of X on Y. This possibility is a common threat to the accuracy of evaluation designs.[2]

Suppose that an investigator wishes to determine whether the rigidity of instructional curricula affects the achievement of inner-city school children. The investigator should not rely on hearsay that the students in one school face a rigid curriculum and similar students in a nearby school face a flexible curriculum. He should observe firsthand that the so-called rigid curriculum is truly rigid and that the flexible program also lives up to its claims. The investigator will probably notice less difference between the curricula than he might otherwise have thought. Teachers who allegedly use rigid curricula may find it difficult to adhere to such formality and discipline in the classroom. Over the course of the semester, the teacher may lapse into a more casual approach with which he is comfortable. He may also make a professional judgment that the rigid curriculum is wholly inappropriate for one or two students, modifying his approach accordingly. Teachers with flexible curricula may likewise increase classroom formality. What teachers are accustomed to and what they believe is professionally responsible may diminish the variation between programs and thus reduce the variation in X. Indeed, evaluators must always be careful to ascertain that the procedural variation or program change whose effectiveness they investigate is actually implemented in accord with their beliefs about its implementation.[3]

Yet evaluators often fail to verify their presuppositions with empirical observation. The evaluators of the federal Head Start and Follow-Through Planned Variations program pointed to suggestive evidence that educationally disadvantaged children learned better under rigid than flexible curricula. Yet this evidence was far from conclusive, because contractors who promised rigid or flexible curricula apparently were not always able to deliver in the classroom what they promised in theory. Because the actual variations from one classroom to another were probably less than the planned variations, the investigators underestimated the magnitude of the covariation between achievement and type of curriculum (Rivlin and Timpane 1975). By failing to ascertain that X truly varied, they made it more rather than less difficult to detect causal impact.

There are many other instances in which the actual variation in X may be less than the planned variation. An evaluation of educational performance contracting suggested that instructors who are rewarded monetarily for raising achievement scores are no more successful than instructors who are salaried (Gramlich and Koshel 1975). Yet the performance contract lasted only a year; perhaps differences would have appeared had the contract been extended. Failure to maximize the difference between the new and the existing policy may thus elicit the conclusion that performance contracting was not successful when in fact it was incompletely implemented in the field.

In other program areas, maximizing the variation in treatments is also critical. Reassessments of the New Jersey Graduated Work Incentive Experiment suggest that the evaluators should have experimented with a wider variety of treatments.[4] To test the hypothesis that high tax rates will reduce labor force participation, the investigators randomly assigned subjects to one of the three different treatment categories: 30%, 50%, or 70% tax rates. To maximize variation between these treatments, the investigators might have assigned subjects to 0% and 100% tax rates as well, but considerations of cost and practicality foreclosed these options. The investigators excluded extreme tax rates because additional treatments are costly (Kershaw and Skidmore 1974). The investigators also decided to experiment with treatments that were politically realistic, and they judged that tax rates greater than 70% were too high and those less than 30% were too low for the political agenda.

The Work Incentive Experiment also tested the impact of the guarantee level on labor force participation. Even in this instance, critics have alleged that the decision to vary the guarantee from 50% to 125% of the poverty line failed to provide enough variation. Citing the experiment's unexpected results, which showed that variations in guarantee levels and tax rates had little or no impact on labor force participation, critics argue that failure to maximize variation between the treatments produced misleading evidence (Lyall 1975; Anderson 1975). Had variation between treatments been greater, they contend, variation in labor force participation might also have been detected.

Evaluation researchers should thus ascertain that the variation between the treatments they evaluate is as great as possible. Investigators who believe that treatments differ in principle should also verify that they differ in practice. Investigators should also be sure that new treatments or programs last long enough before conclusions are drawn.[5] When investigators must restrict the treatments they study to the realm of what is politically feasible, they should guard against concluding that the treatments make no difference. The conclusion that the treatments did not vary enough to make a difference may sometimes be more accurate.

ESTABLISHING TIME ORDER

The second requisite for valid causal inference is to show that X precedes Y. As a principle of causal inference, this requirement is self-evident, but as a practice of evaluation research, the requirement is often difficult to implement.

Consider the problem of evaluating the impact of Comprehensive Employment and Training Act (CETA) funds on urban unemployment rates. The formula by which the aid is distributed targets funds to cities likely to have the highest unemployment. Cities with the highest unemployment at some arbitrary time (t_1) should thus receive the most aid at some later time (t_2). If CETA is truly effective, receipt of CETA aid at (t_2) should produce a reduction in unemployment at a subsequent time (t_3). Figure 4.1 depicts the entire process from targeting to impact. The figure demonstrates how the passage of time must be an explicit component of this evaluation of CETA, yet evaluators frequently lack adequate time-based information. At worst, they must rely on observations drawn from a single point in time. If Figure 4.1 portrays the actual impact of

FIGURE 4.1

Actual Effect, Knowing Time Order

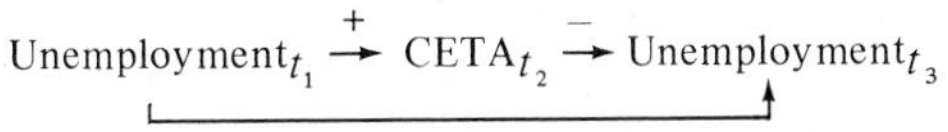

$$\text{Unemployment}_{t_1} \xrightarrow{+} \text{CETA}_{t_2} \xrightarrow{-} \text{Unemployment}_{t_3}$$

CETA, then reliance on cross-sectional information will be misleading. Figure 4.2 reveals that, instead of observing that the receipt of CETA reduces unemployment, the investigator could erroneously conclude that there is little or no covariation between CETA and unemployment. The absence of information about unemployment both before and after the infusion of CETA monies makes it impossible to disentangle the targeting of CETA from the impact of CETA. If targeting produces positive covariation and impact produces negative covariation, then the

FIGURE 4.2
Observed Effect, Not Knowing Time Order

Unemployment $\overset{+}{\underset{-}{\rightleftarrows}}$ CETA

two effects could nearly cancel one another, producing little or no covariation. The investigator, having observed no covariation, erroneously concludes that CETA has no impact.[6]

Similar examples abound. The Westinghouse Corporation's evaluation of Head Start found little or no difference between students who were exposed to the Head Start program and generally similar students who were not exposed (Cicirelli et al. 1969). Since program administrators apparently assigned students with the lowest achievement scores to Head Start, the program was targeted to the most needy. Even if the program improved achievement, the absence of temporal measures of achievement could obscure this effect, leading investigators to the erroneous conclusion that Head Start had no impact. (See Figure 4.3.)

FIGURE 4.3
Effect of Knowing Time Order

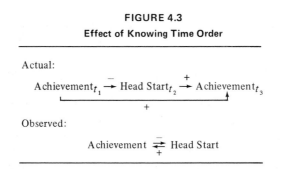

Actual:

$$\text{Achievement}_{t_1} \overset{-}{\rightarrow} \text{Head Start}_{t_2} \overset{+}{\rightarrow} \text{Achievement}_{t_3}$$

Observed:

$$\text{Achievement} \overset{-}{\underset{+}{\rightleftarrows}} \text{Head Start}$$

This problem is most likely to occur when programs to ameliorate a particular condition are also targeted to areas where that condition is the most in need of amelioration. Many programs besides CETA are targeted. Pollution control efforts are likely to be greatest where pollution is worst. Policies to improve the quality of housing are often targeted where housing quality is poor. Many innovative anticrime programs have been launched in portions of cities where crime is highest. In these and similar instances, investigators should strive to measure the level of the condition both before and after the program is implemented lest they erroneously conclude that the program was ineffective.

ELIMINATING VARIATION IN SPURIOUS AND CONFOUNDING VARIABLES

The last requirement for internally valid evaluation research is the elimination of all spurious and confounding variables. This aspect of causal inference is the most important and difficult to secure. An indication of its centrality is that the practical methods for controlling spurious and confounding variables correspond to three basic research designs that evaluators use—the experiment, the quasi experiment, and the nonexperiment.

Modeled after the classical scientific method, the experimental design controls spurious and confounding variables by randomly assigning subjects to treatments. Random assignment means that the process of matching subjects to treatments is essentially blind.[7] When assignment is random, the probability that each person in the study receives one treatment or another is independent of all of his personal characteristics. In the California Community Treatment Project (CTP), investigators first compiled a list of convicted felons who were eligible for the experiment. They then randomly assigned each eligible person to one of two possible treatments: incarceration or release into the custody of a parole officer (Warren 1967). The random assignment process is analogous to coin-tossing. For each subject, "heads" could mean assignment to prison, and "tails" could mean assignment to community treatment. In the case of six treatments, random assignment is analogous to rolling a die, and the roll of the die determines which of the six treatments each subject receives.

When the number of subjects in each treatment is reasonably large, random assignment guarantees that all characteristics of the subjects, measurable or not, will, on the average, be the same from one treatment group to another.[8] In the case of the CTP, the average age, education, work experience, prior earnings, prior record, race, and motivation of the subjects assigned to each treatment will be statistically equal. Investigators can rule out the possibility that personal characteristics like these are spurious or confounding factors that constitute untested rival explanations for the experimental findings. Had the CTP not employed random assignment, a critic could argue that persons who were incarcerated were "tougher" criminals with less education and poorer work histories. He could further argue that these personal characteristics, and not incarceration, account for the observation that incarcerated criminals are more likely to commit another crime upon release than those treated in the community. Without random assignment, the critic can list spurious and confounding variables which the investigator has failed to control. He can plausibly charge that these variables, rather than the treatment differences, account for the findings. Figure 4.4(a) models the critic's argument, and Figure 4.4(b) shows why random assignment rules out these variables—as well as all other characteristics of the subject—as alternative explanations. Random assignment transforms potentially confounding and spurious variables into variables that are unrelated to the treatment. By converting spurious or confounding variables which characterize the subjects of the study into extraneous variables that influence the dependent variable alone, random assignment augments internal validity.[9]

Random assignment cannot convert every confounding variable into an extraneous influence. Specific factors associated with the conditions of the experiment itself may sometimes become confounding variables, and random

FIGURE 4.4
Impact of Random Assignment

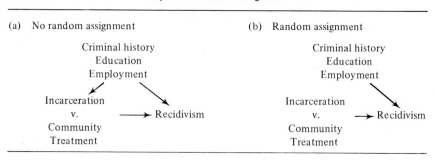

(a) No random assignment

Criminal history
Education
Employment

Incarceration
v.   → Recidivism
Community
Treatment

(b) Random assignment

Criminal history
Education
Employment

Incarceration
v.   → Recidivism
Community
Treatment

assignment cannot eliminate their influence. Investigators could erroneously attribute an observed effect to a particular treatment when in fact, conditions associated with, but not part of, the treatment are the causal agent. An investigator could credit test-score differences between two groups of randomly assigned students to variations in teaching methods; but racial differences between the teachers could also be associated with the different pedagogical treatments. The teacher's race could thus be a confounding variable that random assignment fails to eliminate. Random assignment controls for most but not all confounding variables.

Random assignment is also desirable because it guarantees that the treatment (X) precedes the outcome (Y). When assignment is blind, previous values of Y cannot determine the treatment a subject receives. The temporal precedence of X over Y is thus unambiguous when assignment is random.

Because random assignment defines a true experiment, experimental designs meet two of the three requirements for internal validity. With few exceptions, experiments reduce the possibility that spurious or confounding variables and ambiguous time order can produce misleading causal inferences. Even though experimental designs do not automatically assure that variation in the independent variable will be maximal, properly implemented experiments are the best guarantor of internally valid findings.[10]

The quasi experiment is probably the most popular approach to program evaluation. Instead of random assignment, the quasi experiment is identified by the use of equivalent comparison groups to remove spurious and confounding variables. The ideal comparison groups consist of two naturally occurring sets of individuals. Both sets should be statistically similar on all possibly spurious or confounding variables save the treatment. The Westinghouse Corporation's evaluation of the Head Start program was a quasi experiment. It compared the achievement levels of Head Start children to the achievement levels of untreated children with the same age, sex, race, ethnicity, previous kindergarten attendance, and socioeconomic status as the treated children. The Boston Housing Authority, in another quasi experiment, compared tenants who resided in public housing units that the Authority had recently improved to a similar group of persons who were on a waiting list to get into public housing (Wilner et al. 1962). The untreated group was similar to the public housing tenants on a number of social, demographic, and ethnic characteristics. The study revealed that persons residing in the improved public housing units had lower mortality rates, fewer accidents, and higher proportions of children promoted in school than persons on the waiting list.

These studies qualify as quasi experiments because they compare outcome measures from a treated group to the same measures from an untreated group that is similar on factors which the investigator believes may be spurious or confounding. The comparison group could receive either no treatment or a different treatment. Although all quasi experiments use at least one comparison group, Chapter 7 indicates that the quasi experiment actually encompasses several types of research designs.

Because quasi experiments rely on groups that are equivalent on some but not necessarily all spurious or confounding variables, the internal validity of quasi experiments is frequently questionable. The quasi experiment can remove only those spurious and confounding variables that the investigator thinks of and measures. There is no guarantee that an evaluator can even enumerate all of these variables; if he could, he probably would know so much about his research problem that further study would be unnecessary. Even if the investigator could enumerate all spurious and confounding variables, he would probably be unable to measure them. When spurious and confounding variables represent psychological or motivational qualities, they are particularly difficult to measure.

Not only are quasi experiments unlikely to remove all spurious and confounding influences, but sometimes they also fail to establish the temporal precedence of treatment before outcome. The Westinghouse Head Start evaluation was criticized in this regard. The evaluators compared the achievement scores of Head Start participants to the scores of comparable nonparticipants, but they had no data on the achievement of either group before the inception of Head Start. The absence of time-series measurements on the dependent variable made it impossible for the investigators to distinguish between the two contrasting conclusions depicted in Figure 4.5.

Figure 4.5(a) discloses no difference between participants and nonparticipants at the program's end. Figure 4.5(b) reveals how knowledge of preprogram achievement can alter the interpretation of the postprogram scores in Figure 4.5(a). According to Figure 4.5(b), Head Start raised the normal rate at which achievement improves from the dotted to the solid line. Without Head Start, participants would score less than nonparticipants; with Head Start, participants score equally well.

The presence of preprogram and postprogram information can thus alter inferences about program impact, but acquiring time-series data is often costly and infeasible. Data acquisition usually accompanies and rarely precedes the inception of a new program. When evaluation commences after a program is already operating, preprogram information will be readily available only by

FIGURE 4.5

Impact of Time-Series Information on Conclusion: Head Start

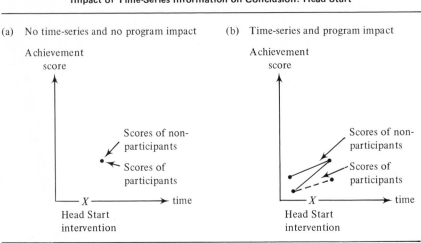

(a)   No time-series and no program impact

Achievement
score

Scores of non-
participants

Scores of
participants

X → time

Head Start
intervention

(b)   Time-series and program impact

Achievement
score

Scores of non-
participants

Scores of
participants

X → time

Head Start
intervention

chance alone. To guard against misleading inferences due to the absence of time-series data, evaluators should strive for quasi experiments that are prospective rather than retrospective.

Chapter 7 shows that all quasi experiments are subject to the charge that potentially spurious and confounding variables have not been removed, while only some quasi experiments fail to control for the passage of time. Like experiments, the quasi-experimental design does not guarantee that variation in the independent variable will be maximized.

The nonexperiment is the third design that evaluators often use. The nonexperiment is characterized by the use of statistical procedures to remove confounding influences, but it differs from the quasi experiment in degree rather than kind. The nonexperiment shares the same limitations as the quasi experiment. Like the quasi experiment, nonexperiments are always subject to the charge that spurious or confounding variables are present; nor do all nonexperiments measure the passage of time and maximize variation in independent variables.

The process of controlling spurious and confounding variables differentiates the two designs. The quasi experiment compares average scores on outcome measures for two or more groups constructed to be similar on possibly spurious and confounding variables and different on the treatment variable. The investigator thus identifies the characteristics of those in the treatment group and deliberately constructs an identical untreated group. The nonexperiment analyzes scores on an outcome measure for a single set of individuals who vary in respect to their treatment and in respect to spurious or confounding variables as well. Statistical methods for analyzing categorical and continuous data then remove differences among these individuals on spurious and confounding variables.[11] Chapters 8 and 9 discuss these procedures in some detail.

Because nonexperiments rely on statistical analysis, they tend to require many observations on large numbers of individuals. Coleman's *Equality of Educational Opportunity* is a prominent example of nonexperimental research (Coleman et al. 1966). In contrast, quasi experiments tend to incorporate a limited number of observations on a few carefully selected groups. The Westinghouse Corporation's evaluation of Head Start is an illustrative quasi experiment. Careful statistical analysis is critical to the internal validity of nonexperiments, while careful selection of comparison groups is critical to the internal validity of quasi experiments.

The distinctive characteristics of the three designs for evaluating program impact should not be overemphasized. The best designs involve multiple approaches. The Westinghouse Head Start study compared Head Start participants to a group of non-Head Start students with the same ethnic background, sex, race, and kindergarten attendance, but statistical methods were used to remove the influence of socioeconomic status. Thus, the Westinghouse study combined quasi-experimental and nonexperimental approaches. The New Jersey Graduated Work Incentive Experiment employed all three designs (Kershaw and Skidmore 1974; Pechman and Timpane 1975). The researchers randomly assigned subjects to treatments, making the study a true experiment. Only male-headed families with at least one dependent, income less than 150% of the 1968 poverty line, and residence in one of four New Jersey urban industrial cities were allowed to participate in the experiment. Consistent with principles of quasi-experimentation, each treatment group was comparable on these variables. Finally, the earnings and labor force participation differences between families with access to the negative income tax program and families with access only to Aid to Families with Dependent Children (AFDC) were computed using multiple regression analysis. Based on principles of nonexperimental design, this procedure controlled statistically for age, education, number of adults in the family, number and ages of children, sites, and preexperimental family earnings and labor supply (Kershaw and Skidmore 1974:61–62).

Experiments can even be included within quasi experiments, and quasi experiments can be part of experiments (Boruch 1975). Thus, although it is possible to analyze experiments, quasi experiments, and nonexperiments in separate detail, the pursuit of one approach does not preclude the use of another.

FOOTNOTES

1. Economists use a different term for internal validity. To them, internally valid conclusions are unbiased. See Cain (1975) for a discussion of the equivalence between these terms.

2. Technically, the failure to maximally vary the treatments does not contribute to internally invalid results. Instead, it reduces the precision surrounding estimates of program impact and makes it more difficult for investigators to establish statistical significance. From a practical standpoint, the failure to maximize variation in X makes it difficult to detect

covariation. We consequently consider this issue in Chapter 4 rather than in the discussion of random error in Chapter 5.

3. See Rossi (1978) for a similar point.

4. For some of these reassessments see Rossi and Lyall (1976), Lyall (1975), and Anderson (1975).

5. This *caveat* may sometimes conflict with the need for timely results and possibly increases the chance for the appearance of confounding variables. On the danger of inferring long-term results from short-term treatments, see Metcalf (1974).

6. This consideration of time order indicates that using temporal information regarding unemployment at time 1 (t_1) and time 3 (t_3) is actually equivalent to treating unemployment at time 1 (t_1) as a confounding variable. Problems of time order are thus conceptually equivalent to problems of eliminating spurious or confounding variables.

7. It is not necessary to deprive subjects of a treatment to conduct an experiment. Chapter 6 amplifies this point.

8. The number of subjects assigned to each treatment must be large enough so that the investigator has a reasonably good chance of rejecting the null hypothesis that observed differences in Y between subjects assigned to each treatment are equal. See Glass, Willson, and Gottman (1975) on the importance of securing enough subjects.

9. Chapter 5 shows that variables which affect the dependent variable alone constitute "experimental error." Experimental error is random and makes statistical significance more difficult to attain.

10. Forthcoming chapters reveal that it is not always easy or practical to implement random assignment properly. When it is not possible to implement random assignment properly, other approaches may be more desirable. For a more detailed consideration of some trade-offs involved in selecting designs for evaluation research, see Abt (1978).

11. This text makes an explicit distinction between quasi experiments and nonexperiments whereas in other studies, their meaning is usually implicit. Some authors use the term quasi experiment to cover any design that is not a true experiment, while others use the term nonexperiment to mean the same thing. Still other authors use the same definitions of experiments and quasi experiments as those in this text, but they entirely ignore statistical issues. In this volume, the definition of experiment, quasi experiment, and nonexperiment is explicit and consistently applied.

LIST OF REFERENCES

Abt, Wendy Peter. "Design Issues in Policy Research: A Controversy." *Policy Analysis* 4 (1978):91-122.

Anderson, Andy B. "Policy Experiments: Selected Analytic Issues." *Sociological Methods and Research* 4 (1975):13-30.

Boruch, Robert F. "Coupling Randomized Experiments and Approximations to Experiments in Social Program Evaluation." *Sociological Methods and Research* 4 (1975):31-53.

Cain, Glen G. "Regression and Selection Models to Improve Nonexperimental Comparisons." Ch. 4 in Bennett, Carl A., and Lumsdaine, Arthur A., eds. *Evaluation and Experiment*. New York: Academic Press, Inc., 1975.

Cicirelli, V. G., et al. *The Impact of Head Start: An Evaluation of the Effects of Head Start on Children's Cognitive and Affective Development* Vol. 1. U.S. Dept. of Commerce, National Bureau of Standards, Institute for Applied Technology. Springfield, Va.: Clearinghouse, 1969.

Coleman, James S.; Campbell, Ernest Q.; Hobson, Carol J.; McPartland, James; Mood, Alexander M.; Weinfeld, Frederic D.; and York, Robert L. *Equality of Educational Opportunity*. Washington, D.C.: U.S. Government Printing Office, 1966.

Glass, Gene V.; Willson, Victor L.; and Gottman, John M. *Design and Analysis of Time-Series Experiments.* Boulder: Colorado Associated University Press, 1975.

Gramlich, Edward M., and Koshel, Patricia P. *Educational Performance Contracting: An Evaluation of an Experiment.* Washington, D.C.: The Brookings Institution, 1975.

Kershaw, David N., and Skidmore, Felicity. *The New Jersey Graduated Work Incentive Experiment.* Mathematica Policy Analysis Series, no. 1 Princeton, N.J.: Mathematica, Inc., 1974.

Lyall, Katherine C. "Some Observations on Design Issues in Large-Scale Social Experiments." *Sociological Methods and Research* 4 (1975): 54–76.

Metcalf, Charles E. "Predicting the Effects of Permanent Programs from a Limited Duration Experiment." *The Journal of Human Resources* 9 (1974): 530–555.

Pechman, Joseph, and Timpane, P. Michael, eds. *Work Incentives and Income Guarantees: The New Jersey Negative Income Tax Experiment.* Washington, D.C.: The Brookings Institution, 1975.

Rivlin, Alice M., and Timpane, P. Michael, eds. *Planned Variation in Education: Should We Give Up or Try Harder?* Washington, D.C.: The Brookings Institution, 1975.

Rossi, Peter H. "Issues in the Evaluation of Human Services Delivery." *Evaluation Quarterly* 2 (1978): 573–599.

Rossi, Peter H., and Lyall, Katherine C. *Reforming Public Welfare: A Critique of the Negative Income Tax Experiment.* New York: Russell Sage Foundation, 1976.

Warren, M. O. "The Community Treatment Project: History and Prospects." In *Law Enforcement, Science, and Technology*, edited by S. A. Yefsky. Washington, D.C.: Thompson, 1967.

Wilner, D. M.; Glassner, Marvin N.; Walkley, R. P.; Pinkerton, T. C.; and Taybeck, M. *The Housing Environment and Family Life: A Longitudinal Study of the Effects of Housing on Morbidity and Mental Health.* Baltimore: The Johns Hopkins University Press, 1962.

Chapter 5

EXTERNAL VALIDITY: Problems of Random Selection, Statistical Interaction, and Experimental Error

THE PROBLEM OF GENERALITY

An "internally valid" research design accurately describes the impact of a treatment or program. Results from internally valid designs are said to be "unbiased." Unbiased causal inference is necessary if the results of an evaluation are to be credible. Evaluations should also be externally valid. Externally valid findings are general; they are applicable to other times and places.

Just as previous chapters suggested some pitfalls that jeopardize internal validity, this chapter centers on factors that affect external validity, or generality. The issue of generality is basically one of portability or transferability. When the conclusions from an evaluation accurately depict how a particular program in a particular setting affected a particular population, such conclusions may be unbiased, but they lack generality because they do not apply in conditions that differ from those in which they first emerged.

Although evaluators should strive for the most general results possible, they will often find that external validity is not as important as internal validity. Highly general results are desirable, but they are not always necessary. The degree to which results need to be portable from one time or setting to another depends on the purpose and the audience of the evaluation. The head of a statewide Professional Standards Review Organization may be concerned about the impact of his own organization on the quality of hospitals that serve state residents. He is unlikely to commission research whose results apply elsewhere in the U.S. The chief of police in a large central city could demand an accurate evaluation of his policy allowing police officers to drive city police cars home. The chief has little incentive to ensure that the results of such a study also apply to other jurisdictions. In contrast, federal organizations with national constituencies, like the National Science Foundation and the National Institute of Education, require research results to be applicable to many different users and areas.

A degree of generality is always essential. Even when they are concerned with a single program in a single community, analysts should always ascertain that their results will be applicable in at least the near future. While no methodological procedures guarantee that the future will resemble the past, investigators should strive to verify that the site of their study and the conditions of the program they are evaluating resemble those that are likely to pertain in the near future.

Three factors conspire to jeopardize the external validity of a study. First, failure to select observations randomly from a well-defined universe makes it impossible to apply sample results to the entire population. Sometimes the statistical advantages of random selection conflict with the practicalities of evaluation research. Second, situational peculiarities threaten external validity. We call these peculiarities "statistical interaction," and suggest that the undetected presence of interaction also mars internal validity. Finally, efforts to remove random or experimental error can improve internal validity while threatening external validity.

NONRANDOM SELECTION

In evaluation research, the statistical advantages of random selection may be more apparent than real. As a result, the selection of subjects is usually not random. One of the most common instances of nonrandom selection occurs when investigators confine their analysis to persons (or sites) who voluntarily consent to be studied. The New Jersey Graduated Work Incentive Experiment initially selected a random sample of subjects, but the study included only persons who agreed to participate. As long as persons who give their consent resemble the entire population to which the investigator wishes to apply his findings, analyzing volunteers does not threaten external validity.[1] If the investigator fears that relying on volunteers alone seriously jeopardizes external validity, he could consider paying persons (or sites) for their participation. He could also offer nonmonetary incentives. In no instance should the investigator compel the unwilling to participate. Forcing participation is foolish, because it jeopardizes internal validity by altering the behavior of participants.

Sometimes investigators select a special sample of subjects for study because they are extremely needy or extremely able. Evaluators may also scrutinize programs reputed to be especially well-managed. Conclusions from evaluations like these apply only to the unique population from which they were derived. Most often, researchers choose sites according to convenience and political expedience. While expedient sampling appears to reduce generality, random selection could jeopardize internal validity. Evaluating programs in sites that are reluctant to be inspected may alter the behavior of program administrators and participants, sensitizing them in undesirable ways. Results drawn from resistant but randomly selected sites thus lack credibility.

Nonrandom selection of sites is also advisable when the pressure of time or money precludes random samples. Consider a study of the ability of a new counseling program to promote the prompt repayment of federal education loans. Investigators constrained by time will want to select sites where loan activity is high. Areas where loan activity is low will yield an insufficient number of loan applications to study in a short time.

In each of these instances, nonrandom selection procedures jeopardize external validity. Nonetheless, the reduction in generality is not always substantial, and generality is not always important. The advantages of achieving generality by random selection may thus be outweighed by considerations of cost and practicality and by a reluctance to sacrifice internal validity.[2]

THE PROBLEM OF INTERACTION

Situational peculiarities also affect external validity. The formal term for the impact of situational variations on generality is statistical interaction, or, more simply, interaction. Interaction exists whenever the impact of a program depends on the conditions under which it is administered. There are many instances of interaction. Evidence from the Work Incentive Experiment indicates that the impact of negative income tax payments on labor force participation depends on sex. Among intact families, the negative income tax reduced participation among women but had little or no impact among their spouses. Statistical interaction exists because the impact of the type of income guarantee (X) on labor force participation (Y) varies with the value of a third variable (sex). The availability of a negative income tax causes a reduction in labor force participation. This reduction is larger in rural areas than in urban areas. The urban or rural character of an area is thus an interactive variable.

The presence of interactive effects like these makes generalization impossible. Interaction limits the applicability of an investigator's findings to particular subgroups, sites, or times. For the analyst concerned with generality, the problem is to anticipate and detect interaction.

The need to generalize makes the detection of interaction critical because the undetected presence of interaction mars internal validity. If a program (X) has positive effects on an outcome (Y) in one setting and negative effects on an outcome in another, then the average effect could be zero. Should the investigator fail to examine the separate impact of X and Y in each setting, he might erroneously conclude that X has no impact at all when in fact its impact is merely contingent on the setting in which it occurs. The possibility of interaction means that evaluators who seek general results must identify, measure, and control for possibly interactive variables.

Chapter 4 showed that there are three ways to control for the influence of spurious or confounding variables on the relation between program and outcome. There are, however, only two ways to control the influence of interactive variables. Researchers can use random assignment, comparison groups, or statistical controls in the former instance, but they cannot use random assignment to detect interaction effects. Instead, the investigator must actually identify and measure interactive variables before he can detect their influence.

Suppose that an investigator randomly assigns a large number of psychiatric patients to two different treatments. If the investigator does not actually record the personal characteristics of the patients, he may fail to detect potentially interactive effects. Even though he has a true experimental design, he could conclude that there is no difference between the treatments, when in fact the treatments have opposite effects depending on the patients' income. As Figure 5.1(a) reveals, Treatment 1 is clearly superior to Treatment 2 for low-income patients; the opposite characterizes the high-income patients. Figure 5.1(b) shows that income and treatment are independent, which is the relation that random assignment should produce. Failure to examine the impact of type of treatment on improvement for separate income groups would produce the misleading table in Figure 5.1(c), where the treatments appear equally effective.

Investigators have two choices when they anticipate interactive effects. If the investigator does not need to apply the results to the full range of variation in the interactive variable, he should simply examine behavior within the relevant category of that variable. If high-income patients were ineligible for the psychiatric program in the example above, the analyst need examine only low-income patients. Such a strategy is practical and less costly than examining high-income patients as well.

Investigators concerned with the generality of their findings must anticipate the likelihood and source of interaction.[3] If its effects go undetected, interaction produces inaccurate and misleading findings. If it is detected, it makes sweeping statements about the transferability of results to other settings impossible.

Sources of interaction are so ubiquitous that they can be codified. History is one kind of situational peculiarity that affects the generality of findings from an evaluation. The results of a study carried out in 1960 may not be applicable in 1970 or 1980. Similarly, the findings from an evaluation carried out during a time of economic growth may not apply to the same program implemented during periods of economic stagnation or decline.

The unique properties of the setting of an evaluation can also restrict its generality. Programs administered in rural areas may produce different results than similar programs located in urban areas. Programs administered in large northern cities may have different effects than programs administered in small

FIGURE 5.1

Interactive Findings: Hypothetical Cell Frequencies

(a) Improvement by treatment controlling for income

Low income patients

	Treatment 1		Treatment 2	
Improvement	*Frequency*	*Percentage*	*Frequency*	*Percentage*
Yes	20	80%	5	20%
No	5	20%	20	80%
Total	25	100%	25	100%

High income patients

	Treatment 1		Treatment 2	
Improvement	*Frequency*	*Percentage*	*Frequency*	*Percentage*
Yes	5	20%	20	80%
No	20	80%	5	20%
Total	25	100%	25	100%

(b) Treatment by income: frequencies only

	Income	
Treatment	*High*	*Low*
1	25	25
2	25	25

(c) Improvement by treatment

	Treatment 1		Treatment 2	
Improvement	*Frequency*	*Percentage*	*Frequency*	*Percentage*
Yes	25	50%	25	50%
No	25	50%	25	50%
Total	50	100%	50	100%

southern towns. Confining an evaluation to a single site can thus remove inter-action variables and reduce external validity at the same time.

The process of measurement itself can also reduce the transferability of results from an "evaluation" setting to a "real world" setting (Bernstein et al. 1975). The need to achieve internal validity in an evaluation sometimes necessitates the use of a "pretest." In quasi experiments, pretests are often used to ascertain that comparison groups are truly comparable. Unfortunately, the very process of pretesting may make the whole design reactive. Reactive measurements make subjects aware that they are being studied, and this awareness may alter their behavior.[4] Pretests and other activities associated with evaluation make subjects cognizant of their participation in a study. The results from such a study may apply only to persons who are similarly sensitized. As an illustration, consider a group of criminals which has been released to one of two forms of community treatment in a special study. Even though both groups receive different treatments, each group also gets special attention. Special attention could make any between-treatment differences disappear. Only when the treatments are part of the "ordinary" environment will their impact vary.

The process of posttesting can also sensitize the participants in evaluations. Consider a set of subjects who have been exposed to two different methods for presenting local news on TV. The posttest requires asking subjects about their awareness of local events. The very process of administering the posttest itself may create awareness in both groups, thereby masking differences between the two treatments.

The time at which the measurement of program effects takes place is another source of interaction. Some programs do not have lasting effects. Observations of program impact recorded immediately after participation may not be applicable months, or even years, hence, if effects are not long-lasting. In contrast, other programs may have delayed effects. Investigators concerned with these issues should therefore posttest their subjects at several points in time. Of course, such a procedure could also increase posttest sensitization. The investigator must weigh the advantages of increasing generality by using several posttests against the disadvantages of reducing it by the additional sensitization that could occur as a result.

External validity, of course, is more important in some of these instances than others. Evaluators should always design studies that are as nonreactive as possible. Findings that apply only to "pretested" or otherwise sensitive subjects are not ordinarily useful. Evaluators should seek temporal generality since conclusions that apply only in the very near future will rarely be helpful to program managers. In contrast, if the sponsors of an evaluative study are concerned only with a single site, generalizing to other sites is clearly unnecessary.[5]

PROBLEMS DUE TO EXPERIMENTAL ERROR

Like problems due to interaction, problems due to experimental or random error affect both the internal as well as the external validity of evaluation designs. To understand these effects, it is necessary to conceptualize and specify the sources of random error. Random error represents the effects of "extraneous" variables on Y, the dependent variable. By definition, extraneous variables refer to variables that affect Y but are independent of X, the program itself. Extraneous variables represent all of the variables not already measured by X, the program or treatment, and Z, which represents potentially spurious or confounding variables, that also affect Y.

Consider an evaluation of the impact of a personal patrol vehicle program (X) on crime rates (Y). Figure 5.2 depicts some possibly spurious or confounding variables, including neighborhood income and the residential or commerical character of an area. Policemen drive personal patrol vehicles to their homes, which tend to be located in less wealthy residential areas of a municipality. The income and residential character of an area also affect crime and are thus potentially spurious or confounding Z-variables. Figure 5.2 also depicts age as an extraneous or W-variable affecting crime. Crime tends to predominate in areas populated by youth. Age is a W-variable because it affects Y and because there is little reason to believe that it is related to the presence of personal patrol vehicles (X).[6]

FIGURE 5.2

Extraneous Variables

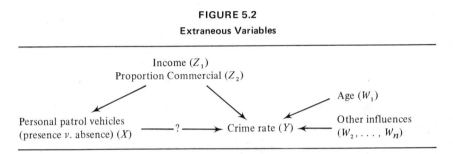

Figure 5.2 does not list all of the Z- and W-variables that could possibly affect crime. Its purpose is to explain the difference between Z- and W-variables. Spurious and confounding variables directly affect both X and Y, whereas extraneous (W) variables affect Y alone. The influence of extraneous variables is said to be random because, unlike Z-variables, the presence of uncontrolled W-variables does not produce biased estimates of program impact. Internal validity requires the investigator to remove the influence of Z-variables and to identify and measure the influence of interactive variables. Failing to control W-variables does not threaten internal validity. Randomized experiments, in fact, attain internal validity by changing Z-variables into W-variables. Experiments do not remove the influence of confounding or spurious variables by holding them constant. Rather, the process of random assignment transforms a confounding or spurious influence into a random one. Only confounding and spurious effects, but not random effects, produce biased inferences.

Random influences are still important, because their presence increases the likelihood of deciding that a program has no impact when in fact it does. In statistics, this is called a Type II error. Figure 5.3 reports the two types of statistical error that an investigator could make. If the statistical hypothesis is that the program had no impact, the investigator could decide that this hypothesis is either right or wrong. The accuracy of his decision depends on what is "really" true. The investigator's problem is to decide from data what this "truth" is. Figure 5.3 shows the four possible outcomes of the investigator's decision. Two of the outcomes are correct, and two are erroneous.

FIGURE 5.3

Aᴺ

Outcomes of Testing Hypothesis That Program Has ~~No~~ Impact

	Real World	
Decision	*Program has no impact*	*Program has impact*
No impact (Reject ~~Accept~~ hypothesis)	No error	Type II error
Impact (Accept ~~Reject~~ hypothesis)	Type I error	No error

Large random errors affect this decision-making process by augmenting the chance of concluding that the program has no impact. By augmenting the probability of this decision, random influences also make one type of error more likely than the other. Factors which increase the chance of deciding that a program has no impact or that a treatment makes no difference also increase the chance that such a decision is wrong. In statistics, these are Type II errors.

Scrutinizing the impact of random influences on the variance of Y suggests why they enlarge the probability of a Type II error. By definition, W-variables affect Y alone; they thereby increase the variance of Y relative to the variance of X or Z. Anything that increases the relative variance of Y makes it more difficult to reject the statistical hypothesis that a treatment has no impact.

As an illustration, consider a study of the influence of two modalities for primary medical care—treatment by a physician (MD) versus treatment by a medical paraprofessional (PP)—on the incidence of illness. Assume further that confounding and spurious influences have either been removed or transformed into random influences, so that the estimate of treatment differences will be un-biased. Figure 5.4 displays two hypothetical instances in which the unbiased per-cent difference is 4%. The two cases diverge only in respect to the variance of the dependent variable, proportion ill. The variance of a proportion across two categories is estimated by the formula $\hat{p}_u\hat{q}_u$, where $\hat{p}_u$ = estimated proportion in the population who are ill, and $\hat{q}_u = 1 - \hat{p}_u$. In both cases of Figure 5.4, the difference between the proportions who are ill is 0.04; the number of subjects (N) in both instances is 200. But in the first case, the variance of Y, or $\hat{p}_u\hat{q}_u$, is 0.25; in the second, it is 0.07. The formula for the Z-test for the difference between proportions reveals that as $\hat{p}_u\hat{q}_u$, which is the variance in Y, increases, the value of Z decreases:

$$Z = \frac{P_1 - P_2}{\sqrt{\hat{p}_u\hat{q}_u}\ \sqrt{(N_1 + N_2)/N_1 N_2}}$$

The smaller the value of Z, the more likely it is that the investigator will decide there is no difference between the treatments. Increasing the chances of reaching such a conclusion also enlarges the possibility that the conclusion is erroneous.

FIGURE 5.4

**The Impact of Variance in Y on Z-test for
Difference of Proportions**

Case I: Large variance			*Case II:* Small variance		
	Type of care			Type of care	
	PP	MD		PP	MD
Proportion ill	0.50	0.46	Proportion ill	0.10	0.06
	$N_1 = 100$	$N_2 = 100$		$N_1 = 100$	$N_2 = 100$
Difference of proportions = 0.04			Difference of proportions = 0.04		

$$\hat{p}_u = \frac{N_1 P_1 + N_2 P_2}{N_1 + N_2} \qquad\qquad \hat{p}_u = \frac{N_1 P_1 + N_2 P_2}{N_1 + N_2}$$

$$= \frac{100(0.50) + 100(0.46)}{200} \qquad\qquad = \frac{100(0.10) + 100(0.06)}{200}$$

$$= 0.48 \qquad\qquad\qquad\qquad\qquad\qquad = 0.08$$

$$\hat{p}_u \hat{q}_u = 0.25 \qquad\qquad\qquad\qquad\qquad\quad \hat{p}_u \hat{q}_u = 0.07$$

This property is not unique to the Z-test for the difference of proportions. It also characterizes t-tests for the difference of means and for the significance of regression coefficients. Consider the difference of means test, which an investigator could use to decide whether the mean earnings of persons who had participated in training programs $(\overline{Y}_1)$ was significantly higher than the earnings of comparable nonparticipants $(\overline{Y}_2)$. The appropriate significance test is:

$$t = (\overline{Y}_1 - \overline{Y}_2)/\hat{\sigma}_{(\overline{y}_1 - \overline{y}_2)}$$

where

$$\hat{\sigma}_{(\overline{y}_1 - \overline{y}_2)} = \sqrt{\frac{\Sigma(Y_{i_1} - \overline{Y}_1)^2/N_1}{N_1 - 1} + \frac{\Sigma(Y_{i_2} - \overline{Y}_2)^2/N_2}{N_2 - 1}}$$

Inspection of these formulas discloses that large variations in Y-scores increase $\sigma_{(\overline{y}_1 - \overline{y}_2)}$ and thereby reduce the value of t. The smaller the value of t, the more likely the investigator is to decide that the treatments make no difference.

Even in the case of regression coefficients, increasing the variance of Y reduces the value of the t-statistic. This contention is easiest to illustrate using bivariate regression coefficients, but the point is valid even for instances involving more than two variables. In the bivariate case, the t-statistic is:

$$t = \frac{\hat{b}_{yx}\sqrt{\Sigma(X_i - \overline{X})^2}}{\sqrt{\Sigma(Y_i - \hat{Y}_i)^2/(N - 2)}}$$

Large random errors augment the value of $\Sigma(Y_i - \hat{Y}_i)^2$ and thereby diminish the value of t. Small values of t enlarge the likelihood of deciding that the regression coefficient is not significantly different from zero.

These instances reveal how the presence of random or experimental error increases the probability of deciding that X and Y do not covary when in fact they do covary. The absence of covariation is usually sufficient evidence for concluding that the program had no impact.[7] Investigations of important issues such as negative income taxes, housing allowances, education and manpower programs, parole supervision, work release, and seat belt regulations have shown little or no impact.[8] Although these findings may be accurate, the presence of random influences magnifies the likelihood that these conclusions are erroneous. Program managers who fear statements like "no impact" and inferences of "ineffective" will resist evaluation. Evaluators should therefore be particularly aware of the steps they can take to reduce the chance of Type II errors.

Increasing Internal validity

REDUCING RANDOM ERRORS

There are several ways to reduce the influence of random errors. Taking these steps will diminish the likelihood of erroneously concluding that programs or treatments are ineffective. None of these steps, however, are without cost.

Inspection of the formulas for the Z- and t-tests mentioned in the last section discloses an obvious way to reduce the relative influence of random errors: increase the number of subjects (N) in the study. In each formula, enlarging N simultaneously increases the value of t or Z. As the value of t and Z increase, investigators are more likely to conclude that the program is effective.[9]

Augmenting the number of observations adds to the cost of an evaluation and may also delay findings. Increasing the number of observations is often a practical way to reduce the threat of Type II errors, but evaluators who have tight budgets and time constraints may find this solution difficult to implement.

Another way to reduce random influences is to maximize variation between treatments. Inspection of the t-statistic for the bivariate regression coefficient reveals that increasing the variance of X increases the t value as well. This suggestion must be considered in light of Chapter 4, which disclosed that practical concerns sometimes preclude maximizing variation between treatments. Maximizing between-treatment variation may require untreated control groups or additional treatment groups. Despite the statistical rationale, withholding or adding treatments can introduce questionable ethics, add to costs, and consign a study to political irrelevance.

Random measurement error in the dependent variable also adds to its variance and thus makes statistical significance more difficult to attain. There are many practical ways to reduce these errors, and investigators should take advantage of them. Verifying the accuracy of data and of keypunching is one way to reduce random error. Applying statistical procedures that correct for unreliability is particularly important when a survey instrument or paper and pencil test are used to measure the dependent variable. Recent evidence suggests that achievement tests and attitude measures have a very large random component that statistical techniques can remove. It is prudent for investigators concerned with reducing the presence of random measurement error to use statistical methods of correcting for unreliability.[10]

The influence of unmeasured W-variables on the dependent variable is another source of random error. These variables are unrelated to the treatment; if they were related, they would, by definition, be spurious or confounding. Measuring these variables and removing their influence by quasi- or nonexperimental techniques is another way to reduce experimental error. Although it is often difficult to ascertain what these influences are, the following examples are instructive. Consider a study of the influence of different training methods in the Work Incentive (WIN) program on the employment prospects of WIN recipients. Variables such as the race, sex, age, and previous earnings of the recipient are probably confounding influences. Trainers are likely to assign WIN recipients whose previous earnings were relatively high to the same training programs; these recipients are also more likely than others to find employment even without training. In an experiment, confounding variables like these become random influences. There are other random influences which no design can automatically eliminate. The impact of factors like the prospective employer's mood, his aversion to tall women, and the local economy on-the-job prospects of WIN recipients, are representative of random influences on employment.

Some of these random influences increase the chances of employment and others have the opposite effect. Their net effect is zero. One way to reduce the influence of extraneous variables like these is to identify, measure, and control them by selecting appropriate comparison groups or by applying appropriate statistical procedures. If an investigator can remove variation in most of the factors that affect Y, the impact measure, while simultaneously maximizing the variation between treatments (X), the easier it is to detect even small effects of X on Y.

Statistically eliminating the influence of extraneous factors may be simpler in principle than in practice. Statistical controls for W-variables necessitate their measurement, which may be costly. If the investigator believes that the height of WIN recipients is an important extraneous influence, he must gather and record data on recipients' height. This could be expensive and time consuming. If height also turns out to be an unimportant extraneous influence, its measurement and control will do little to reduce random error. Resources used to measure extraneous influences that turn out to be important will be poorly spent. The measurement of extraneous variables must also be accurate. The process by which extraneous variables themselves are measured may be subject to random or nonrandom errors. The presence of measurement error in extraneous variables that are statistically controlled threatens internal validity.[11] Efforts to control extraneous variables for the purposes of reducing experimental error can thus introduce new sources of measurement error that mar internal validity.

Investigators must also be concerned with the number of extraneous influences they measure and control. In any particular study, there are many extraneous factors. While measuring all of them is probably never practical, investigators concerned with detecting possibly small program effects may seek to control many of them. No matter what kind of design the analyst uses, measuring and controlling for an increasingly large number of extraneous influences requires the investigator either to sacrifice external validity or to incur the additional costs of more observations. To illustrate, suppose that the analyst believes that height is an important extraneous factor which he needs to control. The analyst could restrict his study to tall WIN recipients, for instance, thereby sacrificing external validity. Alternatively, the analyst could examine the impact of WIN on employment among separate groups of short, average, and tall women. This choice necessitates having a large number of observations within each of these groups. Failure to increase the number of observations when more control variables are added increases the chance of Type II errors. Adding more observations augments the cost of an evaluation.[12]

Carefully selecting sites for conducting an evaluation can also reduce random influences. There are three basic strategies that investigators concerned with external validity can use to select the individuals or other units of analysis. In a study of the impact of WIN training programs on the employment of WIN recipients, an analyst could randomly sample from a national listing a set of recipients for analysis. Because the sample is random, it would be broadly representative of all WIN recipients in the U.S. Alternatively, the investigator could select either a representative or random sample of sites, and randomly select recipients separately within each site. Finally, the investigator could simply examine recipients within a single site.

Figure 5.5 outlines each of these selection strategies. Of the three, the last is most suitable for investigators unconcerned with generality. Conducting research at a single site where outside factors are unlikely to change during the course of the evaluation helps reduce random error. But the conclusions from such an investigation are unlikely to be applicable in other settings. Replicating the same study in many different sites in accord with the second strategy diminishes random error and achieves generality at the same time. Replication also allows the investigator to detect situational sources of interaction. Offsetting these benefits, replication is the most costly of the three strategies. High costs are incurred because each sample in each site must be large enough to scrutinize sites independently. Nonetheless, independent analyses of each site are worthwhile for investigators who seek generality and who anticipate large random errors or different impacts in different sites.

The extraordinary costs of replication mean that investigators who need general results should also consider selecting a simple random sample across all sites. This strategy is advisable for analysts who do not fear Type II errors and for analysts who do not expect findings that vary from one site to another.

FIGURE 5.5
Alternative Sampling Strategies*

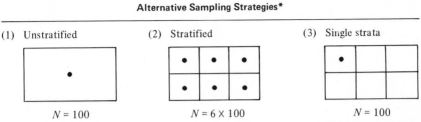

(1) Unstratified	(2) Stratified	(3) Single strata
$N = 100$	$N = 6 \times 100$	$N = 100$

*Each dot represents 100 subjects.

For investigators concerned with Type II errrors, reducing experimental error necessitates either incurring higher costs or sacrificing external validity. But eliminating random error is not always essential. If the analyst believes on an *a priori* basis that a program will have large impact, then costly efforts to remove random error may be unnecessary. The presence of random error makes it more difficult to detect small effects than large effects. When small effects are anticipated, random errors increase the chance of erroneously concluding that a program has no effects when instead it has small effects. The chances of drawing this type of erroneous inference diminish as the probable impact of a program increases.

FOOTNOTES

1. The act of volunteering can jeopardize internal as well as external validity. Investigators should avoid comparing persons who voluntarily participate in a program to nonvolunteers whose treatment is no program at all. In this instance, the act of volunteering is confounded with the treatment itself. Such self-selection ordinarily introduces many spurious and confounding variables.

2. For another discussion of the relation between random selection and generality, see Bernstein, Bohrnstedt, and Borgatta (1975).

3. Examining previous research on the topic is particularly helpful in this regard.

4. See Webb et al. (1966) for a detailed discussion of nonreactive measurement strategy.

5. Both Bernstein, Bohrnstedt, and Borgatta (1975) and Clark (1976) list threats to external validity. Their codification resembles this discussion in most respects. However, some factors that they cite are actually threats to internal validity.

6. If age affected both X and Y, it would, by definition, be a Z- and not a W-variable.

7. Undetected interaction and confusion about the time order between X and Y can also account for the absence of covariation.

8. See Kershaw and Skidmore (1974), Rivlin and Timpane (1975), Gramlich and Koshel (1975), U.S. Department of Housing and Urban Development (1978), Cicirelli et al. (1969), Waldo and Chiricos (1977), Berman (1978), Hinrichs and Taylor (1969: 311–321), and Peltzman (1975).

9. Increasing the likelihood of reaching this conclusion also increases the chance that the conclusion is erroneous. From a practical standpoint, the problem of Type I errors does

not seem to characterize evaluation research today. The conclusion that programs have no impact seems considerably more common than the opposite.

10. Among the best discussions of procedures for removing random measurement error that are relatively accessible to the statistical amateur are Aachen (1975) and Heise (1969). We see in Chapter 10 that random measurement error in independent variables (X and Z) can bias evaluation results. Random measurement error in Y makes estimates imprecise.

11. See Blalock (1964) and Chapter 9.

12. Chapter 9 shows that statistical controls are more efficient in this respect than comparison groups. Adding another control variable necessitates a smaller increase in the number of observations when the control is statistical than when it is based on comparison groups.

LIST OF REFERENCES

Aachen, Christopher H. "Mass Political Attitudes and the Survey Response." *American Political Science Review* 69 (1975):1218–1231.

Berman, John J. "An Experiment in Parole Supervision." *Evaluation Quarterly* 2 (1978): 71–90.

Bernstein, Ilene N.; Bohrnstedt, George W.; and Borgatta, Edgar F. "External Validity and Evaluation Research: A Codification of Problems." *Sociological Methods and Research* 4 (1975):101–128.

Blalock, Hubert M., Jr. *Causal Inferences in Nonexperimental Research.* Chapel Hill: University of North Carolina Press, 1964.

Cicirelli, V. G., et al. *The Impact of Head Start: An Evaluation of the Effects of Head Start on Children's Cognitive and Affective Development.* Vol. 1. U.S. Dept. of Commerce, National Bureau of Standards, Institute for Applied Technology. Springfield, Va.: Clearinghouse, 1969.

Clark, Lawrence P. *Designs for Evaluating Social Programs.* Croton-on-Hudson, N.Y.: Policy Studies Associates, 1976.

Gramlich, Edward M., and Koshel, Patricia P. *Educational Performance Contracting: An Evaluation of an Experiment.* Washington, D.C.: The Brookings Institution, 1975.

Heise, David R. "Separating Reliability and Stability in Test-Retest Correlation." *American Sociological Review* 34 (1969):93–101.

Hinrichs, Harley H., and Taylor, Graeme M. *Program Budgeting and Benefit-Cost Analysis: Cases, Text, and Readings.* Pacific Palisades, Calif.: Goodyear Publishing Co., 1969.

Kershaw, David N., and Skidmore, Felicity. *The New Jersey Graduated Work Incentive Experiment.* Mathematica Policy Analysis series, no. 1. (Princeton, N.J.: Mathematica, Inc., 1974.

Peltzman, Sam. "The Effects of Automobile Safety Regulation." *Journal of Political Economy* 83 (1975):677–725.

Rivlin, Alice M., and Timpane, P. Michael, eds. *Planned Variation in Education: Should We Give Up or Try Harder?* Washington, D.C.: The Brookings Institution, 1975.

U.S. Department of Housing and Urban Development, Office of Policy Development and Research. *A Summary Report of Current Findings From the Experimental Housing Allowance Program.* Washington, D.C.: U.S. Government Printing Office, 1978.

Waldo, Gordon P., and Chiricos, Theodore G. "Work Release and Recidivism: An Empirical Evaluation of a Social Policy." *Evaluation Quarterly* 1 (1977):87–108.

Webb, Eugune J., et al. *Unobtrusive Measures: Nonreactive Research in the Social Sciences.* Chicago: Rand McNally and Co., 1966.

Chapter 6

EXPERIMENTAL DESIGNS

PROPERTIES OF EXPERIMENTS

True experimental designs always assign subjects to treatments randomly.[1] As long as the number of subjects is sufficiently large, random assignment guarantees that the characteristics of subjects in each treatment are statistically equivalent. In this fashion, the true experiment removes all confounding and spurious (Z) variables associated with the subjects themselves. The experiment also ensures the precedence of the treatment over the effect. Since the investigator deliberately assigns subjects and subsequently observes their behavior, he can ascertain that the treatment actually preceded the effect. Two properties of an experiment thus help to achieve internal validity: the experiment controls important Z-variables and also guarantees that X, the program, precedes Y, the effect. Experimental designs do not necessarily maximize variation in X. Nor does random assignment necessarily reduce random error, detect interaction, or achieve generality.

The most important property of an experimental design is random assignment. Random assignment means that the treatment or program to which a subject is assigned bears no relation to any characteristics of the subject himself. Random assignment, however, is different from random selection. To illustrate the distinction, consider an experiment to determine whether on-the-job training, vocational training, or simple orientation to job-searching and interviewing techniques is the best way to increase the future earnings of WIN recipients. The investigator must first select the subjects for his study. Chapter 5 has already suggested several strategies for selecting subjects. To achieve external validity, the investigator should select subjects at random from the population of persons accepted to the WIN program. But random selection is often costly. A less expensive alternative is to randomly select persons accepted to the WIN program in two cities, for instance, whose WIN administrators are willing to cooperate with the evaluator. This procedure reduces the generality of findings, but it also reduces costs and random error. Random selection, however, is not a requisite for a true experimental design. The investigator could abandon random selection entirely and still have an experiment. For instance, cooperating WIN administrators could request WIN recipients to volunteer for the study. The evaluator could then randomly assign the volunteers to one of the three treatments. How the investigator selects the subjects for his study affects external validity. How he assigns them to treatments affects internal validity. While random selection together with random assignment go far to assure the overall validity of results, only the latter is necessary for true experiments.

Random assignment is a major element of internal validity. Randomization guarantees that the particular training program a WIN recipient receives does not depend on the recipient's sex, income, age, education, race, previous training, or motivation. Random assignment makes the personal characteristics of recipients in each training group statistically equivalent. It thus goes far to remove potentially spurious and confounding (Z) variables—even those that the researcher has not thought of or believes he cannot measure. Random assignment accomplishes this by transforming possible Z-variables into extraneous W-variables. As Figure 6.1 shows, experiments do not actually eliminate the influence of the personal characteristics of subjects; instead, they change this source of systematic error into a source of random error.

FIGURE 6.1

Random Assignment

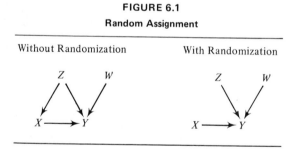

To illustrate, suppose that without random assignment, WIN administrators would ordinarily assign WIN recipients with the most prior work experience to vocational training, those with the least to orientation, and the rest to on-the-job training (OJT). In the absence of random assignment, prior work experience and type of treatment (X) are thus related. Since prior work experience undoubtedly influences future earnings (Y), experience should also be regarded as a potentially confounding or spurious (Z) variable. To transform this Z-variable into a W-variable and thereby remove it as a threat to internal validity, the investigator could use a simple random assignment procedure. Assignment to training programs could be based on the roll of a die for each subject such that a 1 or 2 means assignment to OJT, a 3 or 4 means vocational training, and a 5 or 6 means orientation. Assuming that the die is fair, then every subject has a 1/3 chance of getting any given treatment—no matter what his prior work experience, age, race, sex, or any other personal characteristic.[2] If the number of recipients assigned to each treatment is large enough, randomization makes it difficult for the investigator to reject the null hypothesis that there is no association between prior work experience (Z) and type of treatment (X). He will also be unlikely to reject the null hypothesis that there is no relation between type of treatment and sex, age, race, education, or any other personal characteristic of the subjects.[3] Random assignment thus makes potentially spurious and confounding (Z) variables statistically independent of the treatment (X).

Because random assignment makes Z-variables independent of X, pretesting in experiments is usually unnecessary. Pretesting is the measurement of subjects' scores on Y before the treatment is administered. To show why pretesting is needless in experiments, let Y_a be the posttreatment score on Y and let Y_b be a pretreatment score or pretest. Figure 6.2 shows that Y_b is actually a spurious or confounding variable. Random assignment therefore means that all groups in the experiment have statistically equivalent scores on Y_b. Unless the investigator needs to estimate the impact of both X and the pretest process itself, pretesting in experimental designs is unnecessary. Pretesting may even be detrimental, because it can sensitize subjects. The results from experiments using pretests may apply only to similarly sensitized subjects.[4]

FIGURE 6.2

Pretest Scores on Confounding Variables

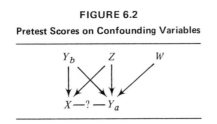

The subjects in an experiment are usually individual people, but they need not be. It is also possible to assign randomly entire neighborhoods or schools or other geographical and institutional units to different treatments. Experimental studies of alternative population control strategies have randomly assigned neighborhoods to treatments (Hilton and Lumsdaine 1975). The Office of Education's evaluation of the Emergency School Assistance Program randomly assigned schools to treatment and control groups (Gilbert, Light, and Mosteller 1975). In these instances, the neighborhood or school or other unit is the unit of observation, rather than the persons within each unit. If the investigator randomly assigns schools to treatments, the number of observations in each treatment group is the number of schools and not the number of students.

Randomly assigning groups to different treatments is sometimes preferable to randomly assigning individuals. Using groups as units of observation helps reduce "contamination" among individuals. Contamination can seriously reduce the difference between treatments, and is therefore a threat to internal validity. For example, an investigator might randomly assign persons living in a single city to different birth control programs. Two neighbors randomly assigned to different treatments who talk to each other will "contaminate" the treatments. By randomly assigning entire neighborhoods to different treatments, the investigator substantially diminishes the likelihood of contamination and thereby helps to assure that variation between the treatments (X) is as large as possible.[5]

Randomly assigning units rather than individuals to treatments sometimes forces the investigator to sacrifice observations from each treatment group. An investigator might have to choose between randomly assigning, say, 500 persons to one treatment and 500 to another or assigning five neighborhoods, each comprised of 100 persons, to one treatment and five 100-person neighborhoods to another treatment. In the former instance the investigator risks contamination but is reasonably sure of eliminating any correlation between the type of treatment and Z-variables. In the latter case, there are only five observations in each treatment. The investigator will have a hard time showing that the treatment is independent of the Z-variables, even though he has mitigated threats from contamination.[6]

Many issues of experimentation are political and moral, not statistical and technical. The challenge most frequently levied at the use of experimental designs to evaluate public programs is that experimentation is unethical.[7] Critics allege that experimentation unfairly deprives persons in the "control" group of potentially helpful treatments. While this charge may sometimes be accurate, two aspects need careful analysis. First of all, even the routine administration of many programs fails to supply enough resources to help everyone who is eligible. For example, the number of persons eligible for low- and moderate-income housing assistance far exceeds the funding levels authorized by Congress. In this instance, policymakers must choose between giving all eligibles an inadequate level of assistance and giving some eligibles a more adequate level of assistance. Policymakers usually select the latter alternative, and they must then separate the actual recipients from the eligible recipients. Head Start administrators apparently choose the most needy of the eligibles. Housing and manpower administrators appear to award the least needy of the eligibles, in a process called "creaming." Some programs rely on "first come, first served." Experimental designs use random assignment to separate the actual recipients from the eligibles. As long as some eligibles will not be served, random assignment is at least as defensible ethically as "creaming" and "first come, first served."[8]

Second, experiments need not deprive anyone of treatment because experiments need not have "control" groups that represent a "no treatment" alternative. The manpower training illustration discussed earlier in this chapter had three different treatments and no control group. Random assignment made the illustration a true experiment, even though no one was entirely deprived of treatment. The need to deprive subjects of a treatment depends on the type of experimental comparison the evaluator chooses to study. Three comparisons are possible (Hilton and Lumsdaine 1975). First, an investigator can compare two or more treatments against each other. Comparisons like these produce evidence regarding the relative effectiveness of program or management alternatives. Second, evaluators can compare one particular program or treatment against no program or treatment. Glennan (1972) calls treatment versus control group comparisons "go-no go" evaluations. Typically these comparisons produce conclusions about the effectiveness of an entire program. The third comparison falls between the first two: it entails comparing three or more treatment alternatives, in which one of the alternatives is no treatment at all.

There are sharp contrasts between the first two types of experimental comparisons. "Go-no go" comparisons may be unethical because they deprive subjects of treatment. They may also fail to meet the needs of program managers (Glennan 1972; Nielsen 1974; Boruch 1974). Because program managers do not like to be told that their program is ineffective, they often refuse to cooperate with evaluations that could produce damaging conclusions. Program managers are much more likely to cooperate with evaluators who compare two or more treatments. Comparing treatments can only disclose which is the best; it cannot uncover the ineffectiveness of an entire program.

Even though "go-no go" comparisions may be ethically and politically sensitive, they may be technically superior to evaluations of the relative effectiveness of two or more treatments. Simply comparing one treatment against no treatment at all makes it easier to maximize variation in X. We saw in Chapter 4 that randomly assigning individuals to different treatments cannot guarantee that between-treatment disparities are preserved once the treatments are implemented in the field. It is technically easier to ascertain that an experimentally induced difference between a particular treatment and none at all is actually carried out.

THE NEW JERSEY GRADUATED WORK
INCENTIVE EXPERIMENT

To show how the interaction among these technical, political, and ethical issues affects the design of experiments, it is instructive to take a close look at the first large-scale social experiment ever conducted in the U.S.—the New Jersey Graduated Work Incentive Experiment (NJGWIE). This experiment was large in several respects. In terms of time, the experiment spanned 6½ years from planning in 1967 to the final report in 1973. In terms of money, the experiment cost eight million dollars. One-third of this sum comprised cash payments to the 1,357 participating New Jersey and Pennsylvania families.[9]

Several factors command close scrutiny of the New Jersey study. Because it was the first large-scale experiment, its design has influenced subsequent experiments. Its design was also relatively complex and consequently illustrates many issues with which practicing evaluators should be familiar.[10] Even though the future of publicly funded large-scale social experiments may be in doubt, the issues with which the designers of the NJGWIE wrestled also face those who design small-scale experiments. The New Jersey study is thus a good vehicle for simultaneously considering the politics and statistics of social experiments.

The NJGWIE tested the influence of a negative income tax on the work effort of the employed poor. This issue was politically salient in the late 1960s when the Office of Economic Opportunity funded the experiment. Critics of income maintenance schemes feared that the poor would cease to work if they could get money without work. These fears were partly based on sound economic theory, which predicts that the higher the level of an income guarantee, the less the work effort. Economic theory also predicts that the rate at which income maintenance payments are reduced as earnings increase also affects work effort. Investigators hypothesized that work effort would decline as tax rates and guarantee levels went up.

Some examples reveal how plausible these hypotheses are. If the government were to guarantee $4,000 per year for a family of four, the government would send $4,000 annually (perhaps spreading the sum into twelve monthly payments) to a family with no earnings. If for each dollar the family earned, the government's payments were reduced a dollar, the implicit tax rate is 100%. Figure 6.3 depicts how a $4,000 guarantee and a 100% tax rate affects the total income of a hypothetical family. If the family's earning capacity less work expenses does not significantly exceed $4,000, then it nets $4,000 with working or without working. Under these circumstances, such a family will rationally prefer leisure to work.

FIGURE 6.3
Negative Income Tax Program:
$4,000 Guarantee, 100% Tax Rate

Earnings	Tax Payment (from government to individual)	Total Family Income (column 1 + column 2)
$ 0	$4,000	$4,000
$1,000	$3,000	$4,000
$2,000	$2,000	$4,000
$3,000	$1,000	$4,000
$4,000	$ 0	$4,000

Suppose now that the family faces a different negative income tax scheme. Let the guarantee level remain at $4,000, but let the tax rate drop to 30%, so that if the family earns $1.00, the government reduces its payment to the family by $0.30. The family keeps $0.70 of each dollar it earns. Figure 6.4 discloses that, by working, the family augments its income.

Although reducing the tax rate should increase work effort, it also makes the program more costly and vertically inequitable. Lowering the tax rate means that even middle-class families will receive negative tax payments. Under the plan in Figure 6.4, families earning as much as $12,000–$13,000 receive income

FIGURE 6.4

Negative Income Tax Program:
$4,000 Guarantee, 30% Tax Rate

Earnings	Tax Payment	Total Family Income
$ 0	$4,000	$ 4,000
$ 1,000	$3,700	$ 4,700
$ 2,000	$3,400	$ 5,400
$ 4,000	$2,800	$ 6,800
$ 6,000	$2,200	$ 8,200
$ 8,000	$1,600	$ 9,600
$12,000	$ 400	$12,400
$13,333	—	$13,333

maintenance payments. Such a prospect disturbs moderate and conservative politicians not only because it is costly but also because they believe that "welfare" should be reserved for "the poor."

Political liberals will also be unhappy with the scheme in Figure 6.4 because the guarantee level is so low: $4,000 was below the poverty line even in 1970, when the NJGWIE was being conducted. But a higher guarantee level would simultaneously reduce work effort, raise costs, and benefit the middle class. A high guarantee and a low tax rate were thus regarded as infeasible. A low guarantee and a high tax rate were equally infeasible. Although less costly to the government, such a plan was regarded as too stingy and as having too few work incentives. No one could devise the proper mix of guarantee level and tax rate that was politically palatable.

These political issues were based on two premises about the employment patterns of the working poor that could be empirically tested. Behind the NJGWIE lay the belief that accurate information regarding the amount of labor force contraction for each $1,000 increase in the guarantee level and for each 1% increase in the tax rate could aid the design of an acceptable welfare reform package. The evaluators actually assumed that increases in guarantee levels and tax rates reduced work effort. Indeed, they regarded their task as one of estimating *how much* work effort changed in response to these policy issues and selected the experimental approach as the best means to obtain accurate estimates.

The basic design was quite simple. Subjects were randomly assigned to one of eight different combinations of guarantee levels and tax rates, or to a control group. Subjects in the control group could obtain any AFDC payments in New Jersey for which they were eligible. The specific treatments to which subjects were assigned are shown by the "x's" in Figure 6.5. Subjects assigned to one of the eight treatments could choose between the particular treatment to which they were assigned and the existing New Jersey AFDC program. This was no real choice; without exception, the experimental treatments were more generous than New Jersey's AFDC program as it existed in 1967. All subjects could obtain

FIGURE 6.5
Treatments in NJGWIE

Guarantee	Tax Rate (%)		
(% of poverty line)	30	50	70
50	x	x	
75	x	x	x
100		x	x
125		x	

any in-kind transfers for which they qualified, including Medicaid, housing, and food stamps. Implicit in this design are two policy or treatment variables: X_1 is the tax rate and X_2 is the guarantee level. The effect measure, Y, is work effort. It was measured by two indicators: hours worked per week and weekly earnings.[11]

The investigators did not anticipate the actual findings. The study discovered little or no relationship between work effort and either of the treatment variables. These findings were disturbing to economists, for they contradicted basic principles—i.e., that work effort would decrease as the guarantee levels and tax rates increased. The findings also had significant policy implications, for they suggested that a negative income tax would not bring about massive withdrawals of the working poor from the U.S. labor force.

The validity of these findings has been controversial ever since they were first released in 1973. In the following pages, we will consider the internal and external validity of the experiment's findings according to the criteria discussed in previous chapters. We will first examine how well the NJGWIE maximized variation in X, controlled Z-variables, and eliminated problems of time order to attain internal validity. We will then scrutinize how the NJGWIE coped with external validity, experimental error, and interaction.

In hindsight, the problem of maximizing variation in the two treatment variables has been a critical issue in reanalyses of the NJGWIE. Critics charge that the "no effect" findings are invalid because the investigators failed to maximize variation in X. Had variation among the treatment groups and between the treatment and control groups been greater, they argue, the study would have disclosed that tax rates and guarantee levels do affect the work effort of the employed poor. Let us examine this charge in greater detail.

First of all, the experimental treatments did encompass a relatively wide range of tax rates—from 30% to 70%—and guarantee levels—from 50% to 125%—of the 1969 poverty line. Even so, not all possible tax rates and guarantee levels were examined. There were two good reasons to omit experimenting with additional treatments: high cost and political irrelevance. It would be costly to include both a 30% and a 32% tax rate. Since each treatment group needs enough subjects if the findings are to be statistically robust, adding more treatment groups requires more subjects. Each subject is eligible for a negative tax payment, depending on his earnings, and the investigators had a limited budget. There was no treatment group with a 100% tax rate, because such a high tax rate had never been on the political agenda. Tax rates lower than 30% were also absent from the political agenda.

Cost and politics also explain why only eight of twelve possible treatment combinations were included in the experiment. No subjects were assigned to a 50% guarantee level in combination with a 70% tax rate because that particular combination was too stingy to be politically acceptable. Incorporating such a treatment into the experiment would drain money from the experimental budget to adduce evidence about a politically irrelevant alternative. The investigators also excluded treatment groups with 30% tax rates and high guarantee levels, because these treatments were costly and their generosity made them politically irrelevant.[12]

These choices reflect a recurring dilemma of experimentation. Internal validity demands that variation between the treatments be as large as possible. But additional treatments are costly, and evaluators typically work within budget constraints. Evaluators also want their results to be politically useful, but politically relevant alternatives tend to be incremental. Investigators must often choose among internal validity, low cost, and political relevance because it may be impossible to attain all three at once.

Failure to maximize variation in treatments is also commonly attributable to the fact that, in practice, the experimenter cannot completely control the treatment to which subjects are assigned. The NJGWIE is no exception to this occurrence, because the assignment of subjects to different tax rates was only partly under the control of the experimenters (Anderson 1975). Consequently, the 40% variation in tax rates (70%-30%) was more apparent than real. Consider first subjects assigned to the three negative tax rate treatment groups—30%, 50%, and 70%. No matter in which group the subject finds himself, as each subject earns more, the government eventually pays nothing. The subject then becomes part of the positive tax system, where he faces a new and different tax rate which is not determined by the experiment. Persons assigned to a treatment group who continue to receive negative tax payments also remain eligible for any in-kind assistance available in New Jersey, including Medicaid, housing, and food stamps. The simultaneous receipt of cash payments from the NJGWIE along with in-kind assistance from New Jersey affects the tax rate facing each subject (Aaron 1973). A subject assigned to the experimental 30% tax rate may also face an implicit 70% tax rate from his housing assistance and food stamps. The subject's effective tax rate may be as high as 100%. Subjects assigned to an experimental 70% tax rate may also face 100% effective tax rates because of in-kind transfers. The net result eliminates the difference among experimentally assigned tax rates.

Nor do persons in the control group face a 0% tax rate. The actual rates confronting those in the control group are entirely self-selected and depend on whether the control subject is on welfare, receives food stamps, or faces the positive tax system. Even though the experimenter randomly assigns subjects to a control group, he cannot determine the tax rate that persons in the control group actually experience.[13]

Because assignment to actual tax rates was partially controlled by the subjects themselves, the NJGWIE also failed to remove completely problems of time order and the possibility of spurious and confounding variables. Both of these constitute threats to the internal validity of the experiment.

The problem of time order is one of ascertaining that the treatment (X) preceded the effect (Y). If the theory of economic behavior that undergirded the NJGWIE were true, then subjects randomly assigned to low tax rates will increase their work effort, and, as a consequence, their earnings. Some will augment their earnings enough to face the positive tax system, whose progressive aspects mean that higher tax rates accompany higher earnings. It is therefore possible that the negative tax rate each subject experiences affects his earnings and that earnings determine the tax rate as well. Figure 6.6 shows how the hypothetical inverse impact of tax rates on earnings could be counteracted by the positive influence of earnings on tax rates. Because these processes may cancel each other, an investigator could underestimate the impact of tax rates on earnings.

FIGURE 6.6
Time Order Problems in NJGWIE

Actual Tax ————⁻————▸ Weekly
Rate (X) ◂————⁺———— Earnings (Y)
(composed of
experimental tax
rate + implicit
tax rate)

It is possible to eliminate problems due to time order by explicitly transforming time-based effects into Z-variables. Measuring the dependent variable (Y) at two points in time changes the time order sequence displayed in Figure 6.6 into the pattern of confounding variables shown in Figure 6.7. One can then control statistically for previous earnings to eliminate the time-dependence.[14] The final report of the NJGWIE actually used this technique and controlled

FIGURE 6.7
Confounding Variable in NJGWIE

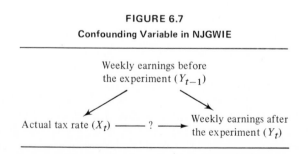

Weekly earnings before
the experiment (Y_{t-1})

Actual tax rate (X_t) ———— ? ————▸ Weekly earnings after
the experiment (Y_t)

prior earnings statistically. Its basic conclusion that there was no relation between the experimental treatments and work effort thus relied on statistical procedures to eliminate the time-dependence effects caused by a faulty random assignment procedure.[15]

The use of statistical controls in experiments is common practice. In theory, internally valid estimates of program impact do not require statistical controls because truly random assignment removes potentially spurious and confounding influences and ensures that the treatment precedes the effect. Experience from the NJGWIE reveals that practical considerations often preclude purely random assignment. In the case of the NJGWIE, complete randomness would have required subjects to waive eligibility for in-kind transfers. No subject would willingly assent to such an arrangement. The experimenters decided instead to use statistical controls to supplement an assignment process that was incompletely random.[16]

From a technical point of view, statistical controls are inferior to completely random assignment. It is always possible that other spurious or confounding variables besides preexperimental earnings affect both the implicit tax rate subjects faced as well as their postexperimental earnings. Failure to identify and measure these variables—if indeed they exist—would make the results of the NJGWIE internally invalid.[17]

Cost considerations dictated another modification of the random assignment procedure in the NJGWIE, and statistical procedures were used again to eliminate as many resulting errors as possible. Because cash payments to subjects comprised a large portion of the experimental budget, investigators feared assigning the poorest people to the most generous plans. The poorest people require the largest cash grants, no matter what treatment they undergo. Assigning them to low tax rate/high guarantee treatments necessitates even higher cash payments. Given a fixed budget, higher cash payments meant that fewer subjects could be included in the experiment. Reducing the number of subjects was undesirable because it would augment experimental error. The NJGWIE investigators decided instead to modify the random assignment procedure. The poorest people, who required the largest cash grants, were overrepresented in the least generous plans and the wealthiest people, who need small or even no payments, tended to predominate in the most generous plans. The experimenters thus deliberately introduced a Z-variable that would not have existed had assignment been completely random. (See Figure 6.8.) To eliminate income as a confounding or spurious variable, the investigators controlled statistically for a variety of variables that account for family income: preexperimental earnings and labor supply, age, education, ethnicity, number of adults, and number and ages of children. The investigators thus hoped to control for as many potentially confounding and spurious variables as possible while preserving the cost reductions and larger sample size that accompanied the modified random assignment procedure.

Systematic error in the measurement process is another confounding factor that could bias the results of the NJGWIE. While completely random assignment

FIGURE 6.8

Modified Random Assignment

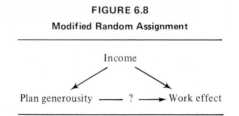

assures investigators that the personal characteristics of subjects in each treatment group are statistically equivalent, it cannot remove any differences in the measurement process among treatment groups. In the NJGWIE, the treated subjects had an incentive to underreport their earnings because subsequent tax payments would increase if reported earnings decreased. The controls, in contrast, had no such incentive. Nonrandom measurement errors like these mean that the actual findings of the NJGWIE could underestimate the difference between the earnings of those in the control and those in the treatment groups. Aware of this threat to internal validity, the investigators verified reported income with employers on a random basis. Nor was reported income the only dependent variable; hours worked were also reported, and there was no differential incentive for those in the treatment group to misreport this value. While results from the NJGWIE may be free of nonrandom measurement error, errors like these are a potential threat to internal validity that even the best random assignment procedure cannot control.

Our consideration of the NJGWIE so far has disclosed that its internal validity has been hotly debated. Internal validity requires that variation in X be as large as possible and that Z-variables be controlled by random assignment. The NJGWIE demonstrates that practical considerations often make both of these requirements unattainable. Strict adherence to these principles might have made the NJGWIE less palatable to the subjects, less relevant to the needs of decisionmakers, more costly, and quite possibly unethical.

Because the NJGWIE was designed to test the national impact of a major policy change, considerations of external validity were as important as those of internal validity. Just as the theoretical and practical requirements for internal validity diverge, the investigators found that considerations of politics, cost, and administrative simplicity necessitated compromises with external validity. A study of the effects of a negative income tax on the work effort of a random sample of all low-income families across the U.S. would theoretically assure a high degree of external validity. However, the actual sites were Patterson, Trenton, and Jersey City, New Jersey; and Scranton, Pennsylvania.[18] These are moderately sized industrial cities located in the northeast, and they all have similar labor markets. The actual subjects were representative of a special subgroup of the poor. Subjects had to be families with able-bodied males between 18 and 58 years of age, incomes below 150% of the poverty line, and at least one dependent.

These decisions reduced the external validity of the study's findings, but the choices were nonetheless justifiable. The investigators wanted to launch their experimental study of an alternative system of delivering welfare in states and cities whose political leaders and top welfare personnel were cooperative. They also wanted subjects to be reasonably proximate to one another and to the investigators; such an arrangement reduces experimental costs. New Jersey was selected because some of the investigators resided in New Jersey, and the state promised to cooperate. The investigators also decided to select subjects from several New Jersey cities rather than from a single city. Selecting a large number of poor persons from a single city threatened contamination, because subjects might talk to one another. It could also unnecessarily sacrifice external validity. On the other hand, selecting subjects from the entire state without regard to their city of residence would increase administrative costs of running the experiment and augment random influences as well. Cooperation of the political leaders in each city affected would also have to be secured. The decision to sample families in four "typical" New Jersey cities was thought to be a reasonable compromise between these extremes. In this fashion, the investigators hoped to provide evidence that would apply to other northeastern industrial cities with declining central city populations.

Another reason was instrumental in choosing New Jersey as a site. At the time the NJGWIE was designed, New Jersey had no AFDC-Unemployed Parent program. The AFDC-UP program resembles a negative income tax because it renders assistance to children in intact families. To maximize the difference between the treatment groups, eligible for a negative income tax, and the control group, eligible for "welfare," the investigators wanted a site where the existing welfare system was as different from a negative tax plan as possible. In this respect, New Jersey appeared at first to be a good choice. During the course of the experiment, New Jersey adopted a very generous AFDC-UP program, thereby reducing the difference between the treatment and control groups. This development led the investigators to expand the study by adding a more generous negative income tax plan (125%/70%) that could compete with New Jersey's AFDC-UP program.[19]

New Jersey was also an imperfect site because only a few white families appeared in the example. The investigators added Scranton, Pennsylvania, as a test site to augment the white sample. In so doing, the investigators also confounded race with city. This became an important problem, since the final results indicated that the impact of a negative tax on work effort depended on race. Since most whites lived in Scranton, it was impossible to disentangle the influence of race from that of city.

The investigators also justifiably restricted external validity by excluding poor households with single (usually female) heads from the study. Politicians and researchers alike feared that a negative income tax would drive the employed poor from the labor market. The possibility that female heads of households might also withdraw from the labor market under a negative income tax was not worrisome, because most of these persons were not in the labor market anyway. AFDC eligibles tend to have only a weak attachment to the labor force, but the failure of the employed poor to work could have major economic consequences.

A serious criticism of the NJGWIE's external validity is based on the investigators' decision to base eligibility for the study on total family income. This decision possibly produced an atypical representation of the employed poor. Most of the employed poor have two breadwinners, and the total income of these families often exceeds 150% of the poverty line, rendering them ineligible for inclusion in the experiment. Lyall (1975) suggests that eligibility should have been determined by the income of the head of the family alone. After selection, payment could be based on total family income.

Another issue of external validity concerns the duration of the experiment. The NJGWIE made payments to eligibles for three years. Some critics argue that this period is too short from which to generalize. Subjects knew the program was temporary, and they may have regarded their payments as temporary windfall gains and altered their behavior accordingly.[20] Similarly, the consciousness of being in the experiment can also alter subjects' behavior in unknown ways.

Hindsight suggests that the NJGWIE, despite its use of random assignment, had only limited success in attaining both internal and external validity. Despite these limitations, the experiment was politically important, for its results appeared to dispel the notion that "welfare reform" would cause massive withdrawals from the labor force. Critics of large-scale social experiments nonetheless point to their huge costs, their compromises with randomization, and their inconclusive results as arguments for ceasing social experimentation.

These charges can more justifiably be levied against large-scale experiments than against all social experiments. Small-scale experiments are less costly and are easier to administer. For example, one social service agency randomly selected and assigned 150 "multiproblem family" cases to one of three treatments: treatment by social workers with more experience and lighter caseloads who were aware of the study, treatment by similar social workers who were not aware of the study, and no special treatment. Treatment lasted two years. Another jurisdiction randomly assigned delinquent girls to special treatments in order to assess their relative effectiveness in reducing delinquency. Many jurisdictions have randomly assigned convicts to community treatment programs in order to determine whether these programs successfully reduce recidivism. The Los Angeles Sheriffs' Academy randomly assigned new police recruits to two different training programs.[21] One federal agency also randomly assigned delinquent mortagees to counseling programs in order to determine whether counseling averts foreclosure (U.S. Department of Housing and Urban Development 1977).

The basic issues of experimentation are thus not ones of scale, feasibility, or cost. Instead, a more fundamental issue characterizes nearly all evaluation designs, including experiments, which, in principle, are the most accurate. Many experiments discussed in this chapter disclose little or no program impact. The NJGWIE revealed that negative income tax payments have only a small influence on work effort. Findings from the Experimental Housing Allowance Program indicate that housing allowances affect neither the quality of housing nor the amount of residential segregation. Many of the small-scale studies we mentioned also disclose that seemingly divergent treatments appear to have distressingly similar impact.[22] There are two explanations for findings like these: either they are correct or they reflect an inadequate experimental methodology.

The propensity of experimental findings to reveal small differences between treatments may be attributable to the difficulty of simultaneously removing experimental error and achieving internal and external validity. While experiments gain internal validity by controlling for spurious and confounding variables, they do not necessarily maximize variation between treatments. Experience from the NJGWIE suggests that costs and political requirements conspire to reduce the between-treatment differences. As variation in X, the treatment, diminishes, the harder it is to reject the null hypothesis that there is no difference between the treatments. Experiments are also subject to random error because random assignment only transforms Z-variables into W-variables. One of the best ways to remove extraneous influences like these is to perform a laboratory experiment; laboratory experiments have little or no generality. In contrast, the field experiment adduces many additional extraneous factors that affect Y. Separating the impact of X on Y from the influence of all the other variables that also affect Y may require more precision than existing methods permit. It is thus not surprising that we so frequently find that X has little effect on Y.

In the NJGWIE, many factors influence work effort besides the tax rates and income guarantee levels that confront a family. Many of these variables were controlled in the experiment—including factors like industrial and economic conditions, previous work experience, sex, race and ethnicity, number of children, and number of workers. Other factors that may have a large impact on work effort were not controlled. Sociologists suggest that the desire for status and recognition in the community, job satisfaction, friends at work, and even problems at home influence work effort. In comparison to all of these factors, the influence of tax rates and guarantee levels might plausibly be quite marginal and very difficult to detect.

Two compromises could make it easier for experiments to detect program impact. One is to increase the difference between the treatments that are tested. This strategy, we have seen, can be costly and politically unsupportable. A second compromise is to eliminate random influences. This strategy can also be costly, and may require the investigator to sacrifice external validity. Even though dilemmas like these have no solution, investigators must nonetheless be aware of the tradeoffs their decisions entail. Investigators who are not cognizant of these tradeoffs are even more likely to produce experimental findings which indicate that divergent policies have identical results.

FOOTNOTES

1. The subjects in an experiment need not be persons. Entire neighborhoods, schools, or city blocks could, in principle, be the subjects in an experiment. No matter what the subjects are, there must be "enough" for statistical generalization. See Campbell and Stanley (1963, Ch. 4–6) and Riecken and Boruch (1974, Ch. 3) for a general discussion of the principles of random assignment and experimental designs.

2. In this example, every subject has an equal chance of receiving each treatment. Random assignment in general does not require equal probabilities. It means instead that the probability of receiving any given treatment is known (and not necessarily equal) and that assignment is by chance alone.

3. The larger the number of subjects randomly assigned to each treatment, the more likely it is that the hypothesis of no relation between X and Z will be accepted. When the number of subjects (N) in a study is very small, random assignment should not be attempted. A quasi-experimental approach will probably be better when N is small. Precisely how large N should be for experimental research depends on a variety of factors, including the number of treatments, the desired level of statistical confidence, and the quality of alternative quasi experiments that are feasible. However, it is probably fair to say that no experiment should have fewer than 20 subjects in each treatment.

4. Ross and Smith (1968) show in detail how pretesting introduces unnecessary complications in experiments.

5. Contamination also reduces the validity of statistical tests of significance, which assume that observations are independent of one another. See Glendening (1977).

6. Hilton and Lumsdaine (1975) point out that randomly assigning groups rather than individuals to treatments also affects experimental error, especially when groups are randomly assigned but individuals within each group are the unit of analysis. If the variation in Y-scores among individuals within each group exceeds the variation in mean scores on Y (or $\bar{Y}$) between each group, then randomly assigning groups increases the relative impact of extraneous (W) variables on the individuals within each group, and makes program effects hard to detect. Randomly assigning groups can have the opposite effect too. When the within-group differences in Y are less than the between-group differences in $\bar{Y}$, randomly assigning groups makes the individuals more homogeneous, and thus reduces random error.

7. The wide variety of circumstances in which experiments have actually been performed and the large sums of public funds that support randomized experiments suggest that many people accept both the logic and ethics of social experimentation. For some examples of experiments, see Boruch, McSweeny, and Soderstrom (1978); Gilbert, Light, and Mosteller (1975); and Riecken and Boruch (1974: 279–324).

8. For a detailed and serious defense of the ethical advantages of experimentation, see Boruch (1974). For a dissent, see Acland (1979). For a discussion of tradeoffs, see Abt (1978). Both Acland and Abt consider the Emergency School Aid Act.

9. For analyses of the NJGWIE in its entirety, see Kershaw and Skidmore, 1974; Rossi and Lyall, 1976; Pechman and Timpane, 1975; and Rees, 1974. Similar experiments were also undertaken in Seattle, Denver, and Gary. We will not consider these related studies here.

10. Nearly all field experiments, no matter what their size, face essentially the same problems of experimental design that the NJGWIE faced. Among the actual field experiments that were influenced by the NJGWIE are the Health Insurance Experiment and the demand portion of the Experimental Housing Allowance Program. See Newhouse (1974) and Buchanan and Heinberg (1972).

11. There were other dependent variables, but work effort was central. Subsequent reanalyses have examined the effect of the treatments on family stability, home ownership, etc. See Baumol (1974) and Rossi (1975).

12. The absence of a 70%/125% treatment group will be addressed subsequently. The 125% treatment was added after the experiment had begun.

13. For a general discussion of problems that investigators can encounter in the random assignment process see Conner (1977). Campbell and Boruch (1975) argue that, despite complications in the random assignment process, the internal validity of experiments exceeds that of quasi-experimental and nonexperimental approaches.

14. Techniques of statistical control are considered in Chapters 8 and 9.

15. If the reciprocal relation between earnings and tax rates operates during the course of the experiment, controlling for preexperimental earnings alone may not entirely remove the time-dependence effect portrayed in Figure 6.6.

16. In addition to controlling for preexperiment earnings, the investigators also controlled statistically for preexperiment labor supply, age, education, number of adults, number and ages of children, and sites. Preexperiment labor supply was controlled for the same reasons preexperiment earnings were.

17. Chapter 9 shows that the presence of random measurement error in statistical controls also alters internal validity.

18. To attain external validity, the NJGWIE has since been replicated in other cities. These comments apply to the New Jersey study alone.

19. For a detailed discussion of the impact of the New Jersey's AFDC-UP program on the NJGWIE results, see Garfinkel (1974).

20. For a detailed discussion of this issue, see Metcalf (1974).

21. Gilbert, Light, and Mosteller (1975) describe these and other experiments in greater detail.

22. See also Waldo and Chiricos (1977), Berman (1978), and Acland (1979) for discussions of experiments that show little or no impact.

LIST OF REFERENCES

Aaron, Henry J. *Why Is Welfare So Hard to Reform?* Washington, D.C.: The Brookings Institution, 1973.

Abt, Wendy Peter. "Design Issues in Policy Research: A Controversy." *Policy Analysis* 4 (1978):91–122.

Akland, Henry. "Are Randomized Experiments the Cadillacs of Design?" *Policy Analysis* 5 (1979):223–242.

Anderson, Andy B. "Policy Experiments: Selected Analytic Issues." *Sociological Methods and Research* 4 (1975):13–30.

Baumol, William J. "An Overview of the Results on Consumption, Health, and Social Behavior." *The Journal of Human Resources* 9 (1974):253–264.

Berman, John J. "An Experiment in Parole Supervision." *Evaluation Quarterly* 2 (1978): 71–90.

Boruch, Robert F. "On Common Contentions About Randomized Experiments for Evaluating Social Programs." Unpublished manuscript, Evaluation Research Program, Dept. of Psychology, Northwestern University, 1974.

Boruch, Robert F.; McSweeny, A. John; and Soderstrom, E. Jon. "Randomized Field Experiments for Program Planning, Development, and Evaluation: An Illustrative Bibliography." *Evaluation Quarterly* 2 (1978):655–695.

Buchanan, Garth, and Heinberg, John. *Housing Allowance Household Experiment Design.* Part I: *Summary and Overview*, working paper 205-4. Washington, D.C.: The Urban Institute, 1972.

Campbell, Donald T., and Boruch, Robert F. "Making the Case for Randomized Assignment to Treatments by Considering the Alternatives: Six Ways in Which Quasi-Experimental Evaluations in Compensatory Education Tend to Underestimate Effects." Ch. 3 in Bennett, Carl A., and Lumsdaine, Arthur A., eds. *Evaluation and Experiment.* New New York, Academic Press, Inc., 1975.

Campbell, Donald T., and Stanley, Julian C. *Experimental and Quasi-Experimental Designs for Research.* Chicago: Rand McNally and Co., 1963.

Conner, Ross F. "Selecting a Control Group: An Analysis of the Randomization Process in Twelve Social Reform Programs." *Evaluation Quarterly* 1 (1977): 195-244.

Garfinkel, Irwin. "The Effects of Welfare Programs on Experimental Responses." *The Journal of Human Resources* 9 (1974): 504-529.

Gilbert, John G.; Light, Richard J.; and Mosteller, Frederick. "Assessing Social Innovations: An Empirical Base for Policy." Ch. 2 in Bennett, Carl A., and Lumsdaine, Arthur A., eds. *Evaluation and Experiment.* New York: Academic Press, Inc., 1975.

Glendening, Linda Kay. "Operationally Defining the Assumption of Independence and Choosing the Appropriate Unit of Analysis." Unpublished Ph.D. dissertation, Michigan State University, 1977.

Glennan, Thomas K., Jr. "Evaluating Federal Manpower Programs: Notes and Observations." Ch. 9 in Rossi, Peter H., and Williams, Walter. *Evaluating Social Programs: Theory, Practice and Politics.* New York: Seminar Press, 1972.

Hilton, Elizabeth T., and Lumsdaine, Arthur A. "Field Trial Designs in Gauging the Impact of Fertility Planning Programs." Ch. 5 in Bennett, Carl A., and Lumsdaine, Arthur A., eds. *Evaluation and Experiment.* New York: Academic Press, Inc., 1975.

Kershaw, David N., and Skidmore, Felicity. *The New Jersey Graduated Work Incentive Experiment.* Mathematica Policy Analysis Series, no. 1. Princeton, N.J.: Mathematica, Inc. 1974.

Lyall, Katharine C. "Some Observations on Design Issues in Large-Scale Social Experiments," *Sociological Methods and Research* 4 (1975): 54-76.

Metcalf, Charles E. "Predicting the Effects of Permanent Programs from a Limited Duration Experiment." *The Journal of Human Resources* 9 (1974): 530-555.

Newhouse, Joseph P. "A Design for a Health Insurance Experiment." *Inquiry* 11 (1974): 5-27.

Nielson, Victor G. "Why Evaluation Does Not Improve Program Effectiveness," *Policy Studies Journal* 3 (1975): 385-390.

Pechman, Joseph, and Timpane, P. Michael, eds. *Work Incentives and Income Guarantees: The New Jersey Negative Income Tax Experiment.* Washington, D.C.: The Brookings Institution, 1975.

Rees, Albert. "An Overview of the Labor-Supply Results." *The Journal of Human Resources* 9 (1974): 158-180.

Riecken, Henry W., and Boruch, Robert F., eds. *Social Experimentation: A Method for Planning and Evaluating Social Intervention.* New York: Academic Press, 1974.

Ross, John, and Smith, Perry. "Orthodox Experimental Designs." Ch. 9 in Blalock, Hubert M., Jr., and Blalock, Ann B., eds. *Methodology in Social Research.* New York: McGraw-Hill, 1968.

Rossi, Peter. "A Critical Review of the Analysis of Nonlabor Force Responses." *Work Incentives and Income Guarantees: The New Jersey Negative Income Tax Experiment,* edited by Joseph Pechman and P. Michael Timpane, pp. 157-182. Washington, D.C.: The Brookings Institution, 1975.

Rossi, Peter H., and Lyall, Katharine C. *Reforming Public Welfare: A Critique of the Negative Income Tax Experiment.* New York: Russell Sage Foundation, 1976.

U.S. Department of Housing and Urban Development, Assistant Secretary for Policy Development and Research, Office of Policy Development and Program Evaluation, Division of Special Studies. *Counseling for Delinquent Mortgagors II, A Staff Study.* Washington D.C.: U.S. Government Printing Office, 1977.

U.S. Department of Housing and Urban Development, Office of Policy Development and Research. *A Summary Report of Current Findings From the Experimental Housing Allowance Program.* Washington, D.C.: U.S. Government Printing Office, 1978.

Waldo, Gordon P., and Chiricos, Theodore G. "Work Release and Recidivism: An Empirical Evaluation of a Social Policy." *Evaluation Quarterly* 1 (1977):87–108.

Chapter 7

QUASI-EXPERIMENTAL DESIGNS

PROPERTIES OF QUASI EXPERIMENTS

The absence of random assignment distinguishes quasi experiments from true experiments. Quasi experiments employ comparison groups that are as similar as possible on all potentially confounding and spurious variables. In theory the comparison groups should differ only in respect to the treatment they receive. Quasi-experimental designs strive to resemble randomized experiments by selecting comparison groups that have the same score on all Z-variables and that differ according to their scores on X alone.

In practice, quasi experiments differ from randomized experiments in several respects. Quasi experiments tend to be retrospective, although they need not be. When the decision to evaluate program impact comes long after the program is in effect, the possibility of experimentation is usually foreclosed. Under these circumstances, quasi-experimental approaches are frequently the only feasible way to estimate program impact. Prospective quasi experiments also require nearly as much advance planning as experiments. Prospective evaluations are therefore equally likely to be experimental or quasi-experimental (or nonexperimental). Even though most quasi experiments are retrospective, the examples in this chapter suggest that the internal validity of a well-designed prospective quasi experiment can sometimes exceed that of an experiment.[1]

Unlike experiments, quasi-experimental designs incorporate several approaches to evaluation, ranging from those that require data for many comparison groups measured for a long period of time to those that resemble simple case studies. Quasi experiments relying on a judicious use of comparison groups tend to require more information. Designs like these also attain the most internal validity. Whenever these designs also require advance planning by program officials, they may be as difficult to implement as true experiments.

The internal validity of most quasi experiments is ordinarily more questionable than that of experiments. Quasi experiments require the construction of groups that are comparable on all potentially confounding and spurious variables without the use of random assignment. Random assignment guarantees that subjects will be statistically comparable no matter what treatment they receive. Randomization also relieves the investigator of identifying every variable that could cause subjects to select one treatment over another. In contrast, the quasi experiment requires the investigator to identify each of these characteristics, measure them, and construct comparison groups accordingly. Successfully executing these tasks may be quite troublesome. If the investigator can accurately identify all of the spurious and confounding variables, he will probably know so much about his topic that there is no need to do the evaluation in the first place. Even if the investigator can identify all the Z-variables, he may not be able to measure them; data may be unavailable, or the variables may be highly abstract concepts that are awkward to measure. If data and measurement are not problematic, it still may be difficult to locate subjects who are comparable on all of the Z-variables and differ with regard to the treatment (X) variable. Once located, the subjects may be such an odd subset of the target population that the sample lacks external validity.

Suppose that an investigator is asked to determine whether burglary prevention programs effectively reduce burglaries. Suppose further that experimentation is unadvisable or impossible and so the investigator selects a quasi-experimental approach. He may decide to compare burglary rates in communities with prevention programs to burglary rates in those without, but he must also assure himself that these communities have equivalent values on potentially confounding and spurious variables. Otherwise, any observed difference in burglary rates could be attributable to preexisting community differences on these variables instead of the prevention program. Selecting comparable communities requires the investigator to enumerate Z-variables such as the residential character of the community, community wealth, the size of the police department, the professionalism of the police chief, and the burglary rate itself. Ascertaining that communities are actually equivalent in these respects necessitates measuring each variable. Some variables are easier to measure than others. Measures of "professionalism" are, at best, accurate only to an ordinal level, and obtaining the value of these variables in each community prior to the community's decision to adopt the prevention program may be impossible. Yet finding historical values of variables is often necessary when evaluation succeeds the inception of the program. Finally, locating communities that are equivalent with regard to spurious and confounding variables but disparate with regard to the treatment could produce an empty or an atypical set. This outcome is most likely when the Z-variables are highly predictive of program adoption.[2] If nearly all communities with burglary prevention programs have high burglary rates, high-income residential areas, and professional police chiefs with a large staff, locating a similar community without a burglary prevention program could be futile. Even when it is possible to locate a few similar communities, so that some have prevention programs whereas others do not, the resulting sample may be extremely atypical. In practice, investigators examine communities that are just roughly comparable on the most important spurious and confounding variables. Reducing comparability sacrifices some internal validity in exchange for a more representative set of communities to examine.

Problems like these plague all quasi experiments, and it is tempting to conclude that quasi experiments are a waste of time. Nonexperimental approaches, however, share the same weaknesses as quasi experiments, and randomized experiments are not always feasible or even completely random. When the number of subjects is small, quasi experiments may even be superior to true experiments. Very often, the effective choice is to select the best possible quasi experiment, or do no evaluation at all.

The variety of quasi-experimental designs discussed in the remainder of this chapter indicates that while all quasi experiments are subject to questions about validity, these questions are likely to affect some quasi experiments more than others. Quasi experiments are actually a family of designs whose shared characteristic is the use of at least one comparison group. The following pages outline only the properties of the most representative members of the entire family. Investigators will often find it useful to combine these basic designs into unique quasi experiemnts appropriate for special situations.

THE INTERRUPTED TIME-SERIES COMPARISON GROUP DESIGN

The interrupted time-series with a comparison group (ITSCG) is among the quasi experiments that, when properly implemented, has the most potential to resist bias. Figure 7.1 shows two ways to conceptualize this design. The curves show that the interrupted time-series compares the change in Y-values over time for two groups. One is the "treated" group and the other is untreated. The use of two groups is purely illustrative. ITSCG designs can also be used to compare the impact of three or more different treatments; for simplicity, the discussion below centers on just two comparison groups.[3]

The interpretation of results from an ITSCG design depends on the pattern of data that emerges as well as on the nature of the intervention. Clark (1976) indicates some of the patterns that an investigator might observe. Patterns like those shown in Figure 7.2(a) and 7.2(b) indicate that the program has had an abrupt and permanent impact. Investigators should not expect patterns like these when program changes are gradual or incremental. Most often, results are not so clear cut. Figures 7.2(c) and 7.2(d) suggest a delayed result, but it is also possible that a major change subsequent to the treatment, rather than the treatment itself, accounts for the delayed response. Figure 7.2(e) could indicate that a gradual intervention was effective, but it could also suggest no impact if the change was abrupt. Figure 7.2(f) suggests that some programs simply increase the instability of outcome measures. Thus, interpreting the results from an ITSCG depends on the type of intervention. The validity of these interpretations also rests on the assumption that there are no threats to the internal validity of the design. It is

FIGURE 7.1

The Interrupted Time-Series with Comparison Group (ITSCG)

(a) Graphic

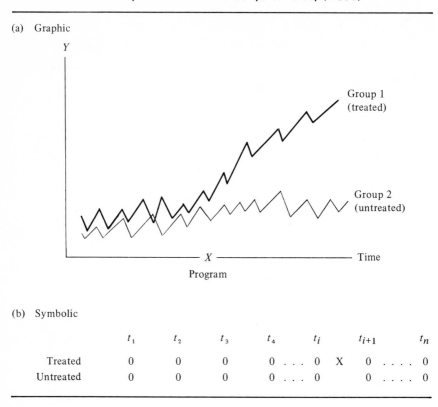

(b) Symbolic

	t_1	t_2	t_3	t_4	t_i		t_{i+1}	t_n
Treated	0	0	0	0 . . . 0	X		0 0	
Untreated	0	0	0	0 . . . 0			0 0	

also necessary to separate program impact from random influences by using appropriate statistical tests.

The best way to develop an ITSCG design that is internally valid, general,
and free of random error is to anticipate what the potentially spurious, confounding, and extraneous variables might be prior to contructing the comparison
groups. Suppose that an investigator wishes to determine whether the Farmers'
Home Administration weatherization loan program (*X*) reduces the borrowers'
utility consumption (*Y*). This program was actually implemented in rural counties where the electric cooperatives volunteered to administer it. An ITSCG could
be used to compare household utility demand in counties without the weatherization program to demand in similar counties before and after adoption of the
program. (See Figure 7.3.) To attain internal validity, comparison counties must
have roughly similar values on potentially spurious and confounding variables. In
order to select the comparison counties, the investigator must enumerate what
these variables might be. Empirical inspection might reveal that electric coopera-

FIGURE 7.2
Possible Results from ITSCG Design

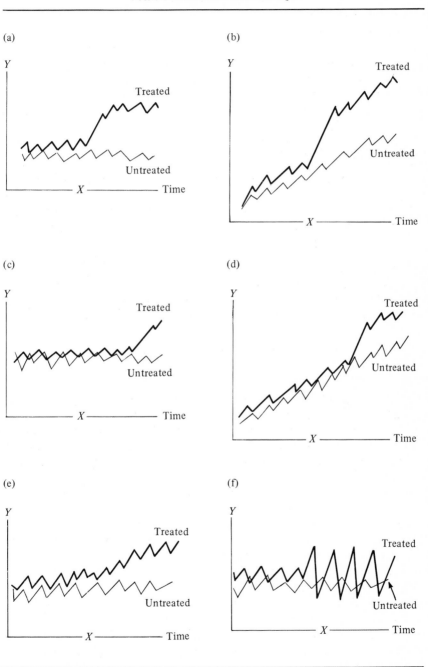

FIGURE 7.3

**ITSCG to Examine Weatherization Program:
Hypothetical Data**

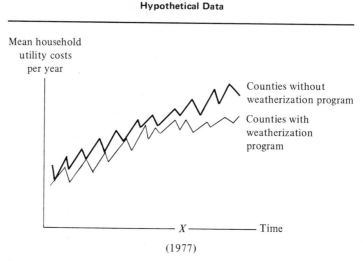

Mean household
utility costs
per year

Counties without
weatherization program

Counties with
weatherization
program

X ———— Time

(1977)

tives in counties with low-income (Z_1), high energy needs (Z_2), and high costs (Z_3) tended to adopt weatherization programs (X) and to have high utility demand (Y). Counties whose utility demand had been creeping upward (Y_{t-1}) may also tend to have the weatherization program (X); these counties are also likely to have high utility demand (Y_t) even without a weatherization program. Figure 7.4 displays these possibly confounding or spurious variables by diagram.

For internal validity, the investigator should locate counties without weatherization programs but with roughly the same income, energy needs, energy costs, and prior pattern of consumption increases as counties with weatherization programs. The investigator should also ascertain that counties with weatherization programs do not also have other energy-related programs which the com-

FIGURE 7.4

Causal Model for Weatherization Program

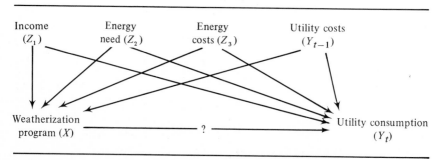

Income
(Z_1)

Energy
need (Z_2)

Energy
costs (Z_3)

Utility costs
(Y_{t-1})

Weatherization
program (X) ———— ? ———— Utility consumption
(Y_t)

parison counties do not also have. Otherwise, these other programs, rather than the weatherization loans, could account for any observed differences in utility usage. Under these conditions, a graph of average annual utility consumption for counties with and without weatherization loans both preceding and following the program's inception should reveal the impact of weatherization on utility demand. If the investigator has accurately identified and measured all of the possible Z-variables, then this design will produce unbiased results. But in practice the investigator can never entirely rule out the possibility that he has overlooked or poorly measured one or more of these variables.

The external validity of this design depends on the investigator's ability to locate subsets of counties which are identical in respect to all of the Z-variables but which differ in respect to X. Suppose that the investigator can only identify a set of low-income counties with high energy needs, large fuel bills, and increasing demand that differ only in respect to a weatherization program. At best, the investigator can apply his results only to counties with these characteristics. To extend his results, the investigator must identify a different set of counties. Sometimes, additional sets may not exist. In all cases, searching for additional sets augments the cost of evaluation. In the context of weatherization loans, the investigator could decide that the need for generality does not warrant its cost.

Random influences also make it difficult to interpret results from the ITSCG design. Computing "moving averages" is one of the easiest ways to smooth a time-series. A three-year moving average, for example, uses the mean for the first three years as the first observation, the mean for the second, third and fourth years as the second observation, the mean for the third to fifth years as the third observation, and so on. If an original time-series spanned twelve years, the corresponding three-year moving average time series would thus have ten observations.[4]

If the groups in an interrupted time-series are truly comparable, the design will be internally valid. Comparability on Z-variables guards against the threat of spurious and confounding variables. The interrupted time-series will also nearly always require comparability on previous trends in the dependent variable. Past behavior is a recurring confounding variable whose influence experiments remove by random assignment. If comparability is attained, the internal validity of the interrupted time-series will be secure at least relative to other quasi experiments.[5] In contrast, attaining external validity using an ITSCG design may not be practical and could be impossible. Nonetheless, in evaluation research, the absence of generality does not necessarily compromise utility.

Although the ITSCG is among the best quasi-experimental approaches, it is not always an appropriate design. To use the design, concurrent time-series data must be available for two groups of subjects—those who were treated and those who were not. These data must also record behavior before and after treatment commences. The design is thus inappropriate for evaluating the impact of policies that have a universal impact. When policies apply universally, comparison groups from which treatment has been withheld do not exist.

Some policies, like Medicaid, which became law in 1965, have a universal impact, but only within a single class of eligibles. Medicaid affected the health care of the entire poverty population in the U.S. No comparison group exists. Unlike the national 55-mph speed limit, Medicaid did not affect the entire nation. In instances such as Medicaid, the investigator can modify the ITSCG by substituting a noncomparable group for the comparison group. One study of the impact of Medicaid on physician use compared low-income Medicaid eligibles to high-income ineligibles.[6] Figure 7.5 reveals that the use of physicians has decreased among all income levels except among those eligible for Medicaid. In this design, income is the primary confounding variable, because income deter-

FIGURE 7.5
Interrupted Time-Series with Noncomparable Groups: Medicaid

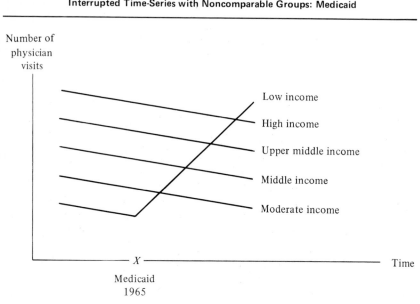

mines Medicaid eligibility as well as physician use. But the comparison groups do not have the same income. The internal validity of this design is difficult to assail, but the design must be selectively used because policy changes rarely have such universal impact on a single class of eligibles.[7]

THE REGRESSION-DISCONTINUITY DESIGN

The regression-discontinuity design is another quasi experiment. This design compares the regression of Y, the outcome measure, on the eligibility criterion, which is usually a Z-variable, both for those who are treated and for those who are not treated. It is appropriate only when the distinction between treated and untreated groups rests on a clear, quantitative eligibility criterion. Both the eligibility criterion as well as the impact measure (Y) must be continuous variables.

The design could be used to evaluate an interest credit program of the Farmers' Home Administration. This program subsidizes low-income homeowners residing in rural areas. One purpose of the program (X) is to improve the housing quality (Y) of low-income homeowners. To apply the regression-discontinuity design, the dependent variable must be continuous. Accordingly, a suitable indicator of housing quality might be the market value of the home. The eligibility criterion is also based on a continuous variable: only households with annual incomes under $10,000 can receive the subsidy.

Figure 7.6 graphs the regression-discontinuity design. The design compares the regression of housing value on income for households with interest credit subsidies to the same regression calculated for ineligible households.[8] The upward slope of both regressions indicates that as income increases, the expected home values do also. Program impact is measured at the eligibility cutpoint. In the example, the expected home value of those whose income is just below the eligibility cutpoint exceeds the expected home value of those whose income is

FIGURE 7.6

**Regression-Discontinuity Design: The Impact
of Subsidized Interest Credit on Home Values**

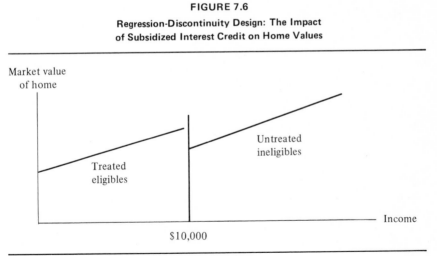

just above the cutpoint. At the cutpoint, the program is successful.[9] Had the regression line for the ineligibles resembled that shown in Figure 7.7, the program would be considered ineffective.

The regression-discontinuity design has a compelling rationale. It assumes that subjects just above and just below the eligibility cutpoint are equivalent on all potentially spurious and confounding variables and differ only in respect to the treatment. According to this logic, if the treated just-eligibles have homes whose value exceed those of the untreated just-ineligibles, then the treatment

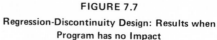

FIGURE 7.7

Regression-Discontinuity Design: Results when
Program has no Impact

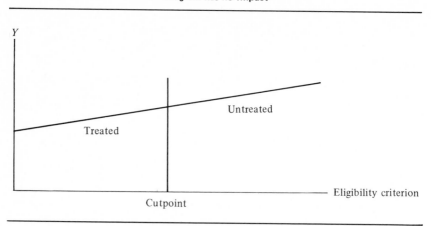

should be considered effective. The linear nature of the regressions makes it possible to extrapolate these results to the rest of the treated and untreated groups.

The limits of the design are also compelling. Its results are ambiguous if the cutpoint for treatment eligibility is also the eligibility criterion for other types of services. Its results are equally ambiguous when regressions are not linear. Figure 7.8 indicates that differentiating between the continuation of a downward trend and a program effect when one regression is nonlinear may be difficult. In addition, the design requires follow-up data on treated and untreated groups. While bureaus often retain data on the outcome measure (e.g., market value of homes) for their clients, they rarely retain comparable data for ineligibles. Data for those not treated must be sought from other sources.

Assuming that treated just-eligibles are comparable on all potentially spurious and confounding variables to untreated just-ineligibles may also be unwise.

FIGURE 7.8

Regression-Discontinuity with Nonlinearities

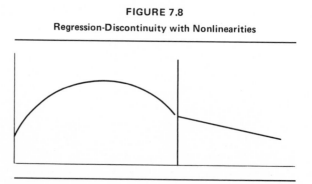

Figure 7.9 depicts two groups of eligibles: those who volunteer and those who do not. Similarly, of those who are ineligible for a program, some will apply and be rejected, while others will refrain from applying. The regression-discontinuity design does not control for this potentially confounding influence. Nor is it clear how the design should address the problem of volunteers. Two comparisons are possible. An investigator could compare eligible volunteers to ineligible volunteers. (See arrow (a) in Figure 7.9.) Ineligible volunteers are persons who applied for the program and were rejected. Eligible volunteers could also be compared to ineligible nonvolunteers. (See arrow (b) in Figure 7.9.) The first comparison is

FIGURE 7.9
Volunteers and Eligibles

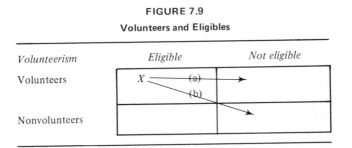

desirable because it contrasts volunteers who are eligible to volunteers who are not. Both groups at least shared enough motivation to apply for the program. It is also possible that persons who applied and were rejected are actually less knowledgeable than persons who applied and were accepted. Because the eligibility criteria in regression-discontinuity designs are so unambiguous, only an atypical subgroup of ineligibles could mistakenly apply. It might be more appropriate to compare eligible volunteers to ineligible nonvolunteers.

It is simply not clear whether it is preferable to compare the treated group in a regression-discontinuity design to subjects who applied and were rejected or to subjects who did not apply at all. Failure to resolve this issue means that "volunteerism" could bias the results of regression-discontinuity designs.

It is also possible to nest an experiment within the regression-discontinuity quasi experiment and thereby eliminate volunteerism as a threat to internal validity (Boruch 1975). Since cutpoints are often arbitrary to begin with, program managers may agree to set a range within which a coin toss could determine eligibility. For the interest credit program, nesting an experiment into the regression-discontinuity design requires randomly assigning interest credits to applicants whose household income, for instance, is between $9,000 and $11,000. A coin toss would determine whether an applicant received credit or not. Building an experiment like this into a range of values that surround the single eligibility criterion is an ethically persuasive means to eliminate the effects of volunteerism. Random assignment thus removes most threats to internal validity, at least for subjects within the range of eligibility considered for experimentation.[10]

THE PRETEST-POSTTEST COMPARISON GROUP DESIGN

The pretest-posttest comparison group (PTPTCG) is an abridged version of the ITSCG design (Riecken and Boruch 1974, 110–112). It is shown schematically and graphically in Figure 7.10. The design compares treated and untreated groups with respect to the difference between their mean scores on Y observed just before and sometime after the treatment commences. To attribute significant differences to the treatment itself, the untreated comparison group must be statistically equivalent to the treated group on all potentially confounding and spurious variables. In Figure 7.10, the posttest between group differences exceeds the pretest difference. If the groups are actually comparable, then the treatment itself accounts for the observed difference of differences.[11]

FIGURE 7.10
Pretest-Posttest Comparison Group Design

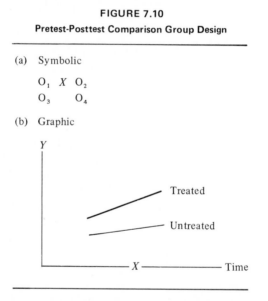

(a) Symbolic

O_1 X O_2
O_3 O_4

(b) Graphic

Making the groups comparable is a critical issue in the PTPTCG design. When the pretest scores are free of random measurement error, the groups need to be matched on the pretest scores alone (Reichardt 1979). Identifying additional spurious and confounding variables is unnecessary. To show why, consider a study of the impact of a special reading program on the achievement levels of educationally disadvantaged first graders. Figure 7.11 identifies some possibly spurious and confounding variables and discloses that these variables influence the pretest as well as the posttest values of Y. By matching on pretest scores alone, the investigator simultaneously makes the treated and untreated groups comparable on all potentially spurious and confounding variables as well.

Matching on pretest scores alone is permissible only in the absence of measurement error (Campbell and Boruch 1975). In most cases, the presence of

FIGURE 7.11
Matching on Pretest Scores: No Measurement Error

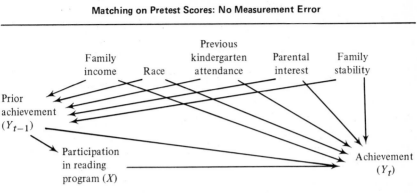

measurement error makes it necessary to match on spurious and confounding variables as well as on pretest scores. As Figure 7.12 indicates, the presence of measurement error in the pretest changes the pretest score into just one of many possibly spurious and confounding influences. Having identified these influences, the investigator must locate nonparticipants who are statistically equivalent to the participants on each. For every participant whose prior achievement score was between 200 and 300, had family income between $6,000 and $10,000, had never attended kindergarten, was black, and so forth, the investigator must locate a similar nonparticipant. If the investigator can identify and measure the spurious and confounding factors, and if he can locate untreated and treated children who are similar in respect to these variables, then, except for the absence of time-series information about the outcome measure, the internal validity of the PTPTCG is reasonably secure.

FIGURE 7.12
Matching on Spurious and Confounding Variables and on Pretests: Measurement Error

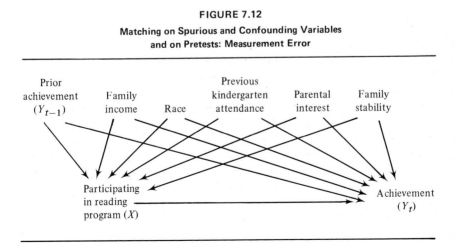

In practice, the investigator may lack data for many spurious and confounding variables. When the design is retrospective, the investigator must obtain historical data. Even if agencies automatically retain historical information on participants, information about nonparticipants can be difficult to secure.

The most important limitation of the PTPTCG design is the absence of longitudinal information about the outcome measure Y. In the face of possible measurement errors, the presence of extreme scores could account for observed differences that might otherwise be erroneously attributed to the program itself. Selection into the reading program, for example, could be a response to a set of achievement test results that seemed abnormally low. Figure 7.13 shows how the actual and observed results might diverge. In the absence of knowledge about prior trends, the investigator cannot differentiate extreme scores from normal patterns. He observes only the last two points for each group. Based on these scores alone, the researcher will conclude that the reading program was successful. Knowledge of the entire trend discloses that the results are attributable to

FIGURE 7.13

The Impact of Extreme Scores on Pretest-Posttest Comparison Group Design

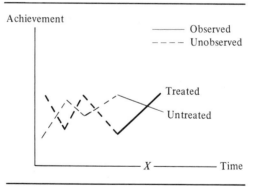

so-called "regression artifacts" and reflect random measurement error rather than a true program effect. Errors of measurement mean that persons who score abnormally low at one time are bound to improve the next time, even without special treatment. Those who score particularly well at one time tend also to score poorly the next. Knowing prior trends makes it possible to distinguish between random deviations like these and true effects. The investigator can then determine if a pretest score is "normal" or extreme.

Because the PTPTCG design contains no record of the changes in Y that occur after the posttest, it is also impossible to determine if a posttest score is "normal" or extreme. Figure 7.14 discloses how follow-up information on changes in Y after a single posttest enables an investigator to determine whether a desired increase in the achievement scores of program participants is a perma-

FIGURE 7.14

Response to Extreme Posttest Scores *v*. True Effects

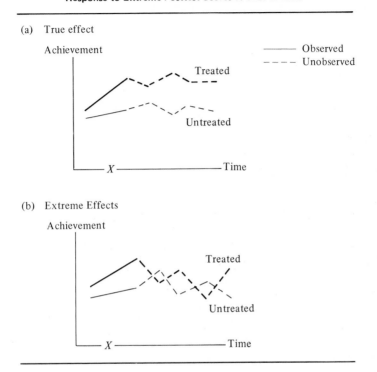

nent or temporary gain.[12] Posttest information in Figure 7.14(a) reveals that the observed gain is permanent; in Figure 7.14(b), posttest data disclose that the observed "effect" is really an extreme score.

The absence of longitudinal information together with the presence of measurement error in pretest scores points to another flaw in the PTPTCG design. Matching on prior trends allows the investigator to detect differences in growth rates. Awareness of differential growth rates reduces the chance of confusing changes in growth rates with program effects. Figure 7.15 shows how confusion can occur. Because the investigator using a PTPTCG design does not observe the long-range trend, he will erroneously conclude that the program had no influence, when in fact it altered the growth rate of the treated group. The investigator who uses a PTPTCG actually sees only the two parallel lines, and they indicate no difference between the treated and untreated groups. Yet the unobserved longitudinal data reveal that treatment has actually altered the growth rate in the treated group.

The absence of time-series information is thus a principle flaw of the PTPTCG design. Even in the absence of measurement error, matching treated and untreated subjects on pretest scores of the outcome measure cannot remove differential

FIGURE 7.15
Differential Growth Rates and True Effects

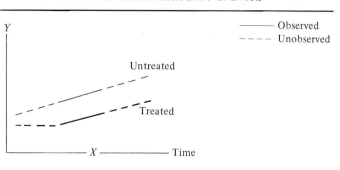

growth rates as a threat to the design's validity. Despite these flaws, investigators use the PTPTCG design with some frequency.[13] Although controversy frequently surrounds its use, the absence of time-series information sometimes makes the PTPTCG the only feasible choice. Compared to other quasi-experimental designs which do not rely on time-series, the PTPTCG is actually the best choice.

THE SINGLE INTERRUPTED TIME-SERIES DESIGN

When investigators cannot locate comparison groups but do have time-series information, they can use a single interrupted time-series design (SITS). Figure 7.16 depicts the single interrupted time-series graphically and schematically. The single interrupted time-series is actually an ITSCG that lacks an explicit comparison group. In the SITS, the comparison group is only implicit; it is the same group before the policy change.

The single interrupted time-series is particularly appropriate whenever the impact of a policy is truly universal. When everyone is a member of the treated group, an untreated comparison group cannot exist. Factors that make comparison groups difficult to construct also make the single interrupted time-series an appropriate choice. Spurious and confounding (Z) variables are often difficult to measure; historical data on these variables is frequently not available; and sometimes truly comparable groups may be an empty set or atypical of the target population. In situations like these, the availability of time-series data recording the values of Y before and after a policy change makes the single interrupted time-series an appropriate choice for measuring program impact.[14]

The SITS is particularly useful when the dependent variable contains random errors of measurement. Observing an entire time-series reduces the chance of confusing true program effects with short-term responses to extreme scores and with unrecognized changes in growth rates.

FIGURE 7.16
Single Interrupted Time-Series

(a)   Graphics

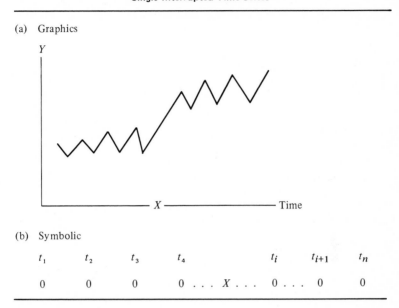

(b)   Symbolic

t_1	t_2	t_3	t_4		t_i	t_{i+1}	t_n
0	0	0	0 ... X ...	0 ...	0	0

Interpreting a time-series demands an understanding of the nature of the intervention. Consider the extreme score in Figure 7.17(a). There are two ways to interpret this pattern. The extreme score could represent a true but short-lived impact that results from a temporary program change. If the program change is permanent, the pattern would not be indicative of program impact. Instead, an investigator would expect a pattern like that in Figure 7.17(b) to emerge when an intervention is permanent.

Even though the single interrupted time-series has no true comparison group, changes in the values of spurious and confounding variables can still account for

FIGURE 7.17
Extreme Scores v. True Effects: Permanent Program Changes

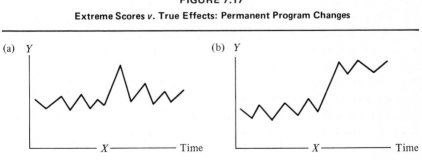

observed changes in the time-series. An investigator could therefore erroneously attribute an observed change to a policy impact. Two types of spurious or confounding influences threaten the interpretation of a SITS. First, many policies may undergo revision at the same time the program being evaluated is altered. It is very difficult to separate the impact of a single program change from other changes with which it is intertwined. Second, the composition of the population may change during the period of the time-series. Populations grow older or younger, richer or poorer. Changes like these must be separated from alterations in policy in order to attribute shifts in time-series to shifts in policy.

Albritton's study of the federal effort to eradicate measles illustrates these issues (Albritton 1978). The measles program began in 1966 and represented a permanent policy change rather than a temporary one-year effort. Figure 7.18 sketches Albritton's findings and indicates the apparent success of the measles program. The validity of such an interpretation rests on the assumption that

FIGURE 7.18
Reported Measles Cases, 1956–1972

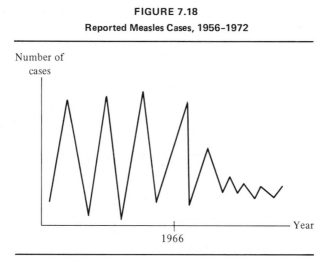

spurious or confounding variables have no impact. One of these variables is the size of the early school-age population. Measles predominates among children in these years. A shrinkage in the size of this population (Z) could confound the analysis if the drop coincides with the inception of the federal program (X) and reduces the number of measles cases (Y) as well. Albritton eliminated this factor as an alternative explanation by ascertaining empirically that the size of this population showed no significant drop in the mid-1960s. He also regarded changes in reporting practices as a possibly confounding influence. Reporting was undoubtedly improved with the introduction of the federal program, and better reporting enlarges estimates of measles incidence. Removing the influence of reporting changes would be extraordinarily difficult; Albritton instead simply argued that better reporting meant his estimate of program impact was actually less than the true effect. Increases in the private use of vaccine accompanied the federal program and constituted another confounding influence. Albritton used statistical (nonexperimental) techniques to eliminate the influence of this factor.[15]

The difficulty of locating comparison groups makes the single interrupted time-series a practical quasi experiment in many instances. As a prospective design, the SITS can sometimes be superior to a true experiment. Studying a time-series before and after a deliberate intervention is especially advisable when the number of subjects available for random assignment in an experiment is small or when experimentation is infeasible (Glass, Willson, and Gottman 1975). Randomly assigning beats that have frequent burglaries to a special burglary prevention program makes little sense if there are only, say, ten beats in the study community whose burglaries are noticeably high. Adding more beats requires involving other jurisdictions and is costly as well. Deliberately introducing the program into one or two carefully selected beats may achieve greater internal validity at less cost. Investigators should select as "demonstration" sites those beats in which spurious and confounding variables are least likely to threaten internal validity. They should thus choose beats with stable populations. Beats near a new juvenile center should not be selected for the demonstration. The inception of the juvenile center may coincide with the burglary prevention program, and both programs could reduce burglaries.

External validity concerns should also influence site selection. The demonstration beat should be typical of high burglary areas in the community. Investigators will usually be able to locate one (or even more) sites suitable for measuring program impact. Using a SITS, they can observe the incidence of burglary over time before and after the inception of the special program.[16]

THE POSTTEST COMPARISON GROUP DESIGN

Compared to other quasi experiments, results from the posttest comparison group (PTCG) design have more competing explanations. This design resembles a PTPTCG that omits the pretest. Figure 7.19 portrays the design symbolically and graphically. This design is nearly always retrospective. Its most popular and controversial example is the Westinghouse Corporation's evaluation of the impact of Head Start on the achievement levels of educationally disadvantaged pupils (Cicirelli et al. 1969).[17] The evaluators were forced to use the PTCG because it is the only design that requires no information regarding values of Y before the program change. The evaluation of Head Start had been commissioned after the program's inception, and historical achievement scores were largely unavailable. The absence of pretest information precluded the use of any design save the PTCG.[18]

The threats to the internal validity of the PTCG design include all those that plague the PTPTCG design plus one additional problem. The internal validity of

FIGURE 7.19

Posttest Comparison Group Design

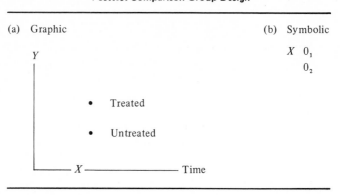

(a) Graphic

(b) Symbolic

$$X \quad 0_1$$
$$0_2$$

both designs requires that treated and untreated groups be comparable on all *Z*-variables, that neither pretest nor posttest scores be extremes, and that prior trends of *Y* be comparable in both groups. The absence of time-series data in both designs makes it impossible to determine empirically whether the last two requirements have been met. Difficulties of measurement and data collection also necessitate compromises with respect to obtaining equivalence on all *Z*-variables. Both designs also require the investigator to identify all potentially confounding and spurious variables.

The PTCG forces the investigator to make one additional assumption which the PTPTCG does not. The PTCG produces misleading inferences whenever there are pretest differences between the *Y*-scores of the treated and untreated groups. As Figure 7.20(a) indicates, an investigator using the PTCG must estimate the

FIGURE 7.20

Measuring Program Impact: Posttest Comparison
Group *v*. Pretest-Posttest with Comparison Group

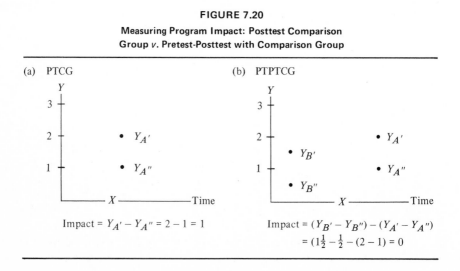

(a) PTCG

Impact $= Y_{A'} - Y_{A''} = 2 - 1 = 1$

(b) PTPTCG

Impact $= (Y_{B'} - Y_{B''}) - (Y_{A'} - Y_{A''})$
$= (1\frac{1}{2} - \frac{1}{2} - (2 - 1) = 0$

magnitude of program impact by subtracting one posttest score from the other. In Figure 7.20(b), the difference between $Y_{A'}$ and $Y_{A''}$ (the posttest scores) equals that in 7.20(a), but in 7.20(b), the difference between the pretest scores is also known. Even though the distance between $Y_{A'}$ and $Y_{A''}$ is the same in both tables, the estimate of program impact is not. The only situation in which $Y_{A'} - Y_{A''}$ gives the correct estimate of program impact is when $Y_{B'} = Y_{B''}$. In the posttest only design, these values are unknown.

THE PRETEST-POSTTEST WITH NO COMPARISON GROUP DESIGN

The pretest-posttest design that lacks a comparison group (PP) is also called a before-and-after design. In form, the design is a single interrupted time-series that has no time-series. Figure 7.21 discloses that the design consists of a pretest and posttest measured for a single group. The design's flaws are multiple, since it shares the weaknesses of the single interrupted time-series, and, in addition, assumes that long-term trends and extreme scores do not account for any observed difference between the pretest and posttest scores.

FIGURE 7.21
Pretest-Posttest with no Comparison Group

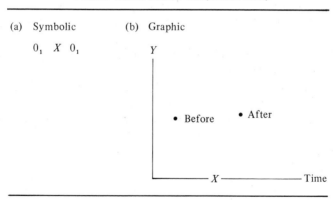

(a) Symbolic

$$0_1 \quad X \quad 0_1$$

(b) Graphic

Consider a claim by a police chief that expansion of his force reduced the city's crime rate by a certain percentage. Implicit in such a claim is a pretest-posttest design. For the claim to have internal validity, several assumptions must be true. There must be no changes in potentially spurious or confounding variables. For instance, a drop in the proportion of youth should not coincide with expansion of the force, because both events could drive the crime rate down. The reduction in crime should not reflect a tendency for extreme scores to return to normal. An alarmingly high crime rate may have prompted the city to support an expanded police force, and the drop in crime could represent a return to statistical normalcy rather than a policy impact. A long-term downward trend could also account for the observed decrease. The PP design makes it impossible to determine whether the trend or the program is the more credible explanation for the drop in crime.

QUASI EXPERIMENTS IN REVIEW

In theory, the internal validity of quasi experiments is considerably more questionable than that of experiments. Yet past experience indicates that truly random assignment may be difficult to achieve. When the number of subjects is small, random assignment can even be inadvisable. Experiments are also inappropriate whenever the need for information is so urgent that designs must be retrospective. While the theoretical supremacy of experimentation is unassailable, its practical advantages must be weighed against those of quasi experiments.[19]

Among the quasi experiments, the best choice depends on the particular situation confronting the investigator. While the ITSCG design may appear to be better than other quasi experiments, failure to implement the design properly can produce misleading conclusions. Before choosing a design like the ITSCG, which requires a comparison group, investigators should realize that choosing a poor comparison group may be worse than having no comparison group at all. Figure 7.22 shows how this can occur. In this diagram, an increasing hospital death rate in community B reverses itself. Community B is the untreated comparison group. In community A, the growing hospital death rate levels off after the inception of an emergency medical vehicle (EMV) program. An investigator who assumed that these two communities were truly comparable would conclude that emergency medical vehicles increase in-hospital deaths. If a change in

FIGURE 7.22
ITSCG with Poor Comparison Group

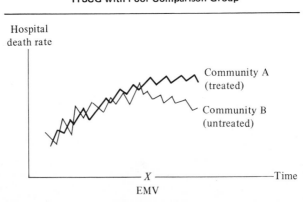

the age structure of community B coincided with the inception of the emergency vehicle program in community A, such a conclusion could be erroneous. The change in age structure and the emergency medical vehicle program are thus competing explanations for the difference between death rates. The unintentional use of an improper comparison group suggests that emergency medical vehicles increase deaths. By contrast, had the investigator used a SITS to examine the treated community alone, a change in the age structure of the untreated community would not be a competing explanation. Assuming that there are no other problems in either design, the inference from the simpler quasi experiment is correct; the inference from the ITSCG is not. The proper use of a simple quasi experiment is thus superior to the improper use of a more elaborate one.

FOOTNOTES

1. Campbell and Boruch (1975) argue that the superiority of a quasi experiment would be an exceptional situation. Glass, Willson, and Gottman (1975) argue in favor of well-designed quasi experiments. For discussion of quasi-experimental approaches in general, see Campbell and Stanley (1963: Ch. 7-16), Riecken and Boruch (1974: Ch. 4), Cook and Campbell (1979), Clark (1976), Campbell (1971), and Hilton and Lumsdaine (1975).

2. In Chapter 8, we refer to this problem as one of "multicollinearity." For a further discussion of this problem, see Blalock (1967).

3. For a discussion of the wide variety of ITSCG designs that are possible, see Glass, Willson, and Gottman (1975: Ch. 2).

4. Statistical techniques for removing random error from time series can get quite complex. A thorough, practical discussion of those techniques can be found in Glass, Willson, and Gottman (1975). For less technical discussions, see Palumbo (1969: Ch. 12) and Wilson (1975).

5. A good discussion of the internal validity of the ITSCG design in the context of studying the impact of mobile intensive care units on deaths from heart attacks can be found in Sherman et al. (1979).

6. Cited in Riecken and Boruch (1974:112).

7. For a more detailed consideration of "most different systems" designs, see Przeworski and Teune (1970).

8. See the Appendix for a discussion of regression.

9. Technically, the difference between Y-values at the cutpoint can be determined by computing $\hat{Y}$ using the equation $\hat{Y} = \hat{a} + \hat{b}_{yx}(10,000)$ for both the eligibles and the ineligibles. If either $\hat{a}$ or $\hat{b}_{yx}$ have different values in the two regressions, then the predicted values of Y at the cutpoint will also differ. To determine if the difference is statistically significant, it is necessary to place confidence intervals around both values of $\hat{Y}$. If the confidence bands do not overlap, the values of $\hat{Y}$ are significantly different. For the exact formula, see Blalock (1972:404).

10. For a more detailed discussion of other designs that nest experiments into quasi experiments, see Boruch (1975).

11. The pretest difference between the comparison groups is not independent of the posttest difference because the subjects in the analysis are the same at both times. For purposes of testing statistical significance, the correct number of observations is the number of pairs. Each observation in the treated group must be matched with a corresponding obser-

vation in the untreated group. The pair's pretest score is the difference between the pretest scores of the treated and untreated subjects comprising the pair. The pair's posttest score is the difference between the posttest scores of the treated and untreated pair. Consider the following scores based on just four matched pairs:

	Before		Pretest	After		Posttest
Pair	Treated	Untreated	Difference	Treated	Untreated	Difference
A	1	1.5	−0.5	5	3	2
B	3	2.5	0.5	7	4	3
C	8	7	1	14	9	5
D	6	7	−1	12	9	3
			Mean = 0			Mean = 3.25

In this example, the posttest difference of means exceeds the pretest difference of means. Observe also that scores for both the treated and the untreated groups have an upward trend, but that the trend for the treated group is larger than that for the untreated group.

12. Glass, Willson, and Gottman (1975).

13. For empirical examples of studies based on the PTPTCG, see Gramlich and Koshel (1975), Abramowitz (1978) and Wortman, Reichardt, and St. Pierre (1978). The latter design actually has two pretest scores and examines three treatments.

14. Maki, Hoffman, and Berk (1978) and Albritton (1978) are empirical studies that use the SITS design.

15. The SITS is sometimes subject to large random fluctuations. It is then necessary to use significance tests to distinguish between systematic and random effects. Using moving averages is a simple way to eliminate random fluctuations. For a discussion of appropriate significance tests, see Albritton (1978) and Glass, Willson, and Gottman (1975).

16. The length of the time-series should be sufficient to allow the investigator to eliminate extreme scores and prior trends as rival explanations. The time-series should not be too long. Lengthy time-series are subject to population changes that could be a confounding influence.

17. For other examples of the PTCG, see Feld (1978), Lewin and Associates (1975), Gray, Conover, and Hennessy (1978), Ahlbrandt (1973), and Ostrom et al. (1973). Feld's study has multiple posttest observations. The study of state certificate of (hospital) need programs by Lewin and Associates has four comparison groups: states with both federal and state programs, states with just one of these programs or the other, and states with no programs. The study does not match states on potentially spurious or confounding variables, but it uses multiple outcome measures.

18. Some school districts probably did have historical data on achievement scores, but the Westinghouse evaluators probably believed that these districts were undesirably atypical for a national evaluation. Hindsight suggests that the Westinghouse investigators should not have sacrificed internal validity for the sake of generality.

19. For a dissenting view, see Boruch, McSweeny, and Soderstrom (1978).

LIST OF REFERENCES

Abramowitz, Alan I. "The Impact of a Presidential Debate on Voter Rationality." *American Journal of Political Science* 22 (1978): 680–690.

Ahlbrandt, Rogers, Jr. "Efficiency in the Provision of Fire Services." *Public Choice* 16 (1973): 1–15.

Albritton, Robert B. "Cost-Benefits of Measles Eradication: Effects of A Federal Intervention." *Policy Analysis* 4 (1978): 1–22.

Blalock, Hubert M., Jr. "Causal Inferences in Natural Experiments: Some Complications in Matching Designs." *Sociometry* 30 (1967): 300–315.

Blalock, Hubert M., Jr. *Social Statistics.* 2d ed. New York: McGraw-Hill, 1972.

Boruch, Robert F. "Coupling Randomized Experiments and Approximations to Experiments in Social Program Evaluation." *Sociological Methods and Research* 4 (1975): 31–53.

Boruch, Robert F.; McSweeny, A. John; and Soderstrom, E. Jon. "Randomized Field Experiments for Program Planning, Development and Evaluation: An Illustrative Bibliography." *Evaluation Quarterly* 2 (1978): 655–695.

Campbell, Donald T. "Reforms as Experiments." *Urban Affairs Quarterly* 7 (1971): 133–171.

Campbell, Donald T., and Boruch, Robert F. "Making the Case for Randomized Assignment to Treatments by Considering the Alternatives: Six Ways in Which Quasi-Experimental Evaluations in Compensatory Education Tend to Underestimate Effects." Ch. 3 in Bennett, Carl A., and Lumsdaine, Arthur A., eds. *Evaluation and Experiment.* New York: Academic Press, Inc., 1975.

Campbell, Donald T., and Stanley, Julian C. *Experimental and Quasi-Experimental Designs for Research.* Chicago: Rand McNally and Co., 1963.

Cicirelli, V. G., et al. *The Impact of Head Start: An Evaluation of the Effects of Head Start on Children's Cognitive and Affective Development.* Vol. 1. U.S. Dept. of Commerce, National Bureau of Standards, Institute for Applied Technology. Springfield, Va.: Clearinghouse, 1969.

Clark, Lawrence P. *Designs for Evaluating Social Programs* Croton-On-Hudson, N.Y.: Policy Studies Associates, 1976.

Cook, Thomas D., and Campbell, Donald T. *Quasi-Experimentation: Design and Analysis Issues for Field Studies.* Chicago: Rand McNally, 1979.

Feld, Scott L. "Deterrence: For the Prevention and Cure of Litter." *Evaluation Quarterly* 2 (1978): 547–560.

Glass, Gene V.; Willson, Victor L.; and Gottman, John M. *Design and Analysis of Time-Series Experiments.* Boulder: Colorado Associated University Press, 1975.

Gramlich, Edward M., and Koshel, Patricia P. *Educational Performance Contracting: An Evaluation of an Experiment* Washington, D.C.: The Brookings Institution, 1975.

Gray, Charles M.; Conover, C. Johnston; and Hennessy, Timothy M. "Cost Effectiveness of Residential Community Corrections: An Analytical Prototype." *Evaluation Quarterly* 2 (1978): 375–400.

Hilton, Elizabeth T., and Lumsdaine, Arthur A. "Field Trial Designs in Gauging the Impact of Fertility Planning Programs." Ch. 5 in Bennett, Carl A., and Lumsdaine, Arthur A., eds. *Evaluation and Experiment.* New York: Academic Press, Inc., 1975.

Lewin and Associates. *Evaluation of the Efficiency and Effectiveness of the Section 1122 Review Process.* Washington, D.C.: Lewin and Associates, Inc., 1975.

Maki, Judith E.; Hoffman, Donnie M.; and Berk, Richard A. "A Time Series Analysis of the Impact of a Water Conservation Campaign." *Evaluation Quarterly* 2 (1978): 107–118.

Ostrom, Elinor; Baugh, William H.; Guarasci, Richard; Parks, Roger B.; and Whitaker, Gordon P. *Community Organization and the Provision of Police Services.* Beverly Hills: Sage Publications, Inc., 1973.

Palumbo, Dennis J. *Statistics in Political and Behavioral Science.* New York: Appleton-Century-Crofts, 1969.

Przeworski, Adam, and Teune, Henry. *The Logic of Comparative Social Inquiry.* New York: John Wiley & Sons, Inc., 1970.

Reichardt, Charles S. "The Statistical Analysis of Data From the Nonequivalent Group Designs." Ch. 4 in Cook, Thomas D., and Campbell, Donald T., eds. *Quasi-Experimentation: Design and Analysis Issues for Field Studies.* Chicago: Rand McNally, 1979.

Riecken, Henry W., and Boruch, Robert F., eds. *Social Experimentation: A Method for Planning and Evaluating Social Intervention.* New York: Academic Press, 1974.

Sherman, Mark A.; Rath, Gustave J.; Schofer, Joseph L.; and Thomson, Charles W. N. "Threats to the Validity of Emergency Medical Services Evaluation: A Study of Mobile Intensive Care Units." *Medical Care* 17 (1979): 127–138.

Wilson, L. A., II. "Statistical Techniques for the Analysis of Public Policies as Time Series Quasi-experiments." Ch. 10 in Scioli, Frank P., Jr., and Cook, Thomas J. *Methodologies for Analyzing Public Policies.* Lexington, Mass.: Lexington Books, Inc. 1975.

Wortman, Paul M.; Reichardt, Charles S.; and St. Pierre, Robert G. "The First Year of The Education Voucher Demonstration: A Secondary Analysis of Student Achievement Test Scores." *Evaluation Quarterly* 2 (1978): 193–214.

Chapter 8

NONEXPERIMENTAL DESIGNS:
Categorical Data

Nonexperimental designs use statistical procedures to remove the effects of potentially spurious and confounding variables. Like experimental and quasi-experimental approaches, nonexperimental research helps investigators determine whether an observed association between variables is causal or spurious.

The nonexperimental approach borrows heavily from the tools of multivariate statistical analysis. The use of multivariate procedures is necessary because program evaluators cannot rely on simple measures of the association between two variables to disentangle the impact of programs from that of other factors on outcome measures. Multivariate procedures can nonetheless be derived from simple measures of bivariate association. Like the choice of bivariate techniques, choosing an appropriate multivariate technique depends on the level of measurement of the variables in an analysis. In this chapter, we consider multivariate tools appropriate for the analysis of categorical data. We show how the simple percentage can be used in multivariate situations to distinguish between spurious and confounding models, and to estimate direct and indirect effects.[1] The next chapter parallels these topics, but concentrates on continuous variables.

SPURIOUS OR CONFOUNDING MODELS

One of the most critical tasks in program evaluation is to determine whether the observed association between a program change and an outcome is spurious. At a conceptual level, the investigator must use his data to decide whether real world phenomena resemble the model shown in Figure 8.1(a) or that shown in Figure 8.1(b). The choice is important, for if the real world looks like Figure 8.1(a), then the program (X) has no effect (Y). In contrast, if the real world

FIGURE 8.1
Spurious *v.* Causal Association

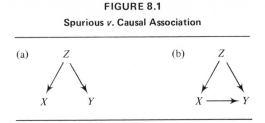

resembles Figure 8.1(b), then the program does have an impact, and the investigator's task is then to estimate its magnitude.

In both cases, the data that the real world generates will display patterns characteristic of each model. Statistical techniques can uncover these unique patterns. They enable the investigator to determine which of the two models best conforms to the real world phenomena he is trying to understand.

The investigator cannot simply observe covariation between program (X) and effect (Y) to choose between these models. No matter whether Z is spurious or confounding, the association between X and Y will be statistically significant. Multivariate analysis, in contrast, can help the investigator to make a choice. In the spurious model, changes in Z make X change; changes in Z also make Y change. Unless Z is invariant, X and Y must covary. In the confounding model, changes in Z also make X and Y change together, but only in that model are changes in X alone also sufficient to make Y change. Even though bivariate percentage differences will be nonzero in both models, the multivariate analysis of percents produces results that depend on whether the real world resembles a spurious or confounding model.

To carry out such an analysis, the investigator must eliminate the influence of variation in Z by making it statistically constant. When Z is invariant, values of Z will be roughly equivalent, no matter to what type of program the subject has been exposed. If X and Y are spuriously related, holding Z constant will also eliminate the original association between X and Y. Figure 8.1(a) suggests why bivariate association disappears when Z is spurious. If Figure 8.1(a) depicts real world phenomena, then changes in Z make both X and Y change. When the investigator prevents Z from changing, X and Y cannot continue to change together. Because the original bivariate association between X and Y is entirely accounted for by their common dependence on variations in Z, eliminating variation in Z makes the original association disappear and indicates that the program has no impact because the model is spurious.[2]

A numerical example illustrates how the investigator can actually hold Z constant. Consider the positive association between quality of school facilities and achievement scores shown by the frequencies in the "total" table in Figure 8.2. Both variables are dichotomies, so the percentage difference is an appropriate and simple way to measure their association. The table shows that students who attend schools with good facilities tend to have higher achievement scores

FIGURE 8.2

**Association Between Quality of School
and Achievement**

| | Quality of School Facilities | | | | Total |
| | High | | Low | | |
Achievement Scores	Frequency	Percent	Frequency	Percent	Frequency
≥ National norms	60	60%	40	40%	100
< National norms	40		60		100
Total	100		100		200

% Difference = 20%

than students who attend schools with poor facilities. If this bivariate association is spurious, good school facilities do not improve achievement.

In fact, the association observed in Figure 8.2 could well be spurious. Previous research has indicated that students with high socioeconomic status (SES) are more likely than low status students to attend schools with good facilities. High SES students also tend to have higher achievement scores. The covariation between school quality and achievement in Figure 8.2 could possibly be due to their joint dependence on a common cause—the student's SES. Figure 8.3 models this possibility.

FIGURE 8.3

Spurious Association: Achievement and School Quality

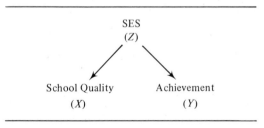

To evaluate this model, it is necessary to hold Z constant statistically. If the model in Figure 8.3 conforms to real world phenomena, then the association between school quality (X) and achievement (Y) will disappear when students with the same SES are analyzed separately. Figure 8.4 shows what happens to the data in Figure 8.2 when this analysis is performed and the model is actually spurious. Figure 8.4 holds the spurious variable Z constant because it separates high and low SES students. Within each group, SES (or Z) is invariant. The percentage difference in each "partial" table is also zero.[3] Controlling for SES reduces original covariation shown in the total table to zero. The partial association has entirely disappeared, which is what the spurious model leads us to expect.

FIGURE 8.4

Association Between Achievement and School Quality,
Controlling for SES

	Low SES				
	School quality				
	High		Low		Total
Achievement Scores	*Frequency*	*Percent*	*Frequency*	*Percent*	*Frequency*
≥ National norm	6	15%	10	15%	16
< National norm	35		57		92
Total	41		67		108

% Difference = 0

	High SES				
	School quality				
	High		Low		Total
Achievement Scores	*Frequency*	*Percent*	*Frequency*	*Percent*	*Frequency*
≥ National norm	54	92%	30	91%	84
< National norm	5		3		8
Total	59		33		92

% Difference = 1

The data are thus more consistent with a spurious model in which school quality does not affect achievement than with a causal model.[4]

These partial tables also demonstrate that the distinction between quasi-experimental and nonexperimental approaches is often difficult to define. The data in these tables actually resemble data that a PTCG design could produce. Each partial table includes students who are comparable on at least one important Z-factor—their SES—yet differ in terms of X (school quality). This similarity means that the internal validity of conclusions based on partial tables from a nonexperimental design depend on the same conditions as conclusions based on a PTCG design. In both instances, the investigator must assume that there are no other possibly spurious or confounding variables besides SES, and that the observed data do not simply reflect ongoing trends or responses to extreme scores.[5]

The partial tables also illustrate how quasi experiments and nonexperiments alike sometimes adduce new errors by constructing groups that are only roughly rather than exactly comparable. When comparison groups are not exactly alike in respect to values of Z, Z will not be entirely invariant. Yet Z must be invariant to determine if associations are spurious. In nonexperiments, the number of partial tables equals the number of categories in the control variable (Z). For a fixed number of observations, increasing the number of categories in the control variable reduces the number of observations in each partial table. Reducing the number of observations in the partial tables increases the likelihood that no significant association will be found and thereby enlarges the chance of erroneously choosing a spurious model.[6] At the same time, adding more categories to the control variable makes the observations in any single partial table more homogeneous and ultimately more comparable.

In the partial tables of Figure 8.4, the so-called "low" SES students may actually encompass considerable diversity; some may come from very poor backgrounds, while some may not. Their only similarity is that they all have lower SES than the 92 "high" SES students. By subdividing the 108 low SES students into smaller, more homogeneous groups, an investigator could gain comparability and thus make a potentially spurious and confounding factor more invariant. Creating smaller, more homogeneous comparison groups, however, reduces the number of observations in each partial table. The investigator must choose between errors due to incompletely controlled confounding or spurious variables and errors due to a small sample. The only way to avoid this dilemma is to add more observations. Although this option reduces the chance of error, it may be either infeasible or too costly to implement.[7]

Besides the number of categories within each variable, the number of control variables also affects the usable number of observations in each partial table. If the number of observations is fixed, adding more Z-variables reduces the N in each partial table. Consider again the association between school quality and achievement. An investigator might decide to control for SES and for the level of interest parents have in their children's education. To test a model of spurious association between achievement and school quality due to their common dependence on SES and parental interest, both variables must be held constant. When data are consistent with this model, portrayed in Figure 8.5, the percentage difference in each partial table will be statistically close to zero. Assuming that the two control variables are measured dichotomously, there must now be four partial tables—one for low SES students with interested parents, one for low SES students with uninterested parents, one for high SES students with uninterested parents, and one for high SES students with parents interested in their work. If

FIGURE 8.5

Spurious Association Due to Two Z-Variables

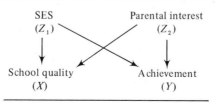

the total number of observations does not increase, then the number of observations in each partial table must decrease, jeopardizing statistical significance.

Adding more control variables always makes it necessary to augment the number of observations. Three dichotomous control variables require 2^3 or 8 partial tables, and 3 dichotomous and 1 trichotomous control variables require a whopping $2^3 \times 3^1$ or 24 partial tables. Investigators who attempt to control for all potentially spurious and confounding variables may rapidly run out of observations. Like the evaluator who wants more homogeneous groups on each control variable, the investigator must choose between errors due to uncontrolled Z-variables and errors due to small samples.[8] Evaluators should always try to anticipate these problems before they design their measurement instruments and collect their data.

Sometimes investigators have very large samples. In this situation, reliance on significance tests alone will nearly always lead the investigator to find significant associations in partial tables, even when percentage differences are as small as 1%. When samples are large, investigators should not substitute statistical for substantive significance. Although no iron-clad rule exists, partial tables with percentage differences as small as 3% or 4% could be indicative of a spurious model even though the association is statistically significant.

We have considered only spurious models so far. In these models, percentage differences in each partial table are nearly or exactly zero. When percentage differences in each partial table are not zero but roughly equal to one another, the investigator should not rush to conclude that Z is confounding and that X causes Y.[9] Two models can actually account for the appearance of nonzero (but equal) measures of association in partial tables, as Figure 8.6 shows. If the investigator controls for the one potentially confounding or spurious variable of which he is aware, both models predict that significant covariation between X and Y will

FIGURE 8.6
Nonzero Association in Partial Tables:
Z Held Constant

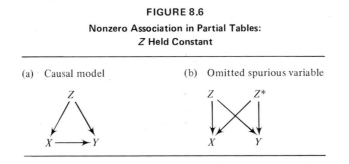

(a)　Causal model　　　　　　(b)　Omitted spurious variable

remain. The investigator could argue that X causes Y; but he cannot rule out the possibility that an omitted variable, Z^*, once it has been identified, measured, and controlled, would, together with Z, completely remove the association between X and Y.

Except in true experiments, the possibility of an uncontrolled variable always exists. Figure 8.7 shows that the investigator who continues to observe a significant association between X and Y in his partial tables even after controlling for both Z and Z^* cannot rule out the possibility that an additional control for Z^{**} would reveal that the association is spurious and not causal. Only random

FIGURE 8.7
Nonzero Association in Partial Tables: Z and Z^* Held Constant

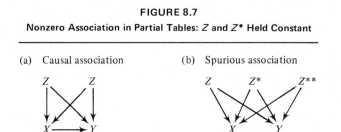

(a) Causal association   (b) Spurious association

assignment can remove the possibility of omitted spurious variables.[10] Investigators who use quasi experiments or nonexperiments can always erroneously conclude that a program has an impact when in fact it does not.[11]

DIRECT AND INDIRECT EFFECTS

The possibility of omitted Z-variables means that nonzero partial associations are not necessarily indicative of causal relationships. The possibility of indirect effects can also alter the interpretation of both zero as well as nonzero partial associations. Consider first the appearance of percentage differences equal to zero in partial tables when the effects of X on Y can be either direct or indirect. Figure 8.8 shows that there are actually two circumstances in which partial tables produce associations equal to zero. In Figure 8.8(a), Z is a spurious variable that jointly causes X and Y to covary. In Figure 8.8(b), however, Z intervenes between X and Y; while X indeed affects Y, it does so indirectly through

FIGURE 8.8
Zero Associations in Partial Tables

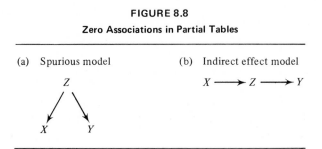

(a) Spurious model   (b) Indirect effect model

the mediating effects of Z. In both models, holding Z constant removes the association between X and Y. In the spurious model, holding Z constant removes the covariation between X and Y; consequently, the partial associations will be zero. When variations in X affect values of Y indirectly through the mediation of Z, removing variations in Z means that changes in X can no longer influence the values of Y. By holding Z artificially constant, changes in X cannot induce changes in Z, and, since Z is constant, Y will remain invariant also. Within each category of Z, the association between X and Y will be zero. Zero partial associations can thus occur no matter whether the total covariation between X and Y is entirely spurious or represents an indirect program effect.

Sometimes this dilemma may not be particularly troublesome. Although there is no statistical difference between the two models of Figure 8.8, the two models imply different temporal orderings of X and Z. In the spurious model, Z must precede X, whereas X must precede Z in the developmental sequence. In the case of school quality and achievement, the interpretation of the zero partial associations observed in Figure 8.4 is not ambiguous, because SES (Z) is clearly antecedent to school quality (X). Attending a good school is unlikely to raise a student's SES, at least in the short run. But a student's status does affect the school he attends. Because Z precedes X, the zero partials indicate that the observed covariation between school quality and achievement is likely to be spurious.

The choice between models of spurious or indirect effects is not always so clearcut. Consider the total association between participation in a job training program (X) and employment status (Y) after the program. Figure 8.9 shows

FIGURE 8.9

Total Table: Association Between Participation and
Employment Status (Low-Income White Males 18–20 Only)

| | Participation | | | | Total |
| | Yes | | No | | |
Employment	Frequency	Percent	Frequency	Percent	Frequency
Employed	120	60%	126	42%	246
Unemployed	80		174		254
Total	200		300		500

that of those who participated, 60% were employed, while only 42% of the nonparticipants were employed. Suppose that the investigator has already held constant potentially confounding and spurious variables such as the subjects' income, race, sex, and age. However, the investigator may also believe that the subjects' motivation may be an additional confounding or spurious factor, because motivation is probably related both to participation and to employment status. According to Figure 8.10, when the level of motivation is held constant,

FIGURE 8.10

Partial Tables: Employment Status by Participation
Holding Motivation Constant

	High motivation				
	Participation				
	Yes		No		Total
Employment	Frequency	Percent	Frequency	Percent	Frequency
Employed	114	64%	75	64%	189
Unemployed	65		43		108
Total	179		118		297

	Low motivation				
	Participation				
	Yes		No		Total
Employment	Frequency	Percent	Frequency	Percent	Frequency
Employed	6	29%	51	28%	57
Unemployed	15		131		146
Total	21		182		203

employment status does not vary with participation. For both highly and poorly motivated subjects, the association between participation and employment status drops to zero.

The ambiguity of the time order between X and Z makes it difficult to determine whether these results correspond to a spurious model in which the training program is ineffective or to a model of indirect effects in which the program is effective. Participation (X) could precede motivation (Z) because job training may improve attitudes as well as skills. Motivation (Z) could also precede participation (X), since people who are motivated to work are more likely to seek out and apply for a job-training program than those who are poorly motivated. In the absence of further evidence, the investigator cannot choose between the two models in Figure 8.11.[12]

FIGURE 8.11

Ambiguous Time Order Between X and Z:
Partial Associations Are Zero

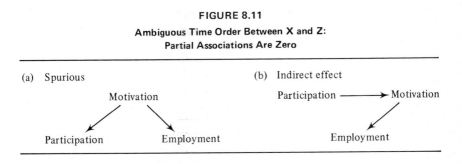

(a) Spurious

(b) Indirect effect

The sequence of X and Z affects estimates of program impact even when partial associations are not zero. When the investigator is reasonably confident that he has eliminated the influence of potentially spurious and confounding variables, and when percentage differences in the partial tables are still not zero, evidence supports the conclusion that the program (X) has a direct causal influence on Y. If the confounding variable (Z) precedes X, then the percentage difference in the partial tables is the correct measure of program impact. In contrast, if X precedes Z, then Z is not a confounding variable; Z is instead intervening, and the program has both a direct and an indirect effect on Y. (See Figure 8.12.) To measure program impact correctly, the investigator should capture both effects. The partial association reflects direct influences alone. When there are direct and indirect effects, the investigator who seeks a measure of total program impact should use the percent difference in the total table. Selecting the correct measure of program impact thus requires the investigator to know the causal ordering between X and Z.

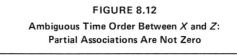

FIGURE 8.12
Ambiguous Time Order Between X and Z:
Partial Associations Are Not Zero

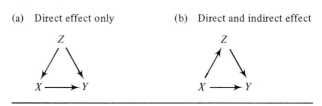

(a)   Direct effect only   (b)   Direct and indirect effect

A priori reasoning can often help to make this choice. In the case of school quality and school achievement, there could be little doubt that acquisition of children's socioeconomic status occurs before the choice of school. When the causal sequence between X and Z is not readily apparent, investigators should try to obtain measures of the value of Z before the inception of the program (X). If values of Z are recorded for time $t - 1$ and the program commences at time t, the investigator can be sure that Z preceded X.[13]

The models discussed so far assume that there is no statistical interaction. Statistical interaction occurs whenever the effect of X on Y depends on the value of Z, and it can be detected whenever the percentage differences in the partial tables differ significantly from one another.[14]

In nonexperimental research, the possibility of undetected statistical interaction is particularly troublesome because it can lead investigators to decide that X and Y do not covary when in fact their association is merely hidden. The appearance of a percentage difference equal to zero in a total table is thus insufficient evidence for concluding that the program has no impact.

Figure 8.13 illustrates this situation.[15] In this figure, covariation between the availability of local affairs broadcasting and knowledge of local events is zero.

An investigator who is unaware of the possibility of statistical interaction might simply stop here, concluding that the absence of covariation constitutes clear evidence that local affairs broadcasting has no impact on the public's knowledge of local events. However, Figure 8.14 reveals that a conditioning variable, the viewer's level of interest in local affairs, masks the association between availability (X) and knowledge (Y). The percentage differences disclose that availability and knowledge are associated only for persons with a high level of interest in

FIGURE 8.13
Local Affairs Broadcasting and Knowledge:
Total Table

| | Broadcasting | | | | |
| | Available | | Not available | | Total |
Knowledge	Frequency	Percent	Frequency	Percent	Frequency
High	140	25%	65	26%	205
Low	410		185		595
Total	550		250		800

FIGURE 8.14
Covariation of Availability and Knowledge,
Holding Interest Constant: Partial Tables

	Low level of interest				
	Availability				
	Available		Not available		Total
Knowledge	Frequency	Percent	Frequency	Percent	Frequency
High	50	13%	15	13%	65
Low	350		105		455
Total	400		120		520

% Difference = 0

	High level of interest				
	Availability				
	Available		Not available		Total
Knowledge	Frequency	Percent	Frequency	Percent	Frequency
High	90	60%	50	38%	140
Low	60		80		140
Total	150		130		280

% Difference = 22%

local affairs. The partial tables have thus uncovered an association that appears only when the interactive variable is held constant.

Even though availability and knowledge are associated just when interest is high, their covariation is insufficient evidence of causation. To determine whether their association is causal, the investigator must control for potentially spurious and confounding factors such as level of education. Only the highly interested subpopulation that displayed covariation needs to be included in this analysis of spurious and confounding variables.

An investigator can thus infer the presence of statistical interaction whenever percentage differences in the partial tables differ significantly from each other. The presence of interaction means that analysis of program impact must be undertaken separately for each subgroup of the interactive variable. Each subgroup must therefore have a sufficient number of cases for independent analysis. Investigators concerned with external validity must anticipate the possibility of interaction and design their study so that cases within each category of the conditioning variable can be analyzed separately. When external validity is not important, scrutinizing total and partial associations within a single category of a conditioning variable will be sufficient.

THE THREAT OF MULTICOLLINEARITY

Multicollinearity exists whenever the association between the treatment and a potentially spurious or confounding variable is very strong. The presence of naturally occurring random errors of measurement and sampling can make multicollinearity a grave threat to valid inference. By exaggerating the effect of random influences, multicollinearity makes it easy for investigators to confuse a random deviation with an overall effect.

To illustrate how this occurs, recall the partial association between school quality and achievement shown in Figure 8.4. If there were complete multicollinearity between school quality (X) and SES (Z), then the investigator would observe that all high SES children attended good schools and that all low SES children attended poor schools. Assuming that the marginal distribution of achievement among high- and low-status children remains just as it is in Figure 8.4, then Figure 8.15 displays the partial tables that complete multicollinearity produces. The frequencies in these tables make the rules of causal analysis completely uninterpretable because these rules require variation in X. Within each partial table in Figure 8.15, X is invariant. Among the low SES children, there is no variation in school quality. Similarly, all of the high SES children attend high-quality schools. The absence of any variation in X makes the possibility of causal analysis moot.

Complete multicollinearity is empirically rare. More common is partial multicollinearity. The tables in Figure 8.16 show that partial multicollinearity can cause a few random errors of sampling or measurement to have radically different effects. In part (a) of Figure 8.16, the percentage differences disclose a slight

FIGURE 8.15
Partial Tables for Complete Multicollinearity

	Low SES School quality		
Achievement	*High*	*Low*	*Total*
⩾ National norm	0	16 (15%)	16
< National norm	0	92	92
Total	0	108	108

	High SES School quality		
Achievement	*High*	*Low*	*Total*
⩾ National norm	84 (91%)	0	84
< National norm	8	0	8
Total	92	0	92

tendency for school quality to raise achievement among low SES children and lower it among high SES children, but neither difference is statistically significant.[16] An investigator would conclude that the relation between achievement and school quality is spurious due to the common dependence of these variables on the students' status. The tables also display substantial multicollinearity between school quality and status because most of the low status students attend poor schools while most of the high status students attend better schools.

Such a high association between X and Z means that a few random errors could radically alter the investigator's inferences. Part (b) of Figure 8.16 illustrates this point. Consider first the low-status students in parts (a) and (b). Recognizing that random errors of measurement are likely to occur in achievement tests, part (b) shows a net movement from part (a) of four low-status students who attend good schools. In part (a), two of eight students have high scores, but in part (b), six of eight score high. Among the 100 low-status students who attend poor schools, there is also a net change in the achievement scores of four people. Thus a net change of eight low-status students distinguishes part (a) from part (b). This has a radical effect on the percentage difference, which increases from an insignificant 11% to a statistically significant 65%. An even larger alteration in the percent difference occurs among the high SES students, where the net movement from part (a) to (b) is only four out of 92 students. Even when these differences are attributable to random errors, they have an extraordinary impact on the percentage difference, which increases from −9% to 93%. Considering both sets of partial tables, part (a) suggests that quality and achievement are spuriously related due to SES, but part (b) indicates the opposite. Multicollinearity accounts for these differences, since it makes statistical evidence especially sensitive to random errors.

FIGURE 8.16
Partial Tables for Partial Multicollinearity

(a)

	Low SES		
	School quality		
Achievement	High	Low	Total
≥ National norm	2 (25%)	14 (14%)	16
< National norm	6	86	92
Total	8	100	108

% Difference = 9%

	High SES		
	School quality		
Achievement	High	Low	Total
≥ National norm	82 (91%)	2 (100%)	84
< National norm	8	0	8
Total	90	2	92

% Difference = −9%

(b)

	Low SES		
	School quality		
Achievement	High	Low	Total
≥ National norm	6 (75%)	10 (10%)	16
< National norm	2	90	92
Total	8	100	108

% Difference = 65%

	High SES		
	School quality		
Achievement	High	Low	Total
≥ National norm	84 (93%)	0 (0%)	84
< National norm	6	2	8
Total	90	2	92

% Difference = 93%

Investigators who anticipate severe multicollinearity have two practical options. When the association between X and Z is extremely high, the investigator should seriously consider a true experiment, because random assignment makes X independent of Z. The effects of multicollinearity can also be mitigated by securing a large number of cases. Random errors have disproportionately large effects when the number of observations is small, and multicollinearity means that some cells will have relatively few observations. Increasing the number of observations should increase the size of these cells and reduce the confusing effects of random error.

SUMMARY

A set of decision rules is sufficient to summarize the causal analysis of categorical data.[17] Figure 8.17 lists these rules, but their practical application is not always obvious. Investigators frequently lack data on potentially spurious, confounding, or interactive variables. Multicollinearity reduces the investigator's

FIGURE 8.17
Rules for Causal Analysis of Categorical Data

If % differences in each partial table are zero and Z precedes X	then	Z with arrows to X and Y	Program has no impact
If % differences in each partial table are zero and X precedes Z	then	$X \rightarrow Z \rightarrow Y$	Total % difference measures program impact
If % differences in each partial table are roughly equal and not zero and Z precedes X	then	Z with arrows to X and Y; $X \longrightarrow Y$	Partial % difference measures program impact
	or	Z Z^* crossing arrows to X and Y	Program has no impact
If % differences in each partial table are roughly equal and not zero and X precedes Z	then	Z with arrows to X and Y; $X \longrightarrow Y$	Total % difference measures program impact
If % differences in each partial table are not equal	then	$Z+: X \xrightarrow{?} Y$ $Z-: X \xrightarrow{?} Y$	Statistical interaction

confidence in his findings. Like the PTCG quasi experiment, nonexperimental designs are usually static; they thus make it possible to confuse program impact with prior trends and reactions to extreme scores.

These hazards can be avoided in many instances. Investigators should identify spurious, confounding, and interactive variables before gathering data. In this way, they can obtain a sample which is large enough for their analytic needs. The static nature of quasi experiments can best be overcome by combining non-experimental approaches with quasi experiments that use time-series. Investigators will also find that techniques for using continuous data, though foreign to the novice, are not difficult. Compared to the causal analysis of categorical data, the analysis of continuous data is more efficient. With continuous variables, augmenting the number of statistical controls necessitates a smaller number of additional cases than the analysis of categorical variables requires. Using continuous data thus makes the need to exchange errors of insufficient statistical control for errors of a small sample much less urgent.

FOOTNOTES

1. The multivariate analysis of contingency tables formed by categorical variables is growing more and more popular, and many new techniques have been developed to meet that demand. The use of percentages is the simplest of these tools. Readers interested in more powerful and efficient methods for analyzing contingency tables should consult Goodman (1965), Goodman (1970), David (1974), Kritzer (1978), and Kritzer (1979). The discussion in this chapter parallels Herzon and Hooper (1976):405–450 in some respects. The techniques we consider in this chapter are also appropriate for controlling the influence of categorically measured W-variables.

2. This discussion assumes that Z causes X. We discuss the situation in which X causes Z below.

3. The partial tables decompose the total table. Adding the frequencies from corresponding cells in the two partial tables yields the cell frequencies in the total table. The 200 students in the total table include 108 low SES students and 92 high SES students.

4. The data in the partial tables also show that SES (Z) is positively associated with both school quality (X) and achievement (Y), as the spurious model leads us to expect. Of the low SES students, 15% scored above national norms, as compared to 91% of high SES students. In addition, 67/108 or 62% of low SES students attended poor quality schools, while only 33/92 or 36% of high SES students attended poor schools.

5. The quasi-experimental version of the partial tables in Figure 8.4 could differ from the nonexperiment in one respect. Quasi experiments sometimes sacrifice external validity by examining just one group of students, say the low SES students. Quasi experiments thus hold Z constant by evaluating the association between X and Y within a single category of Z. Nonexperiments generally consider the full range of Z, and eliminate its variation statistically.

6. Chapter 5 showed how decreasing N augments the chance of a Type II error.

7. The need for enough degrees of freedom in the analysis of $r x c$ tables accounts for the issue of sample size. Statistics texts usually argue that each cell should have at least ten observations. We see below that the analysis of continuous data is less sensitive to issues of sample size.

8. Using continuous data mitigates this dilemma somewhat.

9. We consider situations in which percent differences in each partial table do not equal each other below.

10. Even experiments do not remove all Z-variables, as Chapter 6 showed. Experiments only eliminate the spurious influence of variables that describe characteristics of the subjects who are randomly assigned. Unlike quasi experiments and nonexperiments, experi-

ments do not actually hold *Z*-variables constant. Instead, they transform *Z*-variables into *W*-variables whose influence the investigator can then remove by using statistical or quasi-experimental controls.

11. The chance of detecting program impact when in fact there is none is a theoretical possibility. In practice, evaluators appear more likely to underestimate rather than overestimate program impact.

12. In Figure 8.11(a), the program has no impact. In Figure 8.11(b), the percentage difference in the total table is actually the correct measure of program impact.

13. In the absence of time-based data, the investigator can, under certain circumstances, use statistical procedures appropriate for the analysis of simultaneous equations to determine the causal sequence between *X* and *Z*. Chapter 9 also suggests a simpler approach based on instrumental variables that investigators can use in some situations.

14. Chapter 5 discussed the concept of statistical interaction in some detail, and indicated some situations in which it is likely to occur.

15. The example that follows comes from Herzon and Hooper (1976:420–421).

16. In part (a) of Figure 8.6, $Z = 0.85$ for the low status children and $Z = -0.44$ for the high status children.

17. These rules apply to the analysis of three-variable models. We will consider four-variable models in the next chapter.

LIST OF REFERENCES

Davis, James A. "Hierarchical Models for Significance Tests in Multivariate Contingency Tables: An Exegesis of Goodman's Recent Papers." Ch. 8 in Costner, Herbert L., ed. *Sociological Methodology, 1973-1974.* San Francisco: Jossey-Bass, 1974.

Goodman, Leo A. "On The Multivariate Analysis of Three Dichotomous Variables." *American Journal of Sociology* 71 (1965): 290–301.

Goodman, Leo A. "The Multivariate Analysis of Qualitative Data: Interactions Among Multiple Classifications." *Journal of The American Statistical Association* 65 (1970): 226–256.

Herzon, Frederick D., and Hooper, Michael. *Introduction to Statistics for the Social Sciences.* New York: Thomas Y. Crowell, 1976: 405–450.

Kritzer, Herbert M. "Approaches to The Analysis of Complex Contingency Tables: A Guide for the Perplexed." *Sociological Methods and Research* 7 (1979): 305–329.

Kritzer, Herbert M. "An Introduction to Multivariate Contingency Table Analysis." *American Journal of Political Science* 22 (1978): 187–226.

Chapter 9

NONEXPERIMENTAL DESIGNS:
Continuous Data

The last chapter outlined some statistical procedures that evaluators can use when all of the variables in their analysis are categorical. The analysis of continuous variables requires different statistical methods than the analysis of categorical variables. When variables are continuous, augmenting the number of controls, even when the number of observations is constant, increases the chance of a Type II error much less than it does with categorical variables. The statistical analysis of continuous variables is thus more efficient than the statistical treatment of categorical variables.

No matter whether the investigator confronts categorical or continuous data, he must still use statistical procedures to distinguish between spurious models in which programs have no impact and confounding models in which programs are influential. Even when variables are continuous, selecting the correct measure of program impact depends on whether the effects are entirely direct or only partly direct and partly indirect.

This chapter is divided into three main sections. The first section considers multiple regression analysis, a statistical technique appropriate when all of the variables in an analysis are continuous. The second section outlines some of the assumptions and limitations of multiple regression. The third suggests how investigators can use multiple regression to measure program impact when X is categorical and Y, Z, and W are continuous. Two variations of multiple regression analysis are common in this situation: analysis of covariance and multiple regression using dummy variables. Each section uses numerical examples and centers on the interpretation of regression coefficients in the context of program evaluation.

MULTIPLE REGRESSION ANALYSIS OF
CONTINUOUS VARIABLES

Whether or not all of the variables in an analysis are categorical or continuous, the investigator needs two pieces of information to determine if programs have no causal impact, a direct causal impact, an indirect impact, or direct as well as indirect effects. He must first ascertain the temporal sequence of X and Z. He must then compute an appropriate measure of partial association. When all of the variables in an analysis are continuous, the partial regression coefficient, written $\hat{b}_{yx \cdot z}$, is the most useful measure of partial association.[1] When all of the variables in an analysis are categorical, a percentage difference for each partial table reflects the partial association. Within each partial table, the potentially spurious or confounding (or extraneous) variable is constant. When data are continuous, the investigator controls spurious, confounding, and extraneous variables by a statistical process that yields a single measure of partial association between X and Y, no matter how many control variables there are and no matter how many values or categories each control variable has.[2]

The resulting partial regression coefficient, $\hat{b}_{yx \cdot z}$, has a straightforward interpretation analogous to its bivariate counterpart, $\hat{b}_{yx}$.[3] While the bivariate measure estimates the change in Y associated with a unit change in X, the partial measure estimates the change in Y associated with a unit change in X when the influence of Z is removed. Like the bivariate measure, the value of $\hat{b}_{yx \cdot z}$ can range from $-\infty$ to $+\infty$. Its actual value is determined by the direct impact that X actually has on Y once the influence of Z is removed, and by the units in which X and Y are measured. If X has no influence on Y when the common influence of Z on X and Y has been statistically removed, $\hat{b}_{yx \cdot z}$ will be zero. If X continues to influence Y even when Z has been held constant, then the meaning of $\hat{b}_{yx \cdot z}$ is contingent on the units in which X and Y are measured. When Y = college grade point average (GPA), X = amount of study in hours per week, and Z = family income (in dollars), then $\hat{b}_{yx \cdot z} = 0.1$ means that, if family income were invariant, an additional hour of study per week raises GPA by one-tenth point. If X were "amount of study in minutes per week," then the interpretation of $\hat{b}_{yx \cdot z} = 0.1$ is considerably altered. In this case, an additional minute of study per week raises GPA's by one-tenth point when parental income is constant. The meaning of $\hat{b}_{yx \cdot z}$ thus depends on the units in which X and Y are measured. By contrast, changing the units in which Z is measured (e.g., from dollars to hundreds of dollars) does not alter the meaning of $\hat{b}_{yx \cdot z}$.

There is a conventional way to subscript the partial regression coefficient. The dependent variable (Y) is listed first, and the independent variable (X) follows. The control variable (or variables) is listed after the dot. To measure the impact of X, the program, on Y, the outcome measure, controlling for Z, a confounding or spurious variable, we write $\hat{b}_{yx \cdot z}$ and not, for instance, $\hat{b}_{xy \cdot z}$.

Investigators can compute the value of $\hat{b}_{yx \cdot z}$ from a formula comprised of the bivariate regression coefficients:[4]

$$\hat{b}_{yx \cdot z} = \frac{\hat{b}_{yz} - \hat{b}_{yz}\hat{b}_{zx}}{1 - \hat{b}_{zx}\hat{b}_{xz}}.$$

This simple formula, while useful, displaces attention from the context of multiple regression in which partial regression coefficients can best be understood.

Multiple regression is a statistical technique appropriate for estimating the separate impact of the treatment (X), any confounding variable (Z), and any unmeasured extraneous variable (W) on the outcome measure (Y). Its proper use relies on the validity of the premises for causal inference: X and Y must covary, X must precede Y, and the influence of spurious and confounding variables must be removed by statistical controls. In the simplest case of three continuous variables, the multiple regression equation $Y = \hat{a} + \hat{b}_{yx \cdot z}X + \hat{b}_{yz \cdot x}Z + e$ corresponds to any one of the two causal models shown in Figure 9.1. The first regression coefficient, $\hat{b}_{yx \cdot z}$, is likely to be of greatest interest to program evaluators because it provides an estimate of the direct influence of X and Y when Z is constant.[5] The second regression coefficient, $\hat{b}_{yz \cdot x}$, measures the direct influence

FIGURE 9.1

**Causal Models Underlying a Multiple Regression
of Y on X and Z**

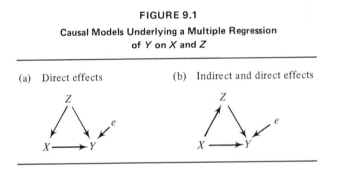

(a)   Direct effects   (b)   Indirect and direct effects

of Z on Y when X is constant. It is an estimate of the change in Y that occurs for each unit change in Z when the influence of X has been removed. This coefficient is ordinarily of secondary interest because it tells the evaluator how much influence spurious and confounding (Z) factors, which he cannot manipulate, have on the outcome measure once the influence of factors he can manipulate (X) have been removed. The first term in the multiple regression, $\hat{a}$, or the Y-intercept, is also of secondary importance. It estimates the value of Y when X and Z are both zero. In situations when Y, X, and Z are continuous, the Y-intercept usually provides information of little relevance to evaluators since zero values of X and Z are empirically rare.

The error term, or e in the multiple regression equation, captures the influence of unmeasured extraneous variables on the outcome measure, Y. No regression coefficient is associated with e because it would be uninterpretable. Regression coefficients require a unit of measurement, and the entire set of unmeasured influences on Y, considered as a whole, has no metric. Consequently a standardized measure of the joint influence of unmeasured variables must be used. The measure is said to be standardized because no matter what variables e represents, the estimate of its impact ranges from 0 to 1.

This standardized measure is $(1 - R^2_{y \cdot xz})$, where $R^2_{y \cdot xz}$ is the coefficient of multiple determination. The value of $(1 - R^2_{y \cdot xz})$ reflects the relative influence of unmeasured variables (e) to measured variables (X, Z). The total influence of measured and unmeasured variables is unity, and $R^2_{y \cdot xz}$ reports the standardized influence of the measured variables X and Z on Y. It can be computed in terms of the simple correlation coefficients discussed in the Appendix:

$$R^2_{y \cdot xz} = \frac{r^2_{yx} + r^2_{yz} - 2r_{yx}r_{yz}r_{xz}}{1 - r^2_{xz}}.$$

The value of $R^2_{y \cdot xz}$ ranges from 0 to 1.00. If $R^2_{y \cdot xz} = 1$, then the unmeasured extraneous variables have no influence on the outcome measure (Y); all of its variance is attributable to the measured program and confounding variables. If $R^2_{y \cdot xz} = 0$, then the measured variables have no influence at all. Usually, $R^2_{y \cdot xz}$ lies between these extremes.

For program evaluators, the value of $(1 - R^2_{y \cdot xz})$ is important. As an estimate of the variance in Y not attributable to the measured X and Z variables, it indicates the influence of random or extraneous variables. When these influences are large, $(1 - R^2_{y \cdot xz})$ may approach unity. Chapter 5 showed that large random influences make regression coefficients look statistically equivalent to zero. When the influence of e relative to X and Z is large, program evaluators may wish actually to measure and control some of the more important extraneous variables for the purpose of reducing random error and making $\hat{b}_{yx \cdot z}$ attain statistical significance.

In this situation, the appropriate multiple regression equation has three measured variables on the right-hand side:

$$Y = \hat{a} + \hat{b}_{yx \cdot zw} X + \hat{b}_{yz \cdot xw} Z + \hat{b}_{yw \cdot xz} W + e.$$

Figure 9.2 depicts the causal models that correspond to this equation. The W-variable in the equation and in the models represents a measured extraneous variable, and e represents the unmeasured random influences. The first partial regression coefficient, $\hat{b}_{yx \cdot zw}$, is most relevant for evaluators. It measures the direct influence of the program on the outcome measure when confounding or spurious (Z) and extraneous (W) factors are held constant.[6] Its value provides an estimate of the change in Y that occurs as a result of a unit change in X when Z and W have been controlled. Its numerical value should not be very different from that of $\hat{b}_{yx \cdot z}$. Its standard error could, however, be smaller, and its value is thus more likely to be statistically significant.[7]

Whether or not the investigator measures and controls the influence of extraneous variables, he must be particularly cautious in his interpretation of partial regression estimates of the influence of X on Y when Z alone, or Z and W

FIGURE 9.2

Causal Models Corresponding to a Multiple
Regression that Measures an Extraneous (W) Variable

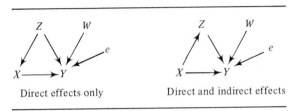

Direct effects only   Direct and indirect effects

together, are controlled. Multiple regressions of Y on X and Z or of Y on X, Z, and W estimate only the direct influence of X on Y. In many situations, program evaluators seek to estimate the total influence of the program on an outcome measure. When the total influence of X on Y includes direct as well as indirect effects, the multiple regression must be altered accordingly.

Consider first the situation in which the computed value of $\hat{b}_{yx \cdot z}$ is statistically no different from zero.[8] Two underlying models could account for such a value. If Z precedes X, then $\hat{b}_{yx \cdot z} = 0$ implies a spurious model in which a change in X has no influence on Y once the influence of Z has been removed. (See Figure 9.3(a).) In the spurious model, holding the common cause, Z, constant removes the covariation between X and Y because they are jointly dependent on Z. The program thus has no impact. By contrast, if X precedes Z, then $\hat{b}_{yx \cdot z} = 0$ implies a model of indirect causation in which an intervening variable, Z, mediates the program's impact. (See Figure 9.3(b).) In this model, changes in X make Y change, but only because X influences Z, which in turn influences Y. Once the

FIGURE 9.3

Models in Which $\hat{b}_{yx \cdot z} = 0$

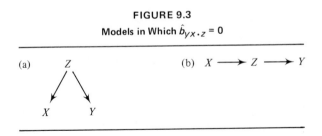

(a) Z

(b) $X \longrightarrow Z \longrightarrow Y$

impact of Z on Y is statistically removed, changes in X no longer affect Y. In both models, the partial regression coefficient will be zero; but only in the spurious model is $\hat{b}_{yx \cdot z}$ a correct estimate of program impact. Using $\hat{b}_{yx \cdot z}$ to estimate total program impact when the true model is indirect indicates that X has no direct effect on Y. As a measure of total impact, $\hat{b}_{yx \cdot z}$ is thus misleading. When X has an indirect influence on Y, $\hat{b}_{yx}$ rather than $\hat{b}_{yx \cdot z}$ is the correct estimate of program impact.

Distinguishing between these two models is therefore critical. The only way to choose is to identify the temporal sequence of X and Z. Sometimes their order is obvious. Consider the following example, in which all of the variables are continuous. Title I of the Elementary and Secondary Education Act distributes federal revenues to school districts on the basis of the relative number of children in poverty. Districts are supposed to use these federal revenues to supplement rather than supplant local education revenues. Districts are thus prohibited from using Title I funds for local tax relief. Locally raised revenues should consequently not decrease upon receipt of Title I. In this example, school districts are the unit of analysis. The program variable (X) is Title I revenues per pupil. The outcome measure (Y) is locally raised revenues per pupil. The school district's wealth is an important confounding or spurious (Z) variable. Low-income districts receive more Title I money than high-income districts, but low-income districts also raise fewer local revenues per pupil than high-income districts.

Income is unlikely to intervene between X and Y. Receiving Title I does not affect the income of school district residents; instead, residents' income influences the amount of Title I. If $\hat{b}_{yx \cdot z} = 0$, Z is thus likely to be a spurious variable. A zero value also indicates that when income (Z) is controlled, an additional dollar of Title I causes neither a reduction nor an increase in local education revenues. If $\hat{b}_{yx \cdot z}$ were negative, Z would be a confounding variable. The negative value would also mean that Title I supplants rather than supplements local education revenues.

Figure 9.4 reports empirical values for the simple regression coefficients needed to compute the partial regression coefficients.[9] The simple regression coefficient, $\hat{b}_{yx}$, is particularly important. It indicates that a decrease in local revenues of $4.20 per pupil is associated with each dollar per pupil increase in Title I revenues. Investigators who ignored the impact of school district income on local revenues and on Title I would conclude erroneously that each Title I dollar causes school districts to substantially reduce their educational revenues. By contrast, controlling for income reveals that school districts do not replace local revenues with Title I. Using the formula on page 133 to hold income constant,

$$\hat{b}_{yx \cdot z} = \frac{-4.20 - (0.05)(-71.45)}{1 - (-71.45)(-0.00266)} = -0.78.$$

This value reveals that when income is invariant, a one dollar per pupil increase in Title I revenues is associated with a $0.78 per pupil decrease in local revenues.[10] The standard error of this estimate is 0.70, and indicates that another sample could produce an estimate which varies by an average of ±0.70 around $b_{yx \cdot z}$. The t-statistic is $\frac{-0.78}{-0.70}$ or −1.11. According to a table of t-values, such a small value means that the partial regression estimate of −0.78 is not significantly different from zero.[11] These results suggest that X (Title I revenues) has no impact on Y (local revenues) and that the underlying model is spurious rather than con-

FIGURE 9.4

**Simple Regression Coefficients: Influence of Title I
on Local Spending (N = 356 School Districts)**

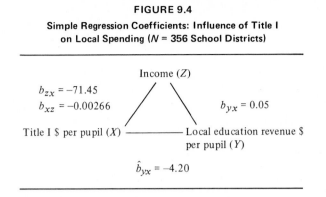

Income (Z)

$b_{zx} = -71.45$
$b_{xz} = -0.00266$ $b_{yx} = 0.05$

Title I \$ per pupil (X) —————— Local education revenue \$
per pupil (Y)

$\hat{b}_{yx} = -4.20$

founding. In this instance, the possibility that Z intervenes between X and Y is not a plausible alternative model, and the statistical evidence thus supports the conclusion that school districts do not use Title I monies to supplant local revenues.

Whenever $\hat{b}_{yx \cdot z} = .0$ and the temporal order of X and Z is ambiguous, the investigator cannot choose between the two models in Figure 9.3. This is a critical shortcoming because the inability to decide whether the spurious or indirect model is valid also makes it impossible to decide whether the program has any influence.[12] It is sometimes possible to determine empirically whether Z precedes X or X precedes Z. A simple way to make this determination requires the investigator to identify an instrumental variable, V. The variable must affect either Z or X directly. If V directly influences both X and Y it is not an instrumental variable.

Suppose that the investigator has identified and measured an instrumental variable V which he knows has a direct effect on Z alone. If X precedes Z, then there will be no association between V and X, as Figure 9.5(a) indicates. If V affects Z and Z precedes X, Figure 9.5(b) shows that V and X will be associated. If the investigator is unable to locate an instrumental variable that directly affects Z, he may be able to find one that directly affects only X. He can then apply the same logic to determine the sequence of X and Z. If V affects X and X precedes Z, then V and Z will be associated. If V affects X and Z precedes X, then V and Z will be independent. (See Figure 9.5(c) and (d).)[13]

FIGURE 9.5

Instrumental Variables (V)

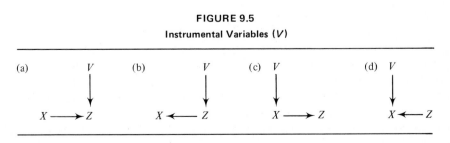

(a) V (b) V (c) V (d) V

$X \longrightarrow Z$ $X \longleftarrow Z$ $X \longrightarrow Z$ $X \longleftarrow Z$

This method is appropriate even when $\hat{b}_{yx \cdot z}$ is not zero. When $\hat{b}_{yx \cdot z}$ is not zero, its causal interpretation requires knowing the time-sequence of X and Z and the conviction that spurious or confounding variables have not been omitted. When $\hat{b}_{yx \cdot z}$ is not zero, four explanations are possible. Assuming that Z is antecedent to X forcloses two of these possiblities. If Z precedes X and if no confounding or spurious variables (besides Z) are present, the investigator can infer that program or treatment differences influence the outcome measure consistent with the model of direct causation shown in Figure 9.6(a). The presence of an omitted Z-variable makes it impossible for the investigator to choose between the model of program impact shown in Figure 9.6(a) and the model in Figure 9.6(b), which indicates no impact.

FIGURE 9.6
Models in Which Z Precedes X and $\hat{b}_{yx \cdot z} \neq 0$

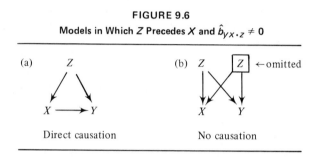

When $\hat{b}_{yx \cdot z}$ is not zero and the investigator believes that X precedes Z, internally valid conclusions regarding program impact depend somewhat less critically on the accuracy of the premise that no variables have been omitted. When intervening variables have been omitted, the investigator can be reasonably certain that the program (X) influences the outcome measure (Y) as long as X precedes Z and $\hat{b}_{yx \cdot z}$ is not zero. The models in Figure 9.7 show, however, that if an intervening variable is neglected, no decision can be made about whether the program's impact is entirely indirect, or if it is both direct and indirect. Only when the investigator must separately estimate the direct and indirect components of a program's total impact is this distinction critical. Otherwise, no matter

FIGURE 9.7
Models in Which X Precedes Z and $\hat{b}_{yx \cdot z} \neq 0$

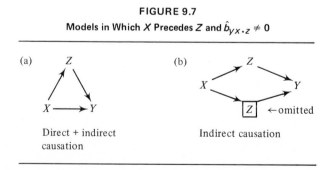

whether Figure 9.7(a) or (b) is accurate, $\hat{b}_{yx}$ is the proper estimate of total program impact.

In most cases, investigators confront a mixture of confounding and intervening variables. This possibility requires us to consider four-variable causal models. In every instance, valid estimates of the total impact of X on Y must control for confounding variables. Only when investigators must obtain separate estimates of direct and indirect influences is it necessary to identify, measure, and control for the impact of intervening Z-variables.[14]

The need to differentiate between confounding and intervening Z-variables means that the four-variable multiple regression equation, $Y = \hat{a} + \hat{b}_{yx \cdot z_1 z_2} X + \hat{b}_{yz_1 \cdot xz_2} Z_1 + \hat{b}_{yz_2 \cdot xz_1} Z_2 + e$, will not always yield correct estimates of program impact. As Figure 9.8 indicates, many different causal models are consistent with this equation. In only two of these models will $\hat{b}_{yx \cdot z_1 z_2}$, the second order partial regression coefficient estimated by the four-variable multiple regression, be the correct estimate of total program impact. This second-order regression coefficient measures the direct effect of X on Y. In Figure 9.8(a) its value will be statistically equivalent to zero; in Figure 9.8(c) its value captures the entire impact of X on Y. Both Z-variables in these models are confounding, and $\hat{b}_{yx \cdot z_1 z_2}$ is thus the correct estimate of total program impact.

FIGURE 9.8

Causal Models Consistent with the Multiple
Regression of Y on X, Z_1 and Z_2

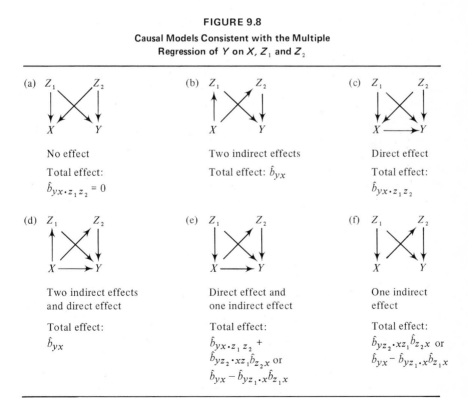

(a) Z_1 Z_2

X Y

No effect

Total effect:

$\hat{b}_{yx \cdot z_1 z_2} = 0$

(b) Z_1 Z_2

X Y

Two indirect effects

Total effect: $\hat{b}_{yx}$

(c) Z_1 Z_2

$X \longrightarrow Y$

Direct effect

Total effect:

$\hat{b}_{yx \cdot z_1 z_2}$

(d) Z_1 Z_2

$X \longrightarrow Y$

Two indirect effects
and direct effect

Total effect:

$\hat{b}_{yx}$

(e) Z_1 Z_2

$X \longrightarrow Y$

Direct effect and
one indirect effect

Total effect:

$\hat{b}_{yx \cdot z_1 z_2} +$
$\hat{b}_{yz_2 \cdot xz_1} \hat{b}_{z_2 x}$ or
$\hat{b}_{yx} - \hat{b}_{yz_1 \cdot x} \hat{b}_{z_1 x}$

(f) Z_1 Z_2

X Y

One indirect
effect

Total effect:

$\hat{b}_{yz_2 \cdot xz_1} \hat{b}_{z_2 x}$ or
$\hat{b}_{yx} - \hat{b}_{yz_1 \cdot x} \hat{b}_{z_1 x}$

By contrast, in Figure 9.8(b) and 9.8(d), both Z-variables are intervening. Using $\hat{b}_{yx \cdot z_1 z_2}$ would misrepresent the influence of programs in those models because it ignores indirect effects. Since these models contain no confounding variables, the bivariate regression coefficient, $\hat{b}_{yx}$, provides an accurate estimate of total program influence.

Expressing the total impact of X is more difficult when the models of Figure 9.8(e) and 9.8(f) are accurate. The bivariate regression coefficient, $\hat{b}_{yx}$, is incorrect because a portion of its value is due to the common dependence of X and Y on Z_1, a confounding variable. This common dependence can be eliminated by breaking the bivariate regression coefficient into its components:

$$b_{yx} = b_{yx \cdot z_1 z_2} + b_{yz_1 \cdot xz_2} b_{z_1 x} + b_{yz_2 \cdot xz_1} b_{z_2 x}.^{15}$$

Inspection of the right-hand side of this equation discloses that $b_{yx \cdot z_1 z_2}$ measures the direct effect of X on Y, once the influence of Z_1 and Z_2 have been removed. The second term, $b_{yz_1 \cdot xz_2} b_{z_1 x}$, expresses the total influence of the path including Z_1 and X on Y, and the third term expresses the total impact of the path including Z_2 and X on Y.

This expression decomposes b_{yx} for any one of the four-variable models in Figure 9.8. In Figures 9.8(a) and 9.8(c), X and Y are dependent on both Z_1 and Z_2. In (a) there is no direct effect, and $b_{yx \cdot z_1 z_2}$ will be zero. In (c), the only impact of X on Y is a direct one, and so the total effect equals the direct effect: $b_{yx \cdot z_1 z_2}$. In Figure 9.8(d), the total effect includes the direct effect as well as two indirect paths through Z_1 and Z_2. In this model, the total effect is thus the sum of all three terms in the equation, which equals b_{yx}. Figure 9.8(b) is similar except that its direct effect is zero. The total effect still equals b_{yx}. In Figure 9.8(e), the total effect includes the direct effect, $b_{yx \cdot z_1 z_2}$, and just one indirect path through Z_2: $b_{yz_2 \cdot xz_2} b_{z_2 x}$. Adding these two terms gives the total effect. In Figure 9.8(f), there is only one indirect effect through Z_2, and the value of that path, $b_{yz_2 \cdot xz_1} b_{z_2 x}$, expresses the total impact of X on Y. The coefficients needed to estimate accurately the total influence of program changes on an outcome measure thus depend critically on the temporal sequence of X and Z. The regression coefficients which are proper when Z is intervening differ from the correct choice when Z is confounding.

The distinction between confounding and intervening Z-variables is important because investigators concerned with total effects alone can actually ignore intervening Z-variables. When estimating total effects, multiple regression equations must include only those Z-variables which are truly confounding. Investigators can thus safely exclude Z_1 and Z_2 from regression equations when Figures 9.8(b) and 9.8(d) apply; there will be no loss of internal validity. In Figures 9.8(a) and 9.8(c), both Z_1 and Z_2 must be included in regression estimates of the impact of X on Y. When there is a mixture of confounding and intervening variables, as in Figure 9.8(e) and 9.8(f), only the confounding variables need to be measured. It is possible to estimate the direct and indirect paths by subtracting the confounding path from the simple regression coefficient b_{yx}. In Figures 9.8(e) and 9.8(f), the total influence of X on Y is thus $\hat{b}_{yx} - \hat{b}_{yz_1 \cdot xz_2}\hat{b}_{z_1 x}$. This expression can be simplified by eliminating Z_2, since $\hat{b}_{yz_1 \cdot xz_2} = \hat{b}_{yz_1 \cdot x}$ in the models of Figures 9.8(e) and 9.8(f).[16] The total impact of X on Y in these figures can thus be estimated without bias by $\hat{b}_{yx} - \hat{b}_{yz_1 \cdot x}\hat{b}_{z_1 x}$ even when data on the intervening variable are unavailable.

This section has illustrated how investigators can use multiple regression to determine if models are spurious or confounding and to estimate total rather than just direct program effects. We have also seen that bivariate regression, together with the identification of instrumental variables, can help the investigator estimate empirically the time sequence of X and Z. This determination indicates whether Z is intervening or confounding. Investigators can then select the correct regression estimate of total program impact.

LIMITS AND ASSUMPTIONS OF MULTIPLE REGRESSION

Multiple regression is indeed a powerful tool for program evaluators. Unless evaluators are aware of the limits of regression analysis, its power can be abused. The accuracy of multiple regression estimates rests on the validity of the premises for valid causal inference. It is easy for investigators who use multiple regression to ignore these premises. Consider first the problem of time order. If X and Y are mutually dependent, mulitiple regression estimates will be faulty. In Figure 9.9, X affects Y in the first time period, but then Y affects X in the next. As a

FIGURE 9.9

**Invalid Causal Models for Multiple Regression:
Simultaneity**

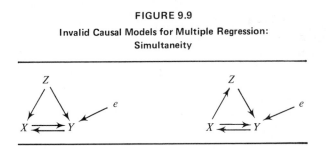

result, X no longer antedates Y, and regression estimates of the impact of X on Y will be internally invalid.[17] Nothing in multiple regression warns the investigator that X and Y are mutually independent. Investigators must consequently rely on *a priori* reasoning, on conjecture, or on behavioral theory to warn them that simultaneity is a possible problem.[18]

Regression estimates will also be misleading if spurious or confounding variables are omitted. The presence of undetected spurious variables will lead analysts to conclude that the program has an impact when in fact it does not. The undetected influence of confounding variables also produces faulty inferences. Even if X causes Y, the omission of a confounding variable produces estimates of program impact that are either too high or too low.[19]

Figure 9.10 depicts such a model. There, the program (X) causally affects an outcome (Y), but a third, confounding variable (Z) has been omitted. To estimate the amount by which the program affects the outcome, the investigator, believing that there are no omitted variables, computes a simple regression coefficient, $\hat{b}_{yx}$. This coefficient yields valid estimates only when the model represented by the variables connected with the solid line in Figure 9.10 is accurate. Unknown

FIGURE 9.10

Invalid Causal Models for a Multiple Regression:
Omitted Confounding Variable

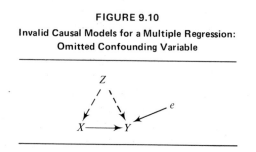

to the investigator is the fact that only $\hat{b}_{yx \cdot z}$ is an accurate estimate of the change in outcome that occurs for a unit change in the treatment. Whether $\hat{b}_{yx}$ underestimates or overestimates $\hat{b}_{yx \cdot z}$ depends on the magnitude and sign of the terms in the expression that relates these two estimates:

$$b_{yx} = b_{yx \cdot z} + b_{yz \cdot x} b_{zx}.^{20}$$

Since the investigator has failed to measure Z, only the bivariate regression coefficient on the left of the equal sign is known. If b_{yx} is positive, and if the partial association between Z and Y as well as the total association between Z and X are either both positive or both negative, then b_{yx} will overestimate $b_{yx \cdot z}$, the "true" value; b_{yx} will underestimate $b_{yx \cdot z}$ if these values are both positive and the last term on the right of the equal sign is negative.

Random measurement errors in either X or Z are an additional source of invalid multiple regression estimates. When $\hat{b}_{yx}$ is the correct estimator of total program influence, random measurement error in the program variable (X) always attenuates estimates.[21] If X is the true level of a treatment and X' is the level that the investigator actually measures, then $\hat{b}_{yx} > \hat{b}_{yx'}$. Random measurement error in the treatment variable thus produces underestimates of program impact.

When a partial regression coefficient is the correct measure of program impact, random measurement error in the controlled confounding variable (or variables) also biases regression estimates, but the direction of bias cannot, in general, be determined. Figure 9.11 depicts a causal model in which X is measured without error, and Z, a confounding variable, is measured with random error. The measured values of the confounding variable, Z', are a function of the

FIGURE 9.11

Random Measurement Error in Z

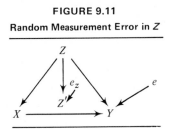

true values (Z), and a random component (e_z). Since Z is a confounding variable, $\hat{b}_{yx \cdot x}$ is the correct estimate of program influence. The investigator cannot actually measure Z. Instead he measures Z' and uses $\hat{b}_{yx \cdot z'}$ rather than $\hat{b}_{yx \cdot z}$ to estimate program influence. The presence of random measurement error means that these two values will never be equal.[22]

Random measurement error in the treatment variable (X) attenuates partial regression estimates just as it attenuates bivariate regressions. Figure 9.12 depicts a causal model in which Z has no measurement error but X contains random error. The measured value is X', and it is a function of the true value, X, as well as a random component, e_x. By using $\hat{b}_{yx' \cdot z}$ instead of $\hat{b}_{yx \cdot z}$ the investigator underestimates program impact.[23] Investigators who fear underestimating the effects of public programs should take particular care to remove as much random error from their measurement of the treatment variable as possible.

FIGURE 9.12

Random Measurement Error in X

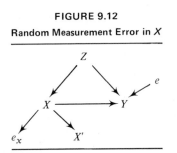

The internal validity of multiple regression estimates thus rests on three important assumptions. There must be no reciprocal dependence between X and Y. Investigators must not ignore confounding variables. They must also measure both confounding (Z) and treatment (X) variables without random error.

Investigators should also strive to make regression estimates as precise as possible. The precision of a regression coefficient depends on the size of its standard error. When the standard error is large relative to the estimated value of the regression coefficient, even large coefficients can look statistically insignificant. Sizable standard errors thus augment the chance of deciding that programs have no influence. Investigators using multiple regression who are concerned with erroneously concluding that treatments make no difference should therefore take steps to reduce the magnitude of standard errors.

The standard error of $\hat{b}_{yx \cdot z}$ can be estimated from the formula:

$$\sqrt{[\Sigma(Y_i - \hat{Y}_i)^2/(N-3)]/[\Sigma(X_i - \bar{X})^2(1 - r_{xz}^2)]}$$

where $\hat{Y}_i$ are the values of Y predicted by the multiple regression equation, $\hat{Y}_i = \hat{a} + \hat{b}_{yx \cdot z}X_i + \hat{b}_{yx \cdot x}Z_i$.[24] Inspection of this formula indicates several strategies that investigators can use to improve the precision of regression estimates and reduce the chance of Type II errors. The previous section of this chapter suggested that adding W variables to the regression of Y on X and Z might reduce the variance in Y. Removing random measurement error from Y also mutes its variance. Reducing the variance in Y reduces the term $\Sigma(Y_i - \hat{Y}_i)^2$ and diminishes the standard error. Adding observations augments the value of $(N-3)$; increasing the variance between treatments enlarges the value of $\Sigma(X_i - \bar{X})^2$. Both of these steps also make the standard error smaller.

One of the most prevalent sources of imprecision in multiple regression estimates is multicollinearity. Multicollinearity exists whenever two (or more) independent variables are highly interrelated. In program evaluation, the association between the treatment (X) and any confounding or spurious variables (Z) determines the amount of multicollinearity in partial regression estimates of the impact of X on Y. As confounding or spurious variables increasingly determine the treatment subjects receive, so does the magnitude of r_{xz}^2. Inspection of the formula for the standard error of $\hat{b}_{yx \cdot z}$ discloses that large values of r_{xz}^2 magnify the standard error of estimate.

Multicollinearity is not an arcane issue for program evaluators. Public programs (X) are frequently targeted to specific populations. Whenever the characteristics of these target populations (Z) also affect performance (Y), the association between X and Z is likely to be high. Targeting programs may be good public policy; but it also makes program evaluation more difficult. Consider the Comprehensive Employment and Training Act (CETA). CETA monies (X) are targeted to areas of high unemployment (Z) for the purpose of reducing unemployment in the future (Y). Targeting means that X and Z will be highly interrelated, and their association increases the chance that the investigator will erroneously decide that $\hat{b}_{yx \cdot z}$ is zero. Ironically, because of multicollinearity, a decision to increase the impact of funds by targeting them may simultaneously augment the likelihood that an evaluator will conclude that the funds have no impact.[25]

Multicollinearity is not always a problem. Recall the analysis of the impact of Title I on local education revenues. In that case, $\hat{b}_{yx \cdot z} = -0.78$; the standard error of this estimate is 0.70. An examination of the separate components of this error indicates that X (Title I revenues per pupil) and Z (family income) are not multicollinear. The first component in the formula for the standard error of $\hat{b}_{yx \cdot z}$, shown above, is the sum of the squared deviations of the actual observations for Y (local education revenues per pupil) from the values of Y predicted by the regression of Y on X and Z. This sum is divided by $(N-3)$, or 353. In the example, $\Sigma(Y_i - \hat{Y}_i)^2 = 22,711,811$; this large value probably explains why the

the standard error is so large relative to the regression coefficient. It represents most (71%) of the total variation in Y, and discloses that the influence of unmeasured variables on Y far exceeds that of the measured variables. The total variation in X, measured by the term $\Sigma(X_i - \bar{X})^2$, is 172,660; the squared correlation between X and Z (r^2_{xz}) is only 0.24. The standard error of the partial regression estimate $\hat{b}_{yx \cdot z} = -0.78$ is thus:

$$\sqrt{[22,711,811/(353)]/[(172,660)(1-0.24)]} = 0.70$$

These components reveal that the influence of unmeasured variables is more likely to explain the imprecision of the regression estimate than multicollinearity between X and Z.

The undetected presence of statistical interaction is another reason for investigators to be cautious in their interpretation of regression estimates. No matter whether bivariate or partial estimates are appropriate, undisclosed interaction makes regression coefficients uninterpretable. If the investigator suspects that the value of $\hat{b}_{yx}$ hinges on the specific value of a third variable that defines the context within which X and Y are associated, then statistical interaction may be present. The procedures for determining whether interaction is present depend somewhat on whether the interactive variable is categorical or continuous. Consider first an example of statistical interaction when it is categorical. Suppose that the regression coefficient relating years of schooling (X) to earnings (Y) among the entire U.S. population is $\hat{b}_{yx} = 1000$. This value means that on the average, an additional year of school is associated with an earnings increase of $1000 per year. The widespread presence of racial discrimination in the U.S. suggests that the impact of an additional year of education on earnings for whites may exceed that for blacks (Miller 1977). If $\hat{b}_{yx} = \$1100$ for whites, and if $\hat{b}_{yx} = \$500$ for blacks, statistical interaction is clearly present. These values indicate that a year of education is worth more to whites than to blacks and suggest that the causes of earnings differences among whites may differ from the causes of earnings differences among blacks.[26] Further analysis of the bivariate associations to determine whether they are spurious or causal thus requires separate computations for each racial group.

When the source of interaction is a continuous rather than a categorical variable, the investigator must devise a specific model of the interactive process. In most instances, the resulting multiple regression will have a multiplicative term. Consider a situation in which the impact of a program (e.g., the amount of emergency assistance funds per pupil given to schools undergoing busing) on an outcome measure (e.g., achievement scores) increases as the value of a third variable (e.g., poverty) increases. All three variables are continuous, but the impact of X on Y depends on the value of the interactive variables, which we denote by I. The influence of X on Y can be represented by a bivariate regression equation:

$$Y = \hat{a} + \hat{b}_{yx}X + e.$$

It is also possible to express the dependence of the value of $\hat{b}_{yx}$ on I by an equation:

$$\hat{b}_{yx} = \hat{c}_{bI}I,$$

where I = poverty of the students. Substituting this expression into the original multiple regression yields a new multiple regression of the form:

$$Y = \hat{a} + \hat{c}_{bI}IX + e.$$

This equation has a multiplicative term. By regressing Y on the term IX, the investigator can use ordinary regression analysis to estimate the value of $\hat{c}_{bI}$. He can then rely on the expression $\hat{b}_{yx} = \hat{c}_{bI}I$ to recover specific values of $\hat{b}_{yx}$ for each value of I.[27]

The accuracy of this procedure depends on the analyst's ability to portray accurately the interactive process itself. Investigators may sometimes find it easier simply to treat continuous interactive variables as if they were categorical variables by subdividing the continuum into categories (e.g., high, medium, low). This procedure is not necessarily accurate either, since it rests on cutpoints which may be arbitrary. In sum, analysts will not find easy solutions when interaction is present. Yet ignoring interaction is also perilous, since its undetected presence can produce misleading evidence.

Many observers argue that exclusive reliance on partial regression coefficients can also yield misleading or partial evidence regarding program impact. They suggest supplementing regression coefficients with standardized measures whose value does not depend on the units in which the variables are measured. Using standardized measures is useful when analysts must compare the relative importance of confounding or intervening (Z) variables to that of the program (X) variable. Using an application of multiple regression aptly termed "path analysis," investigators can compare the strength of the paths marked (a) and (b) shown in the models of Figure 9.13. In models like these, comparing the value of $\hat{b}_{yx \cdot z}$ to that of $\hat{b}_{yz \cdot x}$ is not meaningful, since the units in which variables are measured partly determine the value of regression coefficients. No matter what the outcome measure, if Z is a county's median family income measured in dollars and X is the number of physicians per capita, $\hat{b}_{yx \cdot z}$ and $\hat{b}_{yz \cdot x}$ are not comparable. It

FIGURE 9.13

Causal Models Implicit in Path Analysis

makes no more sense to compare the influence of "number of doctors" to that of "dollars" than it does to compare apples to oranges. Path analysis makes these variables comparable by transforming X, Z, and Y to a common unit of measurement—the standard deviation unit. The "path coefficient" (or Beta weight) is thus the best way to compare the relative influence of X and Z on Y.

To compute the path coefficient $\beta_{yx.z}$, which measures the standardized influence of X on Y, we use the formula:

$$\beta_{yx.z} = \hat{b}_{yx.z} \frac{s_x}{s_y}$$

where s_x and s_y are the standard deviations of X and Y respectively. Similarly, the standardized influence of Z on Y is:

$$\beta_{yz.x} = \hat{b}_{yz.x} \frac{s_z}{s_y}$$

where s_z is the standard deviation of Z.[28]

These are both partial coefficients, and reflect the influence of one variable on another when a third variable is controlled. The values of these path coefficients are also comparable. If $\beta_{yz.x} = 0.90$ and $\beta_{yx.z} = 0.30$, an investigator can conclude that, as measured in standard deviation units, the influence of Z on Y is three times that of X.

Path analysis has actually been a subject of some controversy in the context of program evaluation. Results based on path analyses often indicate that confounding variables have considerably more influence on program outcomes than the program itself. James Coleman's famous study, *Equality of Educational Opportunity* (Coleman et al. 1966) conclude that school quality (X) has little influence on achievement scores (Y) relative to the students' family background (Z) based on a version of path analysis. In a critique of Coleman's study, Cain and Watts (1972) observed that path analysis measures only relative and not absolute importance. The fact that X has little influence on Y relative to Z does not mean that X has no effect on Y at all. Relative to family background, schools are unimportant influences on achievement. Better schools may nonetheless raise achivement scores, and the unstandardized partial regression coefficient, $\hat{b}_{yx.z}$, is the best way to measure this absolute effect. Program evaluators who are concerned with absolute rather than relative effects should thus depend on unstandardized partial regression coefficients.[29]

In this section, we have considered numerous threats to the validity and precision of partial regression estimates. The validity of regression estimates rests on assuming that X and Y are not reciprocally dependent, that confounding and interactive variables have not been omitted, and that X and Z are measured without random error.[30] The precision of regression estimates depends on eliminating variation in Y, maximizing variation in X, amassing large numbers of observations, and reducing multicollinearity. Investigators should be aware that these problems do not inevitably affect every evaluation study. Some studies are free of multi-collinearity; reciprocal dependence between X and Y is not always a problem. These problems are most intractable when investigators ignore them. Carefully designed nonexperimental investigations that explicitly account for the most important threats to the validity and precision of regression estimates can pro-duce useful evidence regarding program impact.

MULTIPLE REGRESSION WHEN X IS CATEGORICAL[31]

Program evaluators frequently encounter situations in which the treatment is a categorical variable, while Z and Y are continuous. Treatments are categorical when they vary in respect to their presence or absence and when they vary in kind. Persons either participate in a training program or they do not. States either require automobile inspection or they do not. WIN recipients participate in three types of training programs; they are trained on-the-job, they attend vocational training, or they receive a special orientation. In each of these examples, the treatment is categorically measured. As long as Z and Y are continuous, multiple regression analysis is still appropriate when X is categorical. The only practical effect of including categorical variables in regression equations is to alter slightly the interpretation of regression coefficients. In all other respects, the strengths and limits of multiple regression are identical no matter whether X is continuous or categorical.

Consider first an analysis of covariance (ANCOVA) model appropriate for estimating the total impact of participation in a program (X) on an outcome measure (Y), controlling statistically for one (or more) confounding variables (Z).[32] The corresponding statistical model is:

$$Y = \hat{a}_{np} + \hat{a}'X_p + \hat{b}_p Z_p + \hat{b}_{np} Z_{np} + e$$

where

  Y = scores on the outcome measure for participants and nonparticipants; Y is thus a vector of scores;

  X_p = 1 if the subject was a participant and 0 if he was a nonparticipant; X is thus a vector of ones and zeros;

  Z_p = score on Z-variable if the subject was a participant and 0 if he was a nonparticipant; Z_p is thus a vector of scores and zeros;

  Z_{np} = score on Z-variable if the subject was a nonparticipant and 0 if he was a participant; Z_{np} is also a vector of scores and zeros.

The only difference between ANCOVA and multiple regression is that ANCOVA models contain variables on the right-hand side with 1s and 0s as well as variables with scores and 0s. This slightly alters the interpretation of the regression estimates, denoted by $\hat{a}_{np}$, $\hat{a}'$, $\hat{b}_p$, and $\hat{b}_{np}$. In multiple regression, the most important coefficient for program evaluators is $\hat{b}_{yx \cdot z}$. In ANCOVA, the regression coefficient $\hat{a}'$ is the most relevant coefficient in the equation. The regression coefficient $\hat{a}'$ is an estimate of the difference in the score on the outcome measure between participants and nonparticipants when Z is held constant. It thus reports the impact of a program once confounding influences have been removed. The intercept $\hat{a}_{np}$ estimates the nonparticipants' score on the outcome measure if the value of Z were zero. The sum $\hat{a}' + \hat{a}_{np}$ is the participants' score on Y if the value of Z were zero. Since confounding variables are rarely zero, the values of $\hat{a}_{np}$ and $\hat{a}' + \hat{a}_{np}$ are not likely to be especially important in the context of program evaluation. The two regression coefficients, $\hat{b}_p$ and $\hat{b}_{np}$, estimate the partial influence of the confounding variable Z on Y when the influence of participation (X) has been removed. They report the adjusted change in Y that corresponds to each unit change in Z for participants and nonparticipants respectively.

Multiple regressions that include categorically measured treatment variables actually represent nonexperimental versions of two quasi-experimental designs— the PTPTCG and the PTCG. In both nonexperiments and quasi experiments, the investigator compares participants to nonparticipants. In quasi experiments, he selects each group so that they are similar in respect to confounding variables. The process of selecting observations is thus the means by which investigators remove confounding influences. In nonexperiments, participants and nonparticipants in the analysis do not necessarily resemble each other. The adjustment for confounding variables is statistical and does not occur in the selection process itself.

Despite these differences, two nonexperimental ANCOVA models correspond to a PTPTCG quasi experiment. In the first, the investigator controls statistically for the pretest score of the outcome measure (Y_t). This is the nonexperimental equivalent of matching subjects on pretest scores alone. The formal model is:

$$Y_t = \hat{a}_{np} + \hat{a}'X_p + \hat{b}_p Y_{(t-1)p} + \hat{b}_{np} Y_{(t-1)np} + e,$$

where Y_t is the posttest score, $Y_{(t-1)p}$ equals 0 for nonparticipants and equals the pretest score of Y for participants, and $Y_{(t-1)np}$ equals 0 for participants and equals the pretest score of Y for nonparticipants. Since $Y_{(t-1)}$ is the only control variable, unbiased estimation of program impact ($\hat{a}'$) necessitates assuming that the pretest score contains no random measurement error. When $Y_{(t-1)}$ is measured with random error, investigators must use the second version of the PTPTCG, which contains at least two confounding variables. One is the pretest score of the outcome measure; the other confounding variables jointly influence the likelihood of participation (X) and the outcome measure (Y). This model is thus nonexperimentally equivalent to quasi experiments that match on pretest scores and on other confounding variables as well. Its formal expression is:

$$Y_t = \hat{a}_{np} + \hat{a}'X_p + \hat{b}_p Y_{(t-1)p} + \hat{b}_{np} Y_{(t-1)np} + \hat{b}_{y_t z \cdot y_{(t-1)}x}Z + e$$

where Z = scores on a confounding variable for participants as well as nonparticipants and where $\hat{b}_{y_t z \cdot y_{(t-1)} x}$ estimates the change in the outcome measure (Y_t)
that corresponds to each unit change in Z once the impacts of X and $Y_{(t-1)}$ have
been held constant.[33] The central measure of program impact is still $\hat{a}'$; it estimates the difference in the outcome measure for participants and nonparticipants
when the influence of $Y_{(t-1)}$ and Z have been removed.

The PTCG quasi experiment also has a nonexperimental version that, like
the PTCG design itself, ignores the previous level of the outcome measure:

$$Y = \hat{a}_{np} + \hat{a}'X_p + \hat{b}_{yz \cdot x}Z + e.$$

The measure of program impact is still $\hat{a}'$. Its value is an estimate of the difference in mean scores on Y between participants and nonparticipants when Z is
constant; $\hat{a}_{np}$ is the value of Y for nonparticipants when Z equals zero, and
$\hat{a}_{np} + \hat{a}'$ is the value of Y for participants when Z equals zero. The regression coefficient $\hat{b}_{yz \cdot x}$ estimates the change in Y per unit change in Z when X is held
constant. Investigators will ordinarily find the value of $\hat{a}'$ to be most important,
since it estimates program influence after confounding and spurious variables
have been controlled.

This equation is not an ANCOVA model, because it has no vectors that
combine scores and zeroes. It includes one vector with ones and zeros (X_p).
Such a variable is called a "dummy" variable, and the equation is a multiple regression with one dummy variable. Dummy variables appear in ANCOVA models
as well as in multiple regressions.[34]

The models we have considered so far have program variables (X) that contain only two categories: participants and nonparticipants. In the case of programs with three categories (e.g., no participation, participation in treatment #1,
participation in treatment #2), the investigator must use two dummy variables,
as the following regression illustrates:

$$Y = \hat{a}_{np} + \hat{a}'_1 X_{p1} + \hat{a}'_2 X_{p2} + \hat{b}_{yx \cdot x}Z + e,$$

where

X_{p1} = 1 if the observation participated in treatment #1 and 0 for all other
observations;

X_{p2} = 1 if the observation participated in treatment #2 and 0 for all other
observations; and

Z = scores for all observations on a confounding variable

and

$\hat{a}_{np}$ = estimated mean score on Y for all nonparticipants, when Z equals
zero;

$\hat{a}'_1$ = difference in mean score on Y between those receiving treatment #1 and nonparticipants, controlling for Z;

$\hat{a}'_2$ = difference in mean score on Y between those receiving treatment #2 and nonparticipants, controlling for Z.

When Z is zero, the mean Y for persons participating in treatment #1 is thus $\hat{a}_{np} + \hat{a}'_1$ and the mean Y for persons participating in treatment #2 is $\hat{a}_{np} + \hat{a}'_2$. The two regression coefficients $\hat{a}'_1$ and $\hat{a}'_2$ are the most important for program evaluators, since they reveal the influence of different treatments on the outcome measure once confounding or spurious factors have been removed.

The specific model that an evaluator uses depends on the number of treatments he investigates and on the availability of data for measuring previous levels of outcome measures and other confounding variables as well. Analysts should try to secure data on previous levels of outcome measures whenever possible.[35] They can then use ANCOVA models to uncover the impact of differential growth rates on estimates of program impact. Examining the simplest ANCOVA model,

$$Y = \hat{a}_{np} + \hat{a}'X_p + \hat{b}_p Y_{(t-1)p} + \hat{b}_{np} Y_{(t-1)np},$$

discloses how investigators can interpret information about growth rates. Figure 9.14 graphs this equation as two regression lines. The participants have slope $\hat{b}_p$ which is steeper on the graph than the nonparticipants' slope $\hat{b}_{np}$. The difference between these slopes is clear evidence of statistical interaction. The presence of interaction makes any single estimate of program impact uninterpretable—includ-

FIGURE 9.14

Differential Growth Rates:
Statistical Interaction with PTPTCG Model

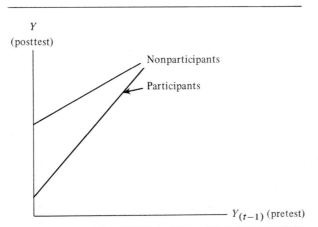

ing $\hat{a}'$. Figure 9.14 reveals that the impact of the program depends on the pretest score; as the pretest score increases, program impact diminishes. The program's influence is thus greatest for persons with the lowest scores.[36] In the absence of information regarding pretest scores, investigators cannot detect contingent effects like these.

Investigators who anticipate contingent effects but who have no information on previous values of outcome measures can sometimes modify the PTCG design to accommodate interaction. Its simple form is a multiple regression with dummy variables; as an ANCOVA model, its form is:

$$Y = \hat{a}_{np} + \hat{a}'X_p + \hat{b}_p Z_p + \hat{b}_{np} Z_{np} + e,$$

where

Z_p = score on Z for participants and 0 for nonparticipants; and
Z_{np} = score on Z for nonparticipants and 0 for participants.

Figure 9.15 depicts a graph of this equation. As long as scores on Z are highly related to scores on $Y_{(t-1)}$, then this equation can account for differential growth rates even in the absence of pretest information.

This chapter has considered two regression models for estimating program impact when the program itself is a categorical variable. The simplest model resembles a PTCG quasi experiment, and casts the program variable as a dummy variable in a multiple regression. The other basic model resembles a PTPTCG. As an analysis of covariance, it not only represents the treatment as a dummy

FIGURE 9.15

Differential Growth Rates:
Statistical Interaction with PTCG Model

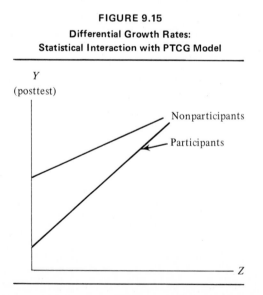

variable, but it also casts pretreatment values of outcome measures and other confounding variables in interactive form. In all other respects, these models are no different from the multiple regression of continuous variables, as the following example illustrates.

Consider an application of the statistical model for a PTCG to the problem of estimating the influence of state requirements for automobile inspection on the automobile accident mortality rate.[37] By 1960, fifteen states had some form of required safety inspection. According to Colton and Buxbaum (1977: 136–138), the mean age-adjusted automobile accident mortality rate in 1960 was lower in states with auto inspection than in states without inspection.[38] There is thus an association between inspection and fatalities, but the association may not be causal. As Tufte (1974) points out, states whose population density is low tend to have higher motor vehicle fatality rates than states where populations are dense. People probably drive faster in sparsely settled states, and emergency medical care may be less available. Both factors could account for higher fatality rates in these states. Sparsely settled states are also less likely to require automobile inspection. Population density is thus a possibly confounding or spurious variable whose influence must be removed before estimating the impact of safety inspection on automobile fatalities.[39] (See Figure 9.16.)

FIGURE 9.16

**Causal Model for Impact of Auto Safety
Inspection on Auto Accident Mortality**

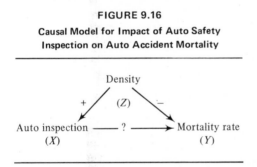

This example requires multiple regression with a dummy variable, since auto inspection is either present or absent. All of the other variables are continuous. The actual equation is:

$$Y = \hat{a}_{NI} + \hat{a}'X_I + \hat{b}_{yz \cdot x}Z + e$$

where

Y = age-adjusted motor vehicle accident mortality rate per 100,000 population for white males 15–64 years old, 1960;[40]

X_I = 1 for all states with motor vehicle inspection requirements in 1960, and 0 otherwise; and

Z = log of population density in each state.[41]

Based on data from the 48 states in 1960, Figure 9.17 lists the value of the intercept and the values of the regression coefficients, their standard errors, and their *t*-statistics.[42] The value of $\hat{a}'$ is most important. Its value is an estimate of the difference in mortality rates between states with and without inspection once the confounding influence of density has been removed. The negative value means

FIGURE 9.17

**Regression Estimates: Auto Safety Inspection
and Accident Mortality, Density Controlled**

Coefficient	Value	Standard error	t
$\hat{a}_{NI}$	84.71		
$\hat{a}'$	−6.34	3.06	−2.07
$\hat{b}_{yz \cdot x}$	−9.08	1.03	−8.82

that states with inspection have lower mortality rates than states without; the specific difference is 6.34. States with auto inspection have 6.34 fewer motor vehicle deaths per 100,000 population than states without inspection. The *t*-statistic is reasonably large. According to a table of probabilities for *t*, the probability of obtaining such a *t*-statistic if the true value of $\hat{a}'$ were zero is very small. The regression estimate is thus significantly different from zero (at the 0.04 level).

In this example, the estimated value for the intercept is not very useful. The 84.71 estimate means that if the influence of density were held constant (at zero) in all states, states without auto inspection would have a fatality rate of 84.71 per 100,000 population. Since $\hat{a}' = -6.34$, it follows that states with auto inspection would have a lower auto fatality rate of 78.37 per 100,000 if population density were zero. Population density, however, cannot be zero. Investigators should thus focus on the difference in fatality rates, measured by $\hat{a}'$, rather than on the level the rates attain under absurd conditions.

It is possible to use another design to analyze the influence of auto safety inspection on motor vehicle accident mortality rates. According to Colton and Buxbaum (1977), five states adopted requirements for automobile inspection between 1950 and 1960. Because accident rates for both 1950 and 1960 are available, the statistical version of a PTPTCG provides an appropriate model with which to reexamine the impact of safety inspection on fatalities. The equation for this design is:

$$Y_{1960} = \hat{a}_{NI} + \hat{a}'_I X_I + \hat{b}_I Y_{(1950, I)} + \hat{b}_{NI} Y_{(1950, NI)} + e$$

where Y_{1960} and X_I have already been defined and where

$Y_{(1950,I)}$ = age-adjusted motor vehicle accident mortality rate per 100,000
population for white males 15–64 years old, 1950, for states

adopting auto inspection between 1950 and 1960, and 0 for states without auto inspection; and

$Y_{(1950,NI)}$ = same 1950 mortality rate as above for states without inspection and 0 for states adopting inspections.[43]

Separating pretreatment levels of the outcome measure for states with and without inspection allows for the possibility that growth rates differ. If $\hat{b}_I$ approximates $\hat{b}_{NI}$, then growth rates do not covary with the adoption of inspection. When $\hat{b}_I$ and $\hat{b}_{NI}$ are equal, investigators can combine the two variates by adding $Y_{(1950,I)}$ and $Y_{(1950,NI)}$.

The results listed in Figure 9.18 suggest that growth rates do not vary greatly with inspection: $\hat{b}_I$ = 1.05 and $\hat{b}_{NI}$ = 0.88. States adopting auto inspection tended to have slightly higher increases in their fatality rates between 1950 and 1960 than states with no inspection, but the difference is not large.[44] Most importantly, $\hat{a}'$, the estimate of program impact, is no longer significant. According to

FIGURE 9.18

Regression Estimates: Auto Safety Inspection and 1960 Accident Mortality, 1950 Accident Mortality Controlled

Coefficient	Value	Standard error	t
$\hat{a}_{NI}$	6.77		
$\hat{a}'$	−9.78	12.63	−0.77
$\hat{b}_I$	1.05	0.22	4.77
$\hat{b}_{NI}$	0.88	0.14	6.29

these results, controlling prior levels of the outcome measure makes the association between auto inspection and lower fatality disappear entirely. This suggests, in sharp contrast to our previous findings, that auto inspection does not reduce fatalities.

Slight modifications of the regression equation fail to alter this result. Adding $Y_{(1950,I)}$ to $Y_{(1950,NI)}$ does not measurably reduce R^2. The resulting equation is $Y_{1960} = \hat{a}_{NI} + \hat{a}'X_I + \hat{b}Y_{1950} + e$. No matter whether the investigator measures prior levels of Y separately for inspection and noninspection states or adds them, the relative influence of measured to unmeasured variables remains unchanged at 0.66. The two equations are thus not substantially different. Figure 9.19 also discloses that this modification fails to alter the conclusion that auto inspection has no impact on auto fatalities.

Even controlling for density as well as prior levels of the outcome measure does not change these findings of no impact. Figure 9.20 discloses the estimates that result from the multiple regression equation:

$$Y_{1960} = \hat{a}_{NI} + \hat{a}'X_I + \hat{b}_1 Y_{1950} + \hat{b}_2 Z + e$$

FIGURE 9.19

**Regression Estimates: Auto Safety Inspection and 1960
Accident Mortality, 1950 Mortality Controlled
(No Allowance for Differential Growth Rates)**

Coefficient	Value	Standard error	t
$\hat{a}_{NI}$	4.43		
$\hat{a}'$	−2.32	4.92	−0.47
$\hat{b}$	0.93	0.12	7.75

FIGURE 9.20

**Regression Estimates: Auto Safety Inspection and 1960
Accident Mortality, 1950 Mortality and Density Controlled**

Coefficient	Value	Standard error	t
$\hat{a}_{NI}$	48.34		
$\hat{a}$	−0.81	3.98	−0.20
$\hat{b}_1$	0.52	0.13	4.00
$\hat{b}_2$	−6.25	1.40	−4.46

The impact of auto inspection on the mortality rate continues to be insignificant, according to the t-statistic associated with $\hat{a}'$.

This example discloses how an investigator's conclusions depend on the design. The example also reveals that time-series information is important, no matter whether the investigator uses quasi-experimental or nonexperimental designs. Designs that include time-series data can yield different conclusions regarding program impact than designs that ignore information based on the passage of time. The PTCG design omits prior levels of the outcome measure as a confounding variable. The PTPTCG design, by incorporating $Y_{(t-1)}$ as well as Y_t, avoids a potentially important source of bias. In the case of auto safety, it appears that both density (Z) and previous fatality levels (Y_{1950}) are important confounding variables. Conclusions based on the coefficients reported in Figure 9.17 are consequently biased by the omission of a confounding variable. Figure 9.21(b) is thus a better model of auto inspection than Figure 9.21(a).[45]

SUMMARY

This chapter outlined techniques for the nonexperimental analysis of continuous data. These techniques are all based on the analysis of partial regression coefficients estimated from multiple regressions that control for confounding and extraneous variables. Regardless of whether they rely on categorical or continuous data, investigators must avoid controls for intervening variables when

FIGURE 9.21

Causal Models for Auto Safety Inspection

(a) Causal impact

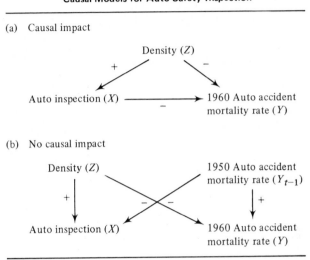

(b) No causal impact

they seek estimates of total program effects. Despite the similarities between the nonexperimental analysis of continuous and categorical data, simultaneously controlling for many variables is far simpler with multiple regression analysis than with the analysis of percentage differences. In fact, investigators who use multiple regression often mistakenly ignore the distinction between direct and indirect effects because controlling for additional variables is so easy.

Users of multiple regression must be cognizant of its limitations and its assumptions. Most of these limitations also apply to the analysis of categorical data. Some of these impediments to nonexperimental analysis are more likely to occur than others. Simultaneous relations between X and Y are quite common. Advanced techniques that we do not consider in this text are available when simultaneity is a problem. Measurement error in X and Z may be more troublesome than evaluators usually recognize because these errors are rarely obvious. There are no simple tests for the presence of measurement error, yet its undetected presence biases estimates of program impact. Large standard errors also plague nonexperimental estimates of program impact. Investigators can reduce standard errors by augmenting the number of observations, maximizing variation in X, and reducing the influence of unmeasured variables. Multicollinearity affects standard errors, but investigators can usually do little to avoid it.

The nonexperimental analysis of models with categorical treatment variables and continuously measured outcome and confounding variables also uncovers the similarity between quasi-experimental and nonexperimental approaches. Multiple regression models with categorical variables have quasi-experimental versions. Explicit consideration of this analogy reveals that time-series information is as important in nonexperimental designs as it is in quasi-experimental approaches.

FOOTNOTES

1. We use the symbol $\hat{b}_{yx \cdot z}$ to denote the estimated value of the population parameter, $b_{yx \cdot z}$. Estimates have a "hat"; parameters, which are the values that occur after repeated random sampling, do not. Under certain circumstances, $\hat{b}_{yx \cdot z}$ is an unbiased and efficient estimator of $b_{yx \cdot z}$, just as $\bar{Y}$, the sample mean, is an unbiased and efficient estimator of μ, the population mean. For a fuller discussion of the terms "unbiased" and efficient," see Blalock (1972: 202–205). The major source of bias in estimates for $b_{yx \cdot z}$ that we consider in this chapter is the failure to control for Z-variables. In all instances, we assume that the time-order requirement for causal inference (X precedes Y) is met. Failure to meet this requirement is another source of bias in estimates for $b_{yx \cdot z}$. For examples of studies that use $\hat{b}_{yx \cdot z}$ to estimate program impact, see Lave and Seskin (1977), Salkever and Bice (1976), Peltzman (1975), and Rosenstone and Wolfinger (1978).

2. For a technical interpretation of $\hat{b}_{yx \cdot z}$, consider the bivariate regression equation $Y = \hat{a} + \hat{b}_{yx}Z + e$. The partial regression coefficient $\hat{b}_{yx \cdot z}$ actually comes from a regression of the error term, e, which measures the values of Y that occur once the influence of Z is removed, on the program variable, X: $e = \hat{a}' + \hat{b}_{ex}X + e'$, where $\hat{b}_{ex} = \hat{b}_{yx \cdot z}$.

3. The Appendix discusses $\hat{b}_{yx}$ in some detail. This chapter centers on the first-order partial regression coefficient, $\hat{b}_{yx \cdot z}$, in which the only control variable is Z. When there is more than one confounding or spurious variable, evaluators must use higher order partials. For two confounding variables, $\hat{b}_{yx \cdot z_1 z_2}$ is the appropriate measure of partial association. To control one confounding and one extraneous variable simultaneously, $\hat{b}_{yx \cdot zw}$ is the appropriate measure of partial association. It is unnecessary to consider these higher order partials in any detail. The case of three variables is perfectly general.

4. For partial regression coefficients in general, $\hat{b}_{ij \cdot k} = \dfrac{\hat{b}_{ij} - \hat{b}_{ik}\hat{b}_{kj}}{1 - \hat{b}_{kj}\hat{b}_{jk}}$. There are many ways to compute the partial regression coefficient. The one shown here is among the easiest for hand computation. This chapter will not dwell on formulas for hand computation. Readers will always find it easier to use packaged statistical routines for computer analysis instead of hand or calculator computation. In packaged routines, the multiple regression of Y on X and Z will provide output reporting the value of $\hat{b}_{yx \cdot z}$.

5. We see below that investigators should not use $\hat{b}_{yx \cdot z}$ to estimate the total (direct plus indirect) influence of X on Y.

6. This coefficient can be computed by the formula $\hat{b}_{yx \cdot zw} = (\hat{b}_{yx \cdot z} - \hat{b}_{yw \cdot z}\hat{b}_{wx \cdot z})/(1 - \hat{b}_{wx \cdot z}\hat{b}_{xw \cdot z})$.

7. In an effort to make $\hat{b}_{yx \cdot z}$ significant, investigators should not include too many W-variables in multiple regression equations. Adding too many variables diminishes the effective number of observations. It may also introduce unnecessary multicollinearity and thus may augment standard errors.

8. The Appendix discusses the t-test for the significance of regression coefficients. For partial regression coefficients, the value of t equals $\hat{b}_{yx \cdot z}$ divided by the standard error of $\hat{b}_{yx \cdot z}$.

9. These values reflect a 7% random sample of school districts from the 1969–1970 School District Data Tapes supplied by the National Center for Education Statistics, U.S. Office of Education. The data on these tapes came from the 1969 Elementary and Secondary General Information Survey (ELSEGIS) and the 1970 Census.

10. The complete multiple regression equation that generated this estimate is $Y = -55.55 - 0.78X + 0.05Z + e$. The Y-intercept is -55.55, and means that districts containing families with zero income and receiving no Title I would spend $-\$55.55$ per pupil in local revenues. Their spending would thus be negative. The value of $\hat{b}_{yz \cdot x}$ is $+0.05$. This figure reveals that a one-dollar increase in family income is associated with a $0.05 per pupil increase in per pupil local education revenues, holding Title I constant. The influence of unmeasured extraneous variables exceeds that of measured variables, since $1 - R^2_{y \cdot xz} = 1 - 0.29 = 0.81$.

11. Increasing the number of observations and identifying, measuring, and controlling for important extraneous influences could alter this conclusion by making $\hat{b}_{yx \cdot z}$ look significant.

12. An empirical evaluation of the impact of habitability laws (X) on rent (Y) illustrates this error. The investigators assume that Z-variables like construction costs and distance from central city precede the imposition of habitability laws. They consequently use $\hat{b}_{yx \cdot z}$ to estimate the influence of these laws on rents. If the presence of habitability laws affects both the choice of construction materials and the location of rental units, which seems likely, then $\hat{b}_{yx}$ rather than $\hat{b}_{yx \cdot z}$ is the appropriate measure of impact. See Hirsch, Hirsch, and Margolis (1977).

13. This method assumes that the relation between X and Z is either $X \rightarrow Z$ or $Z \rightarrow X$ but not $X \rightleftarrows Z$. Estimating the total impact of X on Y when the relation between X and Z is reciprocal also requires the investigator to identify instrumental variables like V, but ordinary regression can no longer be used. See Stokes (1974).

14. This need arises when investigators must examine the process by which a program (X) affects an outcome measure (Y). It may also be necessary to estimate indirect effects when interaction is present. Sometimes the process by which X affects Y may depend on the value of an interactive variable.

15. The derivation of this expression is straightforward. Let $x = (X_i - \overline{X})$, $y = (Y_i - \overline{Y})$, $z_1 = (Z_{1i} - \overline{Z}_1)$, and $z_2 = (Z_{2i} - \overline{Z}_2)$. Then $\hat{b}_{yx} = \Sigma xy / \Sigma x^2$. The multiple regression model associated with Figures 9.8(e) and (f), expressed in deviation form is:

$$y = \hat{b}_{yx \cdot z_1 z_2} x + \hat{b}_{yz_1 \cdot xz_2} z_1 + \hat{b}_{yz_2 \cdot xz_1} z_2 + e.$$

Substituting this expression for y into the right-hand side of the formula for $\hat{b}_{yx}$ and taking expectations yields the required decomposition of b_{yx}.

16. This simplification can only be used when Z_1 and Z_2 are unrelated. It works since

$$b_{yz_1 \cdot xz_2} = \frac{b_{yz_1 \cdot x} - b_{yz_2 \cdot x} b_{z_2 z_1 \cdot x}}{1 - b_{z_2 z_1 \cdot x} b_{z_1 z_2 \cdot x}} .$$

When Z_1 and Z_2 are independent, $b_{z_2 z_1 \cdot x} = 0$ and so $b_{yz_1 \cdot xz_2} = b_{yz_1 \cdot x}$.

17. There are other statistical techniques appropriate for these causal models, including the method of instrumental variables. For a relatively nontechnical introduction to these methods, see Namboodiri, Carter, and Blalock (1975: Ch. 11). For a more advanced treatment, see Hanushek and Jackson (1977: Ch. 9).

18. Microeconomic theories of supply and demand are particularly useful in this regard. For a good illustration of the use of economic theory to predict simultaneity, see Fuchs (1978).

19. Omitting an intervening variable will not bias estimates of total program influence.

20. The derivation of this expression is identical to the derivation of the expression on page 140. Expressing X, Y, and Z in deviation form, let $x = (X_i - \overline{X})$, $y = (Y_i - \overline{Y})$, and $z = (Z_i - \overline{Z})$. The multiple regression implicit in Figure 9.10 can then be written $y = \hat{b}_{yx \cdot z} x + \hat{b}_{yz \cdot x} z + e$. Substituting this into the formula for $\hat{b}_{yx}$, which is $\Sigma xy / \Sigma x^2$, and taking expectations yields the desired result.

21. See Blalock, Wells, and Carter (1970) for a proof and a discussion of this issue. Also see Magidson (1977), Bentler and Woodward (1978), and Magidson (1978) for a discussion of the importance of random measurement error in the context of Head Start evaluations. See also Director (1979) for a consideration of the influence of measurement error in independent variables as applied to manpower training.

22. It can be shown that $b_{yx \cdot z} = \dfrac{b_{yx} - b_{yz} b_{zx}}{1 - r_{zx}^2}$ while $b_{yx \cdot z'} = \dfrac{b_{yx} - b_{yz} b_{zx} r_{z'z}^2}{1 - r_{zx}^2 r_{z' \cdot z}^2}$. The coefficient $r_{z'z}^2$ reflects the association between the true and measured values of Z; when $r_{zz'}^2 = 1$ there is no random measurement error. Whether random measurement error in Z makes $\hat{b}_{yx \cdot z'}$ larger or smaller than the unbiased $\hat{b}_{yx \cdot z}$ depends on the signs of the simple

regression coefficients. The magnitude of its impact also depends on the size of the correlation between X and Z, as Greene (1978) points out. For more discussion, see Namboodiri, Carter, and Blalock (1975: Ch. 12–13).

23. For a formal proof and a discussion of the importance of good measurement in X, see Director (1979). Attenuation occurs because

$$b_{yx'\cdot z} = \frac{r_{xx}{}'(b_{yx} - b_{yz}b_{zx})}{1 - r_{zx}^2 r^2{}_{xx'}}$$

while $b_{yx\cdot z} = \dfrac{b_{yx} - b_{yz}b_{zx}}{1 - r_{zx}^2}$. Since $0 \leqslant r_{xx'}^2 \leqslant 1$, $b_{yx'\cdot z} < b_{yx\cdot z}$.

24. Another way to write the standard error uses the fact that $e_i = (Y_i - \hat{Y}_i) = Y_i - (\hat{a} + \hat{b}_{yx\cdot z}X_i + \hat{b}_{yz\cdot x}Z_i)$. As a result, we can express the standard error in this way:

$$\sqrt{[\Sigma e_i^2/(N-3)]/[\Sigma(X_i - \bar{X})^2(1 - r_{xz}^2)}.$$

25. Randomized field experiments entirely eliminate the problem of multicollinearity, because truly random assignment guarantees that the association between X and Z must be zero.

26. The simplest way to determine if these regression coefficients are significantly different uses the F-test to compare two regression equations. The first equation allows the two regression coefficients to differ: $Y = \hat{a} + \hat{b}_{yx'}X' + \hat{b}_{yx''}X'' + e$, where Y = earnings for entire U.S. population; X' = years in school for blacks and 0 for whites; and X'' = years of schooling for whites and 0 for blacks. The second equation forces the regression coefficients to be equal: $Y = \hat{a} + \hat{b}_{yx}X + e$, where Y = earnings for entire U.S. population and X = years in school for entire U.S. population. The F-test compares the r^2's for both regressions:

$$F = \frac{(r_{y\cdot x'x''}^2 - r_{yx}^2)/1}{(1 - r_{yx'}^2)/(N-3)}$$

For a complete discussion, see Namboodiri, Carter, and Blalock, (1975:195–202).

27. This discussion of interaction rests on Blalock (1968:178–186).

28. In general, $\beta_{ij\cdot k} = b_{ij\cdot k}\left(\dfrac{s_j}{s_i}\right)$. For the second order path coefficient, $\beta_{ij\cdot kl}$, use the formula: $b_{ij\cdot kl}\left(\dfrac{s_j}{s_i}\right)$.

29. The partial correlation coefficient is another way to compare the relative influence of two independent variables on a dependent variable. For program evaluators, it shares the same flaws as the more popular path coefficient, and we do not discuss it here.

30. Aggregation bias is another source for invalid regression estimates. Aggregation biases can occur when investigators use data on groups to make inferences about individual behavior. Irwin and Lichtman (1976) show that the inclusion of confounding variables removes aggregation bias. For a nontechnical discussion of other ways to remove aggregation bias, see Langbein and Lichtman (1978).

31. The material in this section is based on Namboodiri, Carter, and Blalock (1975).

32. Recall that investigators should not control intervening Z variables to estimate total effects.

33. Like $Y_{(t-1)}$, it is possible to write two vectors for Z—one for participants and one for nonparticipants. Investigators who are interested in the possibility that the influence of Z may depend on participation should express Z in two vectors.

34. ANCOVA models thus have both dummy variables and variables composed of scores and zeros. For empirical examples of evaluation studies that use dummy variables, see Director (1979), Barnow and Cain (1977), Colton and Buxbaum (1977), and Hirsch and

Margolis (1977). For a general discussion of multiple regression with dummy variables, see Cain (1975). For a general consideration of ANCOVA, see Alwin and Sullivan (1975).

35. Chapter 6 pointed out how knowing pretest scores can uncover growth rate differences in quasi experiments. Information on growth rates makes the PTPTCG better than the PTCG design.

36. This assumes that $Y_{(t-1)}$ is free of random measurement error.

37. Tufte (1974:5-18) and Colton and Buxbaum (1977) also discuss this example.

38. By using the age-adjusted mortality rate, Colton and Buxbaum have already removed one potentially confounding influence–age.

39. Population density is unlikely to intervene between auto inspection (X) and fatality rates (Y). The presence or absence of auto inspection has no impact on density.

40. The following analysis is restricted to white males. According to Colton and Buxbaum, the impact of auto safety depends on race and sex. These are categorical interactive variables. External validity could be attained by replicating the analysis separately for each race and sex subgroup.

41. The analysis uses the natural logarithm of population density instead of its original value to reduce its variance. The original values of density range from 3.4 to 812.4; the transformed values range from 1.224 to 6.700. Reducing the variance of confounding (Z) variables helps avoid multicollinearity between X and Z and thus reduces the standard error of $\hat{a}'$. The values of Y and X_I come from Colton and Buxbaum (1977:136-137); the values for Z come from the *Statistical Abstract of the U.S.* (U.S. Bureau of the Census, 1962:11).

42. For this equation, $R^2_{y.xz} = 0.68$, indicating that the impact of unmeasured influences on Y is less than that of measured variables.

43. Data for the values of Y in 1950 were computed from the 1960 rates and rate changes listed in Colton and Buxbaum (1977:136-137). The analysis is based on 38 states; it excludes ten states adopting inspection before 1950.

44. Recall that states adopting inspection between 1950 and 1960 had lower mortality in 1960 than those without inspection.

45. The signs on the arrows in Figure 9.21 are also interesting. They indicate the reasons for the failure of auto inspection to save lives. States that began to require inspection in the 1950s were populous and had lower fatality rates than states without inspection. The states that adopted inspection were thus the ones that needed it least.

LIST OF REFERENCES

Alwin, Duane F., and Sullivan, Michael J. "Issues of Design and Analysis in Evaluation Research." *Sociological Methods and Research* 4 (1975): 77-100.

Barnow, Burt S., and Cain, Glen G. "A Reanalysis of the Effect of Head Start on Cognitive Development: Methodology and Empirical Findings." *The Journal of Human Resources* 12 (1977):177-197.

Bentler, Peter M., and Woodward, J. Arthur. "A Head Start Reevaluation: Positive Effects Are Not Yet Demonstrable." *Evaluation Quarterly* 2 (1978):493-510.

Blalock, Hubert M., Jr. *Social Statistics.* 2d ed. New York: McGraw-Hill, 1972.

Blalock, Hubert M., Jr. "Theory Building and Causal Inference." Ch. 5 in Blalock, Hubert M., Jr., and Blalock, Ann B., eds. *Methodology in Social Research.* New York: McGraw-Hill, 1968.

Blalock, Hubert M.; Wells, Caryll S.; and Carter, Lewis F. "Statistical Estimation With Random Measurement Error." Ch. 6 in Borgatta, Edgar F., and Bohrnstedt, George W., eds. *Sociological Methodology,* 1970 San Francisco: Jossey-Bass, 1970.

Cain, Glen G. "Regression and Selection Models to Improve Nonexperimental Comparisons." Ch. 4 in Bennett, Carl A., and Lumsdaine, Arthur A., eds. *Evaluation and Experiment.* New York: Academic Press, Inc., 1975.

Cain, Glen G., and Watts, Harold W. "Problems in Making Policy Inferences from the Coleman Report." Ch. 4 in Rossi, Peter H., and Williams, Walter. *Evaluating Social Programs: Theory, Practice and Politics.* New York: Seminar Press, 1972.

Coleman, James S.; Campbell, Ernest Q.; Hobson, Carol J.; McPartland, James; Mood, Alexander M.; Weinfeld, Frederic D; and York, Robert L. *Equality of Educational Opportunity.* Washington, D.C.: U.S. Government Printing Office, 1966.

Colton, Theodore, and Buxbaum, Robert C. "Motor Vehicle Inspection and Motor Vehicle Accident Mortality." *Statistics and Public Policy*, edited by William B. Fairley and Frederick Mosteller, pp. 131–142. Reading, Mass.: Addision-Wesley Publishing Co., 1977.

Director, Steven M. "Underadjustment Bias in the Evaluation of Manpower Training." *Evaluation Quarterly* 3 (1979): 190–218.

Fuchs, Victor. *The Supply of Surgeons and the Demand for Operations,* working paper No. 236. Washington, D.C.: National Bureau of Economic Research, Inc., 1978.

Greene, Vernon. "Aggregate Bias Effects of Random Measurement Error in Multivariate OLS Regression." *Political Methodology* 5 (1978): 461–468.

Hanushek, Eric A., and Jackson, John E. *Statistical Methods for Social Sciences.* New York: Academic Press, 1977.

Hirsch, Werner; Hirsch, Joel; and Margolis, Stephen. "The Effects of Habitability Laws Upon Rent." Ch. 14 in Nagel, Stuart S., ed. *Policy Studies Review Annual.* Vol. 1. Beverly Hills: Sage Publications, Inc., 1977.

Irwin, Laura, and Lichtman, Allan J. "Across the Great Divide: Inferring Individual Level Behavior From Aggregate Data." *Political Methodology* 3 (1976): 411–439.

Langbein, Laura Irwin, and Lichtman, Allan J. *Ecological Inference.* Sage University Paper Series on Quantitative Applications in the Social Sciences. Beverly Hills: Sage Publications, Inc., 1978.

Lave, Lester B., and Seskin, Eugene P. "Does Air Pollution Save Lives?" *Statistics and Public Policy*, edited by William B. Fairley and Frederick Mosteller, pp. 143–160. Reading, Mass.: Addison-Wesley Publishing Co., 1977.

Magidson, Jay. "Reply to Bentler and Woodward: The .05 Significance Level Is Not All-Powerful." *Evaluation Quarterly* 2 (1978): 511–520.

Magidson, Jay. "Toward a Causal Model Approach for Adjusting for Preexisting Differences in the Nonequivalent Control Group Situation: A General Alternative to ANCOVA." *Evaluation Quarterly* 1 (1977): 399–420.

Miller, Trudi. "Conceptualizing Inequality." Ch. 17 in Guttentag, Marcia, ed. *Evaluation Studies Review Annual.* Vol. 2. Beverly Hills: Sage Publications, Inc. 1977.

Namboodiri, N. Krishnan; Carter, Lewis F.; and Blalock, Hubert M., Jr. *Applied Multivariate Analysis and Experimental Designs.* New York: McGraw-Hill, 1975.

Peltzman, Sam. "The Effects of Automobile Safety Regulation." *Journal of Political Economy* 83 (1975): 677–725.

Rosenstone, Steven J., and Wolfinger, Raymond E. "The Effect of Registration Laws on Voter Turnout." *American Political Science Review* 72 (1978): 22–45.

Salkever, David, and Bice, Thomas. "Impact of State Certificate-of-Need Laws on Health Care Costs and Utilization." NCHSR Research Digest Series. U.S. Public Health Service, Health Resources Administration. Washington, D.C.: U.S. Government Printing Office, 1976.

Stokes, Donald. "Compound Paths: An Expository Note." *American Journal of Political Science* (1974): 191–214.

Tufte, Edward R. *Data Analysis for Politics and Policy.* Englewood Cliffs, N.J.: Prentice-Hall, 1974.

U.S. Bureau of the Census, *Statistical Abstract of the United States.* Washington, D.C.: U.S. Government Printing Office, 1962.

Chapter 10

CONCLUSION

EXPERIMENTAL, QUASI-EXPERIMENTAL AND NONEXPERIMENTAL APPROACHES: AN OVERVIEW

This volume regards causal inference as the central component of program evaluation. Causal inference requires evaluators to gauge the influence of public programs on social and economic outcomes. The first step in evaluating the impact of a program or treatment on an outcome is to select a set of measures that captures the multiplicity of the often conflicting purposes that public policies have. To help evaluators identify a comprehensive list of outcome measures, Chapter 2 developed a general classification of goals and criteria that describe the purposes and values implicit in many public programs. Chapter 3 introduced some labels, denoting the program or treatment as X and the outcome measure as Y. Because evaluations include numerous outcome measures, they also incorporate many dependent (Y) variables. According to Chapter 3, the task of estimating the causal influence of X on Y requires investigators to ascertain that X and Y covary, that X precedes Y, and that no outside factors impinge on both X and Y. Chapter 4 outlined some practical considerations that conspire to reduce the accuracy of causal statements, and Chapter 5 outlined factors that conspire to reduce their precision and generality.

Chapters 6–9 describe the second major decision that evaluators must make after they select measures of program outcome: the choice of an experimental, quasi-experimental, or nonexperimental approach. Detailed consideration of experimental designs indicates that, even in principle, the experimental approach cannot guarantee accurate causal inference. Experiments remove only the effects of spurious and confounding variables associated with the randomly assigned subjects. Experimental designs thus do not automatically control variables associated with the treatment itself. The presence of confounding or spurious variables like these can reduce the validity of experimentally based causal claims.

We also observed that random influences affect experimental designs. Random assignment does not remove random influences, and uncontrolled random influences make it difficult to detect program impact. Scrutiny of the New Jersey Graduated Work Incentive experiment revealed that investigators who use experimental approaches must frequently supplement random assignment with comparison groups and statistical controls to reduce experimental error, to uncover interaction, and to counteract the effects of faulty or incomplete random assignment.

Inspection of quasi-experimental and nonexperimental approaches disclosed that, unlike experiments, these designs force the investigator to identify and measure all potentially spurious and confounding variables. This requirement is probably impossible to implement in its entirety. While careful investigators are unlikely to ignore the most important of these variables, they are always open to the charge of omitting a spurious or confounding influence and of overestimating or underestimating program impact as a result.

Scrutiny of quasi-experimental and nonexperimental designs also disclosed that the need to control spurious and confounding variables requires a large number of observations and the careful selection of comparision groups. Acquiring observations can be costly and locating comparision groups is frequently difficult. The search for generality makes these problems even more awkward to handle. Despite these problems, our discussion also indicated that quasi-experimental and nonexperimental designs are sometimes more appropriate than experimental designs. Quasi-experimental and nonexperimental approaches, moreover, must frequently supplement experiments.

The central theme is that selecting an experimental, quasi-experimental, or nonexperimental approach is not an easy choice, because no single approach assures internal validity, precision, and generality. Investigators must mix designs in a single study, using random assignment where possible, controlling some variables statistically, and removing other influences during the process of selecting observations. Even though no individual approach is consistently superior to any other, the better the research design, the less the need to rely on statistical analysis. Investigators who carefully randomize treatments need not use statistical methods to remove spurious and confounding influences. Investigators who carefully select study sites that are as free of extraneous influences as possible can avoid exclusive reliance on statistical controls and significance tests to uncover program impact. Although statistical manipulation cannot be avoided, carefully designed quasi experiments and well-planned true experiments go far to reduce the need for sophisticated techniques typical in nonexperimental approaches.

PROBLEMS OF UNDERESTIMATING PROGRAM IMPACT

No matter what design or mix of designs the investigator selects, we saw repeatedly that various aspects of all designs share a common danger—that of underestimating program impact. This bias is a property of the methods that evaluators have available to them; it is not a property of evaluators themselves.

Investigators who are aware of this aspect of evaluation methodology can take steps to avoid underestimation.

Our examples suggested that this bias is not trivial. Empirically based estimates of program impact rarely seem exaggerated. On the contrary, practitioners usually believe that their programs have considerably more impact than evaluation research ever detects. Even scientifically based theories usually lead evaluators to anticipate more impact than their own research actually uncovers.

Instances of findings that do not accord with scientific or popular expectations are quite common. Chapter 6 indicated that economic theory predicts that high-income guarantees and high tax rates will reduce work effort, yet the NJGWIE detected only negligible effects. Consideration of Head Start and other compensatory education programs disclosed that the evaluators were as surprised as the program's proponents to find evidence of little or no program impact. Economic theories of crime suggest that rehabilitating criminals with community release programs reduces the deterrent effect of punishment, yet supportive empirical findings are extremely mixed.[1]

Program managers and evaluation researchers nonetheless continue to predict program results that empirical evidence does not confirm. Evaluation research rarely detects influence where none was anticipated. In evaluation research, the chance of underestimating program influence thus seems to exceed that of overstating impact.

Eliminating this bias is politically important for the credibility of evaluation research, because positive findings are far more useful to administrators and politicians than negative findings. Program managers, administrators, and politicians alike will resist, discredit, or ignore evaluations as long as evaluation research repeatedly yields evidence that programs have little or no impact or that divergent treatments make no difference. While conclusions like these may be correct it is also possible to attribute evidence of "no impact" to faulty designs. Eliminating as many flaws as possible can increase the credibility of evaluation research. Reducing the danger of underestimating program impact will thus augment the demand for evaluation research.

Examination of experimental, quasi-experimental and nonexperimental approaches uncovered many reasons for underestimating program impact. One of the most common is the failure to have maximal variation between treatments. We saw that in prospective designs, maximizing between-treatment variation frequently requires withholding treatment entirely, but withholding treatment can be ethically or politically questionable. In retrospective designs, the variation between treatments which exists in theory may far exceed that which exists in the field. Many practical and political considerations reduce the divergence between treatments and thus contribute to understatements of program impact.[2]

Chapter 5 disclosed how random influences also mask program impact by increasing the propensity to decide that a program has no impact and that variations between treatments make no difference. Augmenting the likelihood of this conclusion also increases the chance that it is erroneous. Examining nonexperimental designs disclosed that adding observations can reduce the chance of such an error. When extraneous variables are continuous, statistical controls are also an efficient way to reduce random influences. When extraneous influences are categorical, statistical controls require the investigator to add more observations or sacrifice generality. Removing random measurement errors from the dependent variable can also transform findings of "no difference" into findings of measurable impact.

The undetected presence of statistical interaction is another reason for investigators to underestimate program impact. Failure to control for interactive variables could cause the evaluator to observe little or no relation between variations in X and values of Y when in fact interaction masks or mutes the association.

Some sources of underestimation bias are not present in experimental designs.[3] Experiments are relatively immune from the influence of uncontrolled confounding variables that represent pretreatment values of the outcome measure. Chapters 7 and 9 disclosed how time order problems like these are especially troublesome in quasi-experimental and nonexperimental situations when investigators evaluate programs that target resources to subjects who score poorly on relevant outcome measures. Failure to control completely for the confounding influence of pretreatment values of the outcome measure yields estimates of program impact that are too low. Programs like CETA, which target funds to areas with high unemployment for the purpose of reducing unemployment, and Head Start, which targets programs to low achievers for the purpose of raising achievement, are thus particularly subject to underestimation biases.

We saw that, in nonexperimental evaluations of programs like these, failure to remove the confounding influence of pretreatment values of the outcome measure (Z) means that investigators will use $\hat{b}_{yx}$ to measure program impact when they should use $\hat{b}_{yx \cdot z}$.[4] If the program is actually effective, $\hat{b}_{yx \cdot z}$ will not be zero. Assuming that $\hat{b}_{yx}$ is nearly zero, then ignoring Z means that the absolute value of $\hat{b}_{yx}$ will be smaller than the absolute value of $\hat{b}_{yx \cdot z}$.[5] Evaluators who ignore the effects of time will consequently underestimate program impact. Investigators cannot ordinarily use experimental designs to evalate programs that target resources, but they can nonetheless avoid underestimating program impact by statistically removing the influence of pretreatment scores of the outcome measure.

Chapters 8 and 9 disclosed that the failure to distinguish between direct and total effects can also yield underestimates of program impact when experimentation is impossible. To avoid this bias, investigators must correctly ascertain whether allegedly spurious or confounding variables actually intervene between the program and an outcome measure. If Z actually intervenes between X and Y but the investigator erroneously believes that Z is spurious, he will use $\hat{b}_{yx \cdot z}$ to estimate program impact rather than $\hat{b}_{yx}$. In both instances $\hat{b}_{yx \cdot z} = 0$; but when Z is intervening, $\hat{b}_{yx}$ and not $\hat{b}_{yx \cdot z}$ is the correct estimator of program impact. Using the measure of partial rather than total association thus understates policy influence.

Consideration of nonexperimental designs revealed that underestimation can also occur when $\hat{b}_{yx \cdot z}$ is not zero and investigators fail to distinguish accurately between confounding and intervening variables. When Z is intervening and not confounding, $\hat{b}_{yx}$ rather than $\hat{b}_{yx \cdot z}$ is the correct measure of program influence. Since $b_{yx} = b_{yx \cdot z} + b_{yz \cdot x} b_{zx}$, whenever the term $b_{yx \cdot z}$ and the product $b_{yz \cdot x} b_{zx}$ have the same sign, the absolute value of b_{yx} will exceed that of $b_{yx \cdot z}$.[6] Using the measure of partial association to gauge program impact when the underlying model is intervening can thus yield estimates that are too low.

Consideration of random measurement error in independent variables revealed another reason for investigators to understate program impact. Random measurement error in Z is particularly troublesome whenever persons are selected into programs because they are extremely talented, extremely needy, or extremely unlucky. Whenever these extremes reflect a random occurrence rather than a systematic pattern, confounding variables that describe the selection process will also contain random measurement error. Investigators should use procedures for removing the random element of independent variables in order to avoid attenuated estimates of program impact.

This discussion incorporates only the most likely circumstances in which evaluators could understate the influence of public programs. Other sources of bias can characterize any specific evaluation. Investigators who fear that their design might uncover "no impact" should be particularly cognizant of the variety of underestimation biases that can occur.

PROGRAM EVALUATION AND DECISION MAKING

Even when evaluators uncover evidence that a change in a particular outcome measure is attributable to a particular program change, such evidence alone is insufficient to justify decisions regarding the program's continuation or alteration. In addition to the technology of evaluation, other technical and political issues play a central role in these decisions.

Consider first some of the technical issues. Decision makers cannot act upon valid evidence regarding program impact unless the evidence is supplemented with information regarding program costs. Incontrovertible evidence that ex-criminals released from community treatment facilities have a smaller chance of committing new crimes than similar ex-criminals released from traditional prisons is insufficient grounds for choosing community treatment. Community treatment facilities could be more expensive than traditional facilities, and decision makers may judge that the reduction in crime is not worth the increase in costs. If community treatment were less expensive, then evaluation research supplemented with cost information suggests an unambiguous policy choice.[7]

Even though evaluation research must be supported with economic information about costs and benefits, decision makers and program managers must be aware that analyses of benefits and costs are also incomplete unless they are based on evaluation research. Any ledger of benefits and costs that is not supported with evaluative findings is as uninterpretable as evaluative findings that are isolated from issues of monetary value. Only benefits that are causally attributable to a policy count as a benefit of the policy; only costs that are causally attributable reckon as a cost.[8]

Evaluators will usually find it more difficult to satisfy the political needs of decision makers than to meet the technical needs of formal decision making. Evaluation research applies the tools of social science to a set of questions that social scientists did not ask, in an environment where social scientists are not the principal set of actors. The result is a tension between the demands of good research on the one hand and the demands of politicians and program managers together with the economics of evaluation research on the other.

Consider first some of the differences between social science research and evaluation research.[9] Social science research is directed at testing theories that interest social scientists. In contrast, evaluation research seems atheoretical because it centers on questions that program manangers and politicians ask.

The shorthand causal notation used in previous chapters conveniently summarizes this difference between the theoretical perspectives of evaluation research and social science research. Evaluation research typically considers only the impact of X on Y; the influence of confounding and spurious Z-variables is something to be removed. Evaluators thus separate the relation between X and Y from the larger causal structure. By contrast, social scientists study the entire structure and make no special distinction between manipulable X-variables and nonmanipulable Z variables.

Program evaluation also operates in a different environment than social science. Social science research is constrained by the canons of scientific methodology and by the pressures of peers. Persons engaged in social science research tend to receive their primary income from academic employment; the influence of their peers affects decisions about salary, promotion, and tenure. The canons of science also guide evaluation research, but unlike social science, evaluation research is not primarily judged by peers. While social science research is used by those who practice it, evaluation research is used by those who purchase it. In many instances, these users are also the sponsor of the program being evaluated, and they have a vested interest in the outcome of the research. Government agencies fund studies which evaluate programs they administer, and interest groups fund evaluations of programs they wish to have expanded or removed. Market pressure thus replaces the peer pressure that affects the output of social science.

These differences manifest themselves in a variety of ways. The canons of science demand "truth" and consequently treat Type I and Type II errors with equal severity.[10] Decision makers, in contrast, prefer to avoid Type II errors because such errors make programs look ineffective when in fact they are effective. Efforts to avoid biases of underestimation may thus be more important in evaluation research than in social science research.

The needs of science and evaluation also conflict with respect to the passage of time. While science regards the passage of time as a relatively cheap commodity, decision makers need timely information. According to the canons of science, the best designs require planning. The passage of time is also necessary to guard against confusing program impact with extreme scores and trends, and to separate long- from short-term effects. Despite these requisites of science, time is nonetheless a luxury in evaluation research. Program managers supplement budget requests with evaluation research, and decision makers use evaluation research to plan new programs and defend existing ones. Neither the budget cycle nor the political agenda will wait for the results of evaluation. In evaluation research, findings that are not available when they are needed go unused. In social science research, findings are used whenever they become available.

The role of generality and elegance also distinguishes social science from program evaluation. Even though program evaluation uses the methods of social science, its primary task is not to explain behavior with a parsimonious theory. While the development of explanatory theory is the central task of social science, estimating program impact is the central task of program evaluation. Consequently, evaluation research can accept findings which reveal that X causes Y. Devising a theory to explain why X causes Y is of secondary concern in evaluation research. In social science research, uncovering the reasons for the influence of X on Y is critically important, for the explanation may support one theory but not another. In program evaluation, discovering the impact of X on Y has political but not theoretical connotations.

It is tempting to exaggerate these differences between social science research and evaluation research. The main distinction is the audience: evaluation research is carried out by social scientists for use by decision makers and program managers, while social science research is carried out by social scientists for use by other social scientists. Evaluators are thus social scientists, and they use the tools of social science. Moreover, although evaluation research is rarely the proper vehicle for testing theories, evaluation research should strive to incorporate and use theory. Theories are important to evaluators because they point to possibly spurious and confounding variables as well as to major sources of experimental error.[11]

Evaluators should be particularly cautious when they study program impact in the absence of theory or in the presence of conflicting theories. In these instances, detecting program impact is likely to be especially difficult, and the chance of error will be correspondingly high. The absence of a theory of learning probably goes far to explain why program evaluators repeatedly uncover "no impact" when they study educational innovations. The presence of conflicting theory undoubtedly suggests why empirical evaluations of the impact of punishment on crime are so inconclusive.[12]

The validity and utility of evaluation research thus depends on the quality of social science theory that undergirds evaluation research. Evaluators who avoid the use of available social science theories increase the chances of failing to detect important spurious or confounding variables and of making Type II errors.

Social science theory can also indicate when the relation between X and Y is likely to be reciprocal, and it can shed light on the causal sequence linking X and Z. Research based on the theoretical findings of social scientists is more likely to fulfill both the canons of science and the needs of decision makers at the same time. Using the substance as well as the method of academic social science can thus help evaluators respond to political and market demands.

FOOTNOTES

1. Greenberg (1977) critically surveys some of this literature.
2. The inability to maximize variation in X may explain why it is so difficult to determine whether increasing the severity and certainty of punishment reduces crime. Punishments are quite uniform in the U.S., and investigators find it difficult to detect the impact of small differences. See Greenberg (1977).
3. For an argument favoring the superiority of experiments in this regard, see Campbell and Boruch (1975).
4. This example is based on regression analysis. The bias persists no matter what statistical technique is used.
5. As Chapter 9 showed, $b_{yx} = b_{yx \cdot z} + b_{yz \cdot x} b_{zx}$. In the CETA and Head Start examples, $b_{yx \cdot z} \neq 0$ and $(b_{yz \cdot x})(b_{zx}) > 0$. If $b_{yx} = 0$, then $|b_{yx \cdot z}| > |b_{yx}|$.
6. When $b_{yx \cdot z}$ and $(b_{yz \cdot x})(b_{zx})$ have opposite signs, $b_{yx \cdot z}$ can exceed b_{yx}.
7. For a discussion of this issue, see Gray, Conover, and Hennessy (1978).
8. A detailed consideration of benefit-cost analysis is beyond the scope of this work. For a succinct account of benefit-cost analysis, see Musgrave and Musgrave (1976: Ch. 7–8) and Stokey and Zeckhauser (1978: Ch. 9–10).
9. This discussion reflects many of the points raised by Coleman in his discussion of "discipline" and "policy" research. See Coleman (1972). See also Rossi, Wright, and Wright (1978) for a similar discussion.
10. Some academic social scientists treat Type I errors as slightly more severe than Type II errors. In social science, "nonfindings" are less interesting than "findings." Consequently, detecting a "finding" that is not really true is regarded as a severe error.
11. Microeconomic theories of demand and supply are especially useful in this regard. See also Rossi (1978) and Cline (1976) on the importance of social science theory in evaluation research.
12. Some sociological theories of crime predict that rehabilitation rather than punishment reduces crime, while some economic theories of crime predict that rehabilitation reduces the costs of crime and thereby augments the supply.

LIST OF REFERENCES

Campbell, Donald T., and Boruch, Robert F. "Making the Case for Randomized Assignment to Treatments by Considering the Alternatives: Six Ways in Which Quasi-Experimental Evaluations in Compensatory Education Tend to Underestimate Effects." Ch. 3 in Bennett, Carl A., and Lumsdaine, Arthur A., eds. *Evaluation and Experiment.* New York: Academic Press, 1975.
Cline, Marvin Gerry. "The 'What' Without the 'Why' or Evaluation Without Policy Relevance." In *The Evaluation of Social Programs*, edited by Clark Abt, pp. 367–374. Beverly Hills: Sage Publications, Inc., 1976.

Coleman, James S. *Policy Research in the Social Sciences.* Morristown, N.J.: General Learning Press, 1972.

Gray, Charles M.; Conover, C. Johnston; and Hennessey, Timothy M. "Cost Effectiveness of Residential Community Corrections: An Analytical Prototype." *Evaluation Quarterly* 2 (1978):375–400.

Greenberg, David F. "Crime Deterrence Research and Social Policy." *Policy Studies Review Annual*, vol. 2, edited by Stuart Nagel, pp. 461–475. Beverly Hills: Sage Publications, Inc., 1977.

Musgrave, Richard A., and Musgrave, Peggy B. *Public Finance in Theory and Practice.* 2d ed. New York: McGraw-Hill Book Co., 1976.

Rossi, Peter. "Issues in the Evaluation of Human Services Delivery." *Evaluation Quarterly* 2 (1978):573–599.

Rossi, Peter; Wright, James; and Wright, Sonia R. "The Theory and Practice of Applied Social Research. *Evaluation Quarterly* 2 (1978):171–191.

Stokey, Elizabeth, and Zeckhauser, Richard A. *A Primer for Policy Analysis.* New York: W. W. Norton and Co., 1978.

APPENDIX

MEASURING THE ASSOCIATION BETWEEN TWO VARIABLES*

Covariation has two properties: magnitude and direction. In respect to magnitude, two variables (X and Y) could be strongly or weakly related. In respect to direction, they could be associated positively or negatively. The specific statistical technique that is appropriate for measuring the magnitude and direction of covariation depends on whether the independent and dependent variables are categorical or continuous. The measures of association considered in this Appendix are useful in three instances that program evaluators are likely to confront: categorical independent and continuous dependent variables; categorical independent and dependent variables; and continuous independent and dependent variables.[1]

Consider first the case of categorical independent and continuous dependent variables. An evaluator could compare communities with and without mobile intensive care units (MICU) with respect to heart attack death rates. The presence or absence of MICU is a categorical variable with two categories, while death rate is a continuous variable. Figure A.1 represents a table appropriate for displaying the covariation between these variables. The difference between the means of the continuous variable ($\bar{Y}_1 - \bar{Y}_2$) is a measure of the magnitude and direction

FIGURE A.1

Table to Measure Covariation Between a Categorical Independent and Continuous Dependent Variable

	MICU(X)	
	Present	Absent
Mean death rate	$\bar{Y}_1$	$\bar{Y}_2$

*This Appendix reviews some simple measures of bivariate association. It assumes that readers have some familiarity with statistical inference and hypothesis testing.

172

of covariation between availability of emergency care and death. The larger the difference, the greater the magnitude of covariation. The sign of the difference measures the direction of covariation. Both pieces of information are important. Evaluators must determine if the availability of emergency care is associated with fewer deaths (i.e., direction) and if the difference is very large (i.e., magnitude).

Tests of statistical significance are sometimes useful for making decisions about magnitude. Random influence is a particularly plausible rival hypothesis to that of true association when differences between means are small. Significance tests provide an estimate of the probability that the observed difference could occur if the random influence hypothesis were actually correct. If this probability is low, then the investigator can, with some confidence, reject the random influence hypothesis in favor of the alternative hypothesis of true association.[2]

Like the choice of a measure of association, the choice of a significance test depends on the level of measurement of the independent and dependent variable. When the independent variable is categorical and the dependent variable is continuous, the *t*-test for the difference between means is appropriate.[3]

A numerical example illustrates its use. Figure A.2 provides hypothetical data regarding the mean heart attack death rate (*Y*) for communities with and without Mobile Intensive Care Units (MICU). The table also reports the standard deviation and number of cases in each sample in accord with the requirements for the *t*-test. The table shows that communities without MICU tend to have

FIGURE A.2
Mean Death Rate (per 10,000), by Availability
of MICU: Hypothetical Data

	MICU (X)	
	Present	*Absent*
Mean death rate (*Y*)	14	15
Standard deviation (*s*)	4	6
Number of observations (*N*)	100	200

higher death rates than communities with MICU, but the difference is small and may not be statistically significant. Random influences are thus a plausible alternative explanation for the observed one-death difference between means.

According to the formula for the *t*-statistic,

$$t = \frac{\bar{Y}_1 - \bar{Y}_2}{\sqrt{[s_1^2/(N_1 - 1)] + [s_2^2/(N_2 - 1)]}}.$$

Based on the data in Figure A.2,

$$t = \frac{14 - 15}{\sqrt{(16/99) + (36/199)}} = 1.72.$$

Using a two-tailed t-test, the probability of obtaining $t = 1.72$ if the randomness hypothesis were true is between 0.05 and 0.10. The observed outcome is thus relatively unlikely to occur if the hypothesis of random association were true. Based on the t-test, the investigator can conclude that the presence of a MICU is significantly associated with lower death rates.[4] As Chapter 3 indicates, the presence of significant association is only necessary but not a sufficient condition for attributing causal influence to the MICU.

Another common statistical pattern in program evaluation combines categorical independent with categorical dependent variables. Consider a study of the association between FHA-sponsored default counseling programs and the likelihood of current repayment among FHA's delinquent mortgagors. Participation in default counseling is a categorical independent variable with two categories. The dependent variable also has two categories (payments current or not current). Figure A.3 shows the frequencies that might emerge from randomly assigning delinquent mortgagors to counseling programs. Figure A.4 reports the

FIGURE A.3
Association Between Default Counseling and Currency of Payment: Hypothetical Frequencies

	Participation	
Payments	*Counseled*	*Not counseled*
Current	210	350
Not current	290	550
	500	900

FIGURE A.4
Percent of Delinquent Mortgagors Who Are Current, by Participation in Counseling

	Participation	
	Counseled	*Not counseled*
Percent current	42%	39%
	($N = 500$)	($N = 900$)

corresponding percentages.[5] The difference between these percentages, 3%, measures the magnitude and direction of association between counseling and currency of payment. Because random assignment was used to allocate mortgagors to counseling, this percentage difference, if it is statistically significant, is also indicative of the causal influence of counseling on prompt payment.

In the case of categorical independent and dependent variables that are both dichotomies, the Z-test for the difference of proportions is the appropriate test for statistical significance.[6] According to the Z-test,

$$Z = \frac{p_1 - p_2}{\sqrt{\hat{p}\hat{q}} \sqrt{\frac{N_1 + N_2}{N_1 N_2}}}$$

where

$$\hat{p} = \frac{N_1 p_1 + N_2 p_2}{N_1 - N_2}$$

and

$$\hat{q} = 1 - \hat{p}.$$

Using this formula, $\hat{p} = \dfrac{500(0.42) + 900(0.39)}{1400} = 0.40$, so that

$$Z = \frac{0.42 - 0.39}{\sqrt{(0.4)(0.6)} \sqrt{\frac{1400}{450,000}}} = \frac{0.03}{0.027} = 1.11.$$

If the association between counseling and payment were only random, the probability of obtaining $Z \geqslant 1.11$ is quite high—about 13.35%.[7] Consequently, an evaluator would probably decide to accept the random influence hypothesis and to conclude that counseling delinquent mortgagors does not reduce the chance of late payments.[8]

Program evaluators frequently encounter continuous independent and dependent variables. When X and Y are both continuous, the regression coefficient ($\hat{b}_{yx}$) is an appropriate way to measure the magnitude and direction of their association.[9] The regression coefficient measures the change in Y that is associated with a unit change in X. The sign of $\hat{b}_{yx}$ reflects the direction of association between X and Y, and its value indicates the magnitude of association. When $\hat{b}_{yx} = 0$, X and Y are not associated at all. When $\hat{b}_{yx}$ is positive, X and Y are said to be positively associated, such that high values of X are accompanied by high values of Y. When $\hat{b}_{yx}$ is negative, X and Y are negatively associated, and high values of X will accompany low values of Y.

The regression coefficient can attain any value from $-\infty$ to $+\infty$. Its specific value depends on the units in which X and Y are measured as well as on the magnitude and direction of their association. If X is the price of gasoline (in dollars per gallon) and Y is the annual amount of gasoline purchased (in gallons per household), then $\hat{b}_{yx} = -10$ means that a one-dollar increase in the price of gasoline per gallon is associated with a consumption decrease of 10 gallons. If X is the amount of traffic patrol at a busy intersection (measured in manhours) and Y is the accident rate (measured as accidents per 10,000 vehicles), then $\hat{b}_{yx} = 0.35$ means that a one manhour increase in patrolling is associated with an increase in the accident rate of 0.35 per 10,000 vehicles (or 35 per 1,000,000).[10]

The regression coefficient also records the slope of the straight line that best summarizes a scatterplot of the observed values of X and Y. The equation for such a line is $\hat{Y}_i = \hat{a} + \hat{b}_{yx}X_i$, where $\hat{a}$ is the Y-intercept (the value of Y when $X = 0$) and $\hat{b}_{yx}$ is the regression coefficient or slope. The term $\hat{Y}_i$ indicates the value of Y_i predicted by the quantity $(\hat{a} + \hat{b}_{yx}X_i)$. The difference between the observed and predicted values of Y_i, or $(Y_i - \hat{Y}_i)$, is frequently called an error term and is represented by the symbol "e_i." Figure A.5 portrays $\hat{b}_{yx}$ as the slope of the straight line summarizing a plot of observed values of X and Y, and indicates the location of $\hat{a}$, Y_i, $\hat{Y}_i$, and e_i. This line, called a regression line, is the line that minimizes the sum of the squared, vertical distances between each value of Y_i and $\hat{Y}_i$. The regression line is thus said to minimize the error we make in predicting a value for Y given a value for X.

FIGURE A.5

The Regression Line

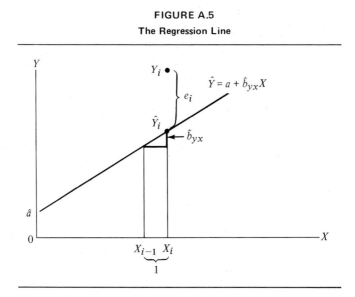

The regression coefficient can be computed according to the formula

$$\hat{b}_{yx} = \frac{N\Sigma XY - (\Sigma X)(\Sigma Y)}{N\Sigma X^2 - (\Sigma X)^2}\text{.}[11]$$

Consider the data in Figure A.6, which reports results from a hypothetical study of the relation between the availability of physicians (X) and the use of hospitals (Y).

FIGURE A.6
Hypothetical Data from Study of Availability of
Physicians and Use of Hospitals: Ten U.S. Counties

County	Number of physicians per 100,000 population (X)	Number of inpatient days per 100 population (Y)
A	193	111
B	0	0
C	96	145
D	137	10.6
E	120	38
F	98	164
G	140	97
H	65	83
I	89	57
J	131	9.7

Figure A.7 illustrates a convenient layout from which to compute $\hat{b}_{yx}$. According to these data,

$$\hat{b}_{yx} = \frac{10(82745.9) - (1069)(715.3)}{10(138145) - 1069^2} = 0.263,$$

which indicates that an increase of one physician per 100,000 population is associated with an increase in inpatient hospital use of 0.263 patient days per 100 population (or 263 per 100,000 population).

FIGURE A.7
Data Layout to Compute $\hat{b}_{yx}$[12]

X	Y	XY	X^2	Y^2
193	111	21423	37249	12321
0	0	0	0	0
96	145	13920	9216	21025
137	10.6	1452.2	18769	112.36
120	38	4560	14400	1444
98	164	16072	9604	26896
140	97	13580	19600	9409
65	83	5395	4225	6889
89	57	5073	7921	3249
131	9.7	1270.7	17161	94.09
1069	715.3	82745.9	138145	81439.45

A significance test helps to determine if this figure reflects random influences or true association. The *t*-statistic indicates whether the computed value of $\hat{b}_{yx}$ differs significantly from a parametric value of zero,

where

$$t = \frac{\hat{b}_{yx}}{\hat{\sigma}_b} \ ,$$

and

$$\hat{\sigma}_b = \frac{\sqrt{\Sigma(Y_i - \hat{Y}_i)^2 / (N - 2)}}{\sqrt{\Sigma(X_i - \bar{X})^2}}$$

The figure, $\hat{\sigma}_b$, is the standard error of the regression coefficient, and its value is 0.387.[13] As a result, $t = 0.263/0.387 = 0.68$, which is not significant. The observed value of $\hat{b}_{yx}$ reflects random influences rather than true association.[14]

It is also possible to estimate the amount of dispersion around the regression line whose slope is $\hat{b}_{yx}$. If there is no difference between $\hat{Y}_i$, which is the value of the outcome measure predicted by the regression equation $\hat{a} + \hat{b}_{yx}X_i$, and Y_i, which is the value of the outcome measure that the investigator actually observes, then there will be no dispersion around the regression line. When there is no dispersion around the regression line, the observed value of X, together with the computed values of $\hat{a}$ and $\hat{b}_{yx}$, predict the value of Y exactly. In this case, knowing X helps reduce error in predicting Y by 100%.

There usually is a considerable amount of dispersion around the regression line, and the difference between Y_i and $\hat{Y}_i$ will not be zero. Figure A.8(a) depicts a regression line with relatively little dispersion, and Figure A.8(b) portrays a line with significant dispersion. The coefficient of determination, denoted r_{xy}^2 or R_{xy}^2, measures the amount of this dispersion relative to the total dispersion in Y. The dispersion of Y around the regression line is $\Sigma(Y_i - \hat{Y}_i)^2$. The total dispersion of Y is its variation: $\Sigma(Y_i - \bar{Y}_i)^2$. Subtracting the quotient of those quantities from unity yields r_{xy}^2.

$$r_{xy}^2 = 1 - \frac{\Sigma(Y_i - \hat{Y}_i)^2}{\Sigma(Y_i - \bar{Y})^2}$$

When there is no dispersion around the regression line, $\Sigma(Y_i - \hat{Y}_i)^2 = 0$ and $r_{xy}^2 = 1$. When the dispersion around the regression line equal the dispersion around the mean of Y, $\Sigma(Y_i - \hat{Y}_i)^2 = \Sigma(Y_i - \bar{Y})^2$, and $r_{xy}^2 = 0$. In this case, knowing values of X does not help predict values of Y at all. These are the two extreme values for r_{xy}^2. In an intermediate case, a value of r_{xy}^2 like 0.30 means that knowing X helps the investigator reduce his error in predicting Y by 30%. Low values of r_{xy}^2 indicate that many variables besides X influence Y; high values mean that X has more relative influence. R_{xy}^2 is thus an indicator of the relative impact of measured variables (X) on Y relative to that of all other variables, which are unmeasured.

FIGURE A.8
Dispersion Around Regression Line

(a) Small dispersion

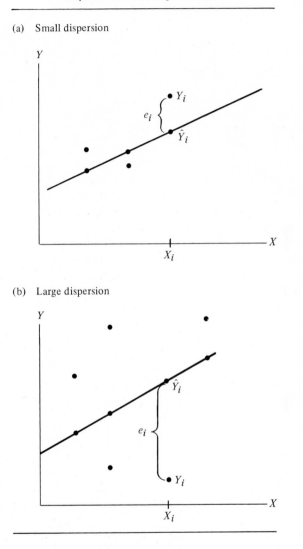

(b) Large dispersion

The simplest way to compute r_{xy}^2 by hand is to use a modification of the formula for the regression coefficient:

$$r_{xy}^2 = \frac{[N\Sigma XY - (\Sigma X)(\Sigma Y)]^2}{[N\Sigma X^2 - (\Sigma X)^2][N\Sigma Y^2 - (\Sigma Y)^2]}$$

Using the data from Figure A.6,

$$r_{xy}^2 = \frac{[10(82745.9) - (1069)(715.3)]^2}{[10(138145) - (1069)^2][10(81439.45) - (715.3)^2]}$$

$$= 0.054$$

This value indicates considerable dispersion around the estimated regression co-efficient. Knowing the number of physicians per 100,000 population helps to reduce the investigator's error in predicting the number of inpatient days per 100 population by just 5.4%. The number of physicians thus accounts for just 5.4% of the total variation in Y; other factors, not captured by X, account for the remaining 94.6%.

Although these measures of association indicate only the magnitude and direction of covariation between X and Y, they also form the basis for testing causal statements regarding the association between X and Y that remains once the influence of outside variables has been removed. We show in the text that measures of the partial association between X and Y can be developed from the measures of association that this Appendix considers. Despite their importance, these measures of association do not span the entire set of topics covered in the statistics texts that social scientists use most often. Evaluators should consult one of these texts when they confront statistical needs.

FOOTNOTES

1. In the case of continuous independent and categorical dependent variables, investigators should use probit or logit analysis. For a discussion of those techniques, see Hanushek and Jackson (1977: Ch. 7).
2. A discussion of error in decisions like these can be found in Chapter 5.
3. The t-test is only appropriate when X has two categories. The F-test for analysis of variance is appropriate when X has $2, \ldots, K$ categories. In the case of 2 categories, $F = t^2$. See Namboodiri, Carter, and Blalock (1975: 77–104) for a discussion of F-tests.
4. There is between a 5% and 10% chance that this conclusion is erroneous.
5. These percentages are similar to those found in a HUD study that reported the results of a default counseling experiment. The frequencies on which the percentages are based differ from those HUD reported (U.S. Department of Housing and Urban Development, January, 1977).
6. When at least one of the categorical variables has more than two categories, the Z-test cannot be used. It is nearly always possible to collapse multicategory variables into dichotomies, so the Z-test can frequently be used. When any one of the variables has more than two categories, the *chi*-square statistic is an appropriate significance test.
7. This is based on a one-tailed test, since the desirable result requires p_1 to exceed p_2.
8. These results are just illustrative. The HUD study cited in footnote 5 found that counseling was effective.

9. The correlation coefficient (r_{yx}) is a more popular measure of association for continuous variables, but $\hat{b}_{yx}$ communicates more information that evaluators need. Its meaning is also analogous to the difference of means and proportions. The symbol $\hat{b}_{yx}$ indicates the estimate of the regression parameter, b_{yx}.

10. This value reflects an association; it does not mean that adding patrol hours increases accidents. The positive association would probably disappear or even become negative once traffic volume was accounted for.

11. The computation of the regression coefficient is the same even when variables are labeled "I" and "J" instead of "X" and "Y." In general,

$$\hat{b}_{IJ} = \frac{N\Sigma IJ - (\Sigma I)(\Sigma J)}{N\Sigma J^2 - (\Sigma J)^2}.$$

By convention, the first subscript denotes the dependent variable.

12. We discuss the values in the column for Y^2 below. These values are not used to compute $\hat{b}_{yx}$.

13. The computational steps to derive this statistic are clearly cumbersome. Packaged computer programs that compute $\hat{b}_{yx}$ also compute its standard error. Chapter 5 considers the standard error in some detail.

14. A larger N could make the same observed value of $\hat{b}_{yx}$ appear to be statistically significant,

LIST OF REFERENCES

Hanushek, Eric A., and Jackson, John E. *Statistical Methods for Social Scientists.* New York: Academic Press, 1977.

Namboodiri, N. Krishnan; Carter, Lewis F.; and Blalock, Hubert M., Jr. *Applied Multivariate Analysis and Experimental Designs.* New York: McGraw-Hill Book Co., 1975.

U.S. Department of Housing and Urban Development, Assistant Secretary for Policy Development and Research, Office of Policy Development and Program Evaluation, Division of Special Studies, *Counseling for Delinquent Mortgagors II: A Staff Study.* Washington, D.C., Jan. 1977.

INDEX